NEW PATHS TOWARD THE SACRED

Awakening the Awe Experience
in Everyday Living

CATHERINE McCANN

Paulist Press
New York/Mahwah, NJ

Cover photograph by Con Brogan

Cover design by Sharyn Banks
Book design by Lynn Else

Library of Congress Cataloging-in-Publication Data

McCann, Catherine.
   New paths toward the sacred : awakening the awe experience in everyday living / Catherine McCann.
      p. cm.
   Includes bibliographical references.
   ISBN 978-0-8091-4551-5 (alk. paper)
   1. Experience (Religion) 2. Christian life—Catholic authors. I. Title.
   BR110.M225 2008
   248.2—dc22

                                                                2008020979

Published by Paulist Press
997 Macarthur Boulevard
Mahwah, New Jersey 07430

www.paulistpress.com

Printed and bound in the
United States of America

Contents

To Charlie,
in gratitude for the sacred gift of our thirty-eight-year friendship

Acknowledgments

I am indebted to many people who have assisted me in different ways in writing this book. First of all, I am grateful to All Hallows College and its accrediting body, Dublin City University, for guiding me through my doctoral project. In particular, I want to thank my tutor Eugene Curran.

I also wish to acknowledge the kindness of Trish Quigley and her helpful staff in Milltown Park Library, and to express my great indebtedness to the Milltown Park Community for the facility of having access to this great library. I want to also acknowledge the help given by Sarah Ball and Colette Edwards for the times I spent in the new National Botanical Garden's library and Jennie O'Connor at the Japanese Embassy for allowing me to borrow books. I want most sincerely to acknowledge my gratitude to the thirteen generous people who participated in the research and especially for their invaluable personal contributions.

I have had mentors along the way. I would especially like to thank Jim Corkery, director of my MA studies, which paved the way for my doctoral project. I am also grateful to Michael Paul Gallagher for his suggestions regarding this book and to Eric Guiry for the encouragement and enthusiasm he gave in urging me to publish. I am deeply grateful to Lawrence Boadt and the Paulist Press board for accepting this book, and in particular to Paul McMahon who guided me through the final editing stage.

I particularly want to thank my friends for their interest and especially to thank Bairbre de Burca who painstakingly proofread my text. I am grateful to my sister, Bridget Suttle, who came to my aid when computer problems arose. Above all, my deepest indebtedness goes to my long-term friend, mentor of heart wisdom, and supreme encourager, Charlie O'Connor.

Introduction

This book focuses on discovering the Sacred within ordinary everyday living. It is especially written for those who want to enliven their faith in an integrated manner. While faith experiencing is very much a matter of the heart, such experience calls for understanding. Our twenty-first century Western world's overly rational and materialistic culture necessitates that we constantly explore ways that enable us to personally make more sense of our faith, of our experiencing the Divine. At the same time, faith is never a private matter but is a gift that contains a "for others" dimension that can enrich both giver and receiver, at local as well as global levels. This requires constantly improving our ability to communicate our faith in ways that are authentic and intelligible. Peter's words are pertinent: "always be ready to make your defense to anyone who demands from you an accounting for the hope that is in you; yet do it with gentleness and reverence" (1 Pet 3:15).[1]

An emphasis in this book is on searching for deeper meaning. A way of achieving this is by becoming alert to life's "ah" moments, so as they arise from within the thoughts, feelings, incidents, and situations that arouse our attention/curiosity we allow ourselves to be moved by the awesome nature of these happenings. This awakening can spring from the simplest reality to the unusual and can come from within our inner self or from our external environment. Readers could include persons of all faith traditions as well as those who claim other systems of meaning. Evidence of my faith, Christianity, is apparent through my reliance on authors, concepts, and terms that are mainly Christian. Since the material presented is foundational to fuller human living, it will hopefully speak to people of varied backgrounds.

The book is a sequel to my doctoral thesis titled *Oasis for the Spirit: Exploring Personal Experiences in a Garden in the Light of the Sacred.* In *New Paths Toward the Sacred: Awakening the Awe Experience in Everyday Living,* I concentrate on the sections from the above work that I consider most significant. This has involved deleting some sections, modifying other passages, and adopting a less academic approach. This has led to a reduction in notes.[2] I have tried to simplify the text by distilling it in an attempt to make the key issues emerge with greater clarity.

Interpreting and weaving together both contemporary and traditional ideas in relation to *human experience* and *the Sacred* are the overall route this book takes. The earlier chapters follow a theoretical approach whereas the chapter on personal experiences uses a format akin to Jeff Astley's description of Ordinary Theology.[3] Each chapter is an entity in itself and readers may choose to go to a specific topic that immediately appeals. The chapters do, however, lead into one another as an unfolding of thought emerges when moving from one chapter to the next.

The first chapter, possibly the most difficult one to read, lays the foundation, since it outlines what is meant by *human experience.* Chapter 2 examines more specifically the meaning of the religious dimension of human experience. The following chapter concentrates on how we can come to some understanding of the core element in religious/faith experience by describing it as an experience of the Sacred. Chapter 4 centers on the aesthetic dimension of human experience and outlines some of the similarities as well as the differences between religious and aesthetical experiencing. The next chapter examines the capacities and dispositions that facilitate our entering deeper levels of religious and aesthetic experiencing.

The significant influence culture and place play in relation to human experience is examined in chapters 6 and 7. Chapter 8 gives an example of how particular places—in this instance gardens have been chosen—can evoke a sense of the Sacred. The personal experiences of thirteen people who spent a reflective day in a particular garden form the basis of chapter 9. Finally, chapter 10 offers some concluding reflections and suggestions.

I conclude this introduction with quotations from two authors whose words struck a deep chord in me as well as provided impetus for my desire to embark, in my seventies, on a doctoral thesis. These words continue to energize me when writing this book. The first two are from Nicholas Lash. "Every Christian [to which I add those of other faiths]...is called to journey in the direction of deeper knowledge of the things of God and the journey is a home-coming, for God is our end as well as our beginning."[4] These words struck a deep chord in me. I received from this same author further encouragement when I read "our public imagination has become, with bewildering rapidity, almost entirely unschooled by Christianity [again I ask those of other faiths to supplement their own]....It requires all of us that we make that truth our own through thought and pain, and argument; through prayer and study and an unrelenting quest for understanding."[5]

Within the same week of reading Lash, I went to an exhibition of the famous Japanese woodblock print designer Katsushika Hokusai (1760–1848) at the Chester Beatty Library in Dublin. Written around the walls of the exhibition gallery was a quotation from the artist:

> I was in the habit of sketching the appearance of things about me from around the age of six. Although I had produced numerous designs by my fiftieth year, nothing I did before my seventieth year was really worth counting. At the age of seventy-three I began to understand the true form of birds, animals, insects and fish and the nature of plants, and trees. If I carry on in this way, by the age of eighty I hope to have made even more progress, and at ninety to have got closer to the essence of art. At the age of one hundred, I will surely have reached a magnificent level and at one hundred and ten each dot and line will be alive. I would like to ask those who outlive me to observe that I have not spoken without reason.[6]

Both authors inspired me, particularly Lash's notion that journeying toward deeper knowledge of the things of God is a kind of homecoming and Hokusai's idea of becoming more alive as we age.

Catherine McCann
25 March 2007

1

Human Experience

This book focuses on two key realities. The first is to understand in greater depth the phrase *personal experience*. The second is to gain insight into how we can experience the Sacred within personal experiences. This opening chapter on what is meant by experience lays the foundation on which all other chapters are built.

Exploring human experience is a difficult task. This is due to many factors such as: the various ways through which human experience can be analyzed; the complex components that make up human experience; the types and levels of experiences; the different range of awareness of experience; the ability to articulate experiences with some level of preciseness. In summary, there are multiple, including imprecise, understandings of what is human experience.

This analysis of the varying issues related to the nature of human experience relies mainly on the views of Bernard Lonergan.[1] When reading especially this first chapter it would be important to take into account the glossary of working definitions given at the end of this book. The key terms offered are: *consciousness, divine, grace, mediate/mediation, mystery, sacrament, spirit, symbol,* and *transcendence.* These definitions are further unpacked as the book unfolds.

Exploring Human Experience

It is worth noting at the outset that while psychologists stress the importance of becoming experientially aware of feelings, not merely in the area of therapy but for fuller living, Lonergan takes a broader spectrum that encompasses thinking as well as feelings when describing human experience.

His approach to human experience is based on nineteen forms of human activities with each of these acting in an interdependent manner. The first five refer to the activities of the senses: seeing, hearing, touching, tasting, smelling; the next six are the operations of understanding: inquiring, imagining, understanding, conceiving, formulating, reflecting; the following three are the operations of judgment: marshalling; then weighing the evidence, judging; and finally the operations of responsible decision making: delivering, evaluating, deciding, speaking, writing. As we activate these operations we become more self-aware and our awareness differs as we progress through these varying types of activities.

He differentiates four qualitatively different levels of experiencing, with each level containing one or more of the nineteen operations.[2] These "fit" in the following ways:

- on the first *empirical* level we sense, feel, imagine, perceive, speak, move;

- on the second *intellectual* level we come to understand through inquiry;

- on the third *rational* level we reflect, gather evidence, pass judgment;

- on the fourth *responsible* level we personalize our goals, evaluate possible courses of action, make decisions about these actions, and then implement these decisions.

Experiencing becomes richer as we move from level to level. The first level is vital since it generates the data that is then processed on further levels. This first level is what is commonly recognized as experience. At this stage the meaning component is absent, something has merely occurred. By moving to the second intellectual level, the initiatory occurrence is deepened through a process of inquiry that involves understanding what actually occurred on the first level. This second level of "coming to understand" is the level at which meaning emerges. This leads to the third level when we try to decide whether "this is so" or "this is not so"—in other words to affirm the truth or authenticity of our understanding. Experience is fuller at these two interior levels since consciousness has been expanded. Finally, at the responsible level, *experience* in its truest sense is arrived at through decisions being made about the truth of facts discovered at the third level. This fourth level also includes the implementation of decisions into personal living. As we move through these various levels of consciousness we can also become aware of a richer experiencing of the self.

This self-transcendental form of experiencing is comprehensive and unrestricted since it constantly leads us to move beyond what we do not yet know or love. Self-transcendence essentially means moving, in a nonspatial sense, from where we are now to another, or further, place such as moving to deeper levels of knowledge and/or love. Transcendence is earthed in the mundane and remains always a movement toward rather than an escape from reality. Rather than lifting us out of the ordinary, transcendence is concerned with attending to the depths that lie within the ordinary as well as the more sublime.

We can be conscious without adverting to what we are experiencing. This happens when the transcendent process largely occurs in a "semi-conscious" manner.[3] When incidents in our lives are lived automatically they remain outside our fuller conscious experiencing of ourselves. Sometimes our awareness remains at the level of sense perception and without any experience of self-awareness. We can easily become so involved in our activities that we remain unaware of ourselves and perhaps also of other people. Truly human experiences are those that happen when we live in awakened states, namely, when we become more consciously aware of the activities we perform. The movement from the semi-conscious type of living that occurs during routine activities toward explicitly conscious ways of sensing, thinking, and willing calls for personal effort. It is when the more conscious state develops that we experience self-transcendence. It is impossible to sustain constantly living at this subjective level of experiencing because the demands of doing so are too difficult. The human spirit needs rest periods apart from times of sleep. The ideal would be to have moments of this depth experiencing while others are lived in a less heightened manner.

Moving from constantly living on automatic pilot, a superficial type of living, toward fuller living becomes possible when the four transcendental precepts are embraced and related to the realities of concrete living. The increased range and depth of awareness that emerges through this self-transcendence journey remains always open-ended so there is always the possibility of further transcendence. At the fourth level of consciousness, the transcendent movement with its unrestricted desire to know and love is open to the possibility of the in-breaking of the Transcendent Other into consciousness. This entrance of the Divine is a full human experience while remaining never fully known.

Experiencing is enhanced when all aspects of our person are involved in the above processes, namely, body, mind, and spirit. Worthy of note at this stage is that the greater the range and depth of our experiencing, the greater is the range and depth of our knowing and loving, since we come to know and love all we know and love only through human experience. Our potential for depth experiences becomes realized when we live with a keener awareness of these four levels within human consciousness.

The Four Transcendental Precepts

How we can better live out these four levels of human experiencing is outlined with some clarity through what Lonergan terms transcendental precepts. He names four: *be attentive, be intelligent, be reasonable, be responsible.*[4]

Be Attentive

Being attentive, the first of these precepts, involves noticing our activities of sensing, perceiving, imagining, feeling, speaking, moving. When, for instance, we are attentive to the different sensations of touch, taste, smell, hearing, or seeing we are more likely to enter into, be present to, these experiences. Partially hearing, feeling, perceiving, imagining, due to a lack of attention, diminishes awareness. Whether the experience is coming from senses, imagination, perceptions, or feelings, attentiveness requires resting in, savoring, or staying with a particular experience. This lingering moment of being present to what we are experiencing needs to be adverted to before moving to reflect on it.

Becoming more fully aware of what is occurring demands being focused on what we are about. It calls for being in the now of each experience. Anthony de Mello in the twentieth century and J. P. de

Caussade writing in the eighteenth century advocate this approach to living.[5] An illustration of not sufficiently attending to present reality is strikingly illustrated in de Mello's "Temple Bells" story. An individual set out to listen for the temple bells yet failed to hear them because he bypassed listening to the immediate sound around him, which was the ocean.[6] The Buddhist way of life is also strongly focused on "mindful" living.[7]

Attention to our feelings plays an important role in enriching human consciousness. Indeed, without them, our knowing, loving, and decision making are impoverished. Carl Rogers, whose approach to therapy became known as "person-centered," saw attentiveness to feelings as recognizing, owning, and expressing them.[8] Growth in awareness of feelings leads toward an ability to notice feelings as they occur, knowingly and acceptingly. Rogers is akin to Lonergan when he indicates that becoming aware of a feeling, particularly to its limits, and having done so in a knowing and open manner, in other words having reflected on one's feelings, an individual has a rich experience of the self.

When awareness of the object of our attention is coupled with an awareness of oneself as the subject of these activities—for example, when we become aware of ourselves as listener, feeler—additional enrichment ensues, providing richer data for the intellect to "work" on.

All experiencing is initiated at this first level. The more we notice what comes to us through the senses, the more alert we are to present feelings, the more open we are in our perceptions, the more awake we are to our imaginings—the richer all this foundational data becomes. This data forms the raw material from which all further transcending levels of consciousness operate.

Today great value is placed on the validity of experience and as a consequence there is a shift in respect toward the "authority of experience" as opposed to a previous emphasis on the "experience of authority." The authority of personal experience becomes more authentic through living this first precept and fuller still when the data that this first precept produces is processed through the activities of the other three precepts.

Be Intelligent

This second precept moves into the area of thinking where the movement of self-transcendence begins. Thinking arises out of our previous levels of attentiveness as our intelligence processes the data that results from our noticings. This is brought about through the operations of inquiring, coming to understand, and expressing what was understood. The goal at this level is insight, which tends to develop out of a conflict of opposites. Insight may come solely through personal effort as in the case of an inventor. Largely, however, insight comes as a result of personal inquiry usually arrived at by listening to other people's inquiries and questionings and by searching through what is available in the environment by means of conversation, books, the media, or the Internet. The epitome of insight experiences is when a *Eureka*[9] cry is evoked.

Growth in intelligence is likely to lead to the realization that answered questions usually lead to further questioning. Remaining receptive to the possibility of further and more enlarged realms opening up may lead to the gifted realm, where unrestricted knowing and loving become manifest as the Unnamable One, or Holy Mystery.

An example of an inquiry process would be the following. The data, such as a negative feeling, is presented to the intellect. The form the inquiry might take could include attempts to discover what aroused that feeling, whether the feeling was linked with our early history, whether the feeling was masked either consciously or unconsciously by some present symptom, or whether the feeling was misplaced in some way. Working out such matters is an experiential reality and it is this added reality of a more intelligible understanding of the original data that considerably expands the initial experience of a negative feeling. "Being intelligent" in this manner is part of the entire transcendental process, which means moving beyond what is known as one strives toward a fuller apprehension of what is yet unknown.

Be Reasonable

Being reasonable requires a further movement of self-transcendence. At this third level, an individual decides on what is true, after inquiring into different possible understandings that have arisen around the initial experience. It takes us beyond the answers that intelligence gave and discerns the validity of these answers. The process at this level is concerned with further reflection, in the sense of gathering the evidence that has been brought forward by the intelligent phase, and then passing judgment on the truth or falsity, certainty, probability, or nonprobability of what has been understood. The goal at this stage is to discover what really is so. The role of reasonableness is to doubt, check, and make sure that our insights and understandings are not faulty. Being reasonable means taking into account that opinions and theories can be many, and therefore sound judgment is called for. "And what is sound judgment? It is to bow to the necessary, to accept the certain, merely to entertain the probable, to distrust the doubtful, to denounce the impossible."[10]

At this level we experience objectively the process of being detached and disinterested as we critically search for what is true. Simultaneously, the subjective experience is one of self-surrender as we search for truth. The process has transcended at this point the what, why, and how of questionings on the second level in an attempt to discern whether the answers to these questions are verifiable. The movement involved in both the intelligible and reasonable levels is from the unknown to the better known.

Be Responsible

The dynamic at this level moves into the area of the will. Having arrived at the truth of what is so this fourth precept is concerned with the choices and commitments that flow from the discerned truth. It involves deliberating in regard to choices, possible courses of action, and how we can implement what has been decided. The goal at this level is for choices of value and ultimately for what is loving and good and then to concretize these choices in living. It is the area where conscious freedom and responsibility enter human living.

Living this fourth precept entails experiencing the objective process of decision making while at the subjective level becoming conscious of experiencing ourselves as a responsible decision maker.

The Unity within the Transcendental Process

While all the processes of being attentive, intelligent, reasonable, and responsible have been described in isolation, the normal form of experiencing is one dynamic process. The dynamic structure of human consciousness is a given and forms a unity in the routines of human living. A sad reality is that our potential for depth experience can remain largely unactivated. This is due to factors such as ignorance, inadvertence, lack of effort, busyness, or other reasons.

Important in all stages of the transcendental process is coming to an awareness of the subjective experiencing of ourselves in the performing of any of our basic operations, be it sensing, feeling, imagining, understanding, judging, deciding, loving. This is achieved by heightening our consciousness at each of these levels. It can be difficult to be at home in these transcendental processes, due to a lack of awareness of this possibility as well as to the pace and largely functional approach to living. However, if the goal of subjective experiencing—richer and fuller living—was recognized and appreciated this could provide the incentive. This form of richer living echoes the heart of Jesus' mission: "I have come that they may have life and have it to the full" (John 10:10), a reference that could be interpreted as relating to all dimensions of human experiencing.

Self-consciousness and self-identity emerge through expanding our levels of experience. Since every experience contains more than each person has the capacity to hold, it is exercising this capacity to live experiences in an ever fuller manner rather than staying on the first level of experiencing that is the significant factor. The depth and implications of some experiences may take time to unfold.

Lonergan summarizes the transcendental processes: "We awake to attend. Observing lets intelligence be puzzled, and we inquire. Inquiry leads to the delight of insight...[that] critical reasonableness doubts, checks, makes sure."[11] Finally, choices have to be made around value where, for instance, we might wonder if what appears attractive is really the good. Finally our choices require implementation.

The Relationship between Experience and Meaning

The dictum "we had the experience but missed the meaning" does not fit easily with the explanation of experience just expanded. As discussed, you cannot really have a truly human experience if the meaning component is missing. Hence, a more apt phrase would be "the event passed and we missed experiencing it." Discovering meaning entails going through the processes of intelligence and reason. While meaning emerges out of the first level it is only truly elicited by the action of understanding and arrives at its fullness in the act of judging. This coming to "what is meant" means moving away from the child's world of immediacy to the adult's world—a world mediated by meaning.[12] An experience is immediate when the object is directly present. But when objects are processed through imagination, language, symbol, memory, and new understandings, experiences become richer. This larger world mediated by meaning is the real world in which we live out our lives.

As our world of experience deepens meanings change. This in turn alters self-consciousness. We inherit particular meaning systems as well as learning from societies. Ultimately, it is through processing such systems through our own experiencing that personal meanings emerge. These change over time and may alter greatly over a lifetime. When our experiences are authentically processed we move toward becoming more human.

Lonergan distinguishes four realms of meaning: the realms of common sense, theory, interiority, and full transcendence and notes that the type of language used in relation to these realms differs. The first, common sense, refers to people and things in relation to oneself. Its meanings arise from an accumulation of experiences that qualify and correct one another. We express such meanings in ordinary everyday language. The second realm, theory, examines the questions of differences, congruences, and relations that emerge from concrete living. It leads to the discovery of answers that enable us to make sense of our lives. The language of this realm is more theoretical and at times even technical. In a third realm, interiority surfaces as we question our own ability to know. Questions such as What am I doing when I am knowing? Why is doing that knowing? What do I know when I do it? arise as we try to discern how we know what we know. The language of this realm can be termed *self-appropriation*.[13]

These first three realms, while moving toward greater self-transcendence as well as predisposing toward full transcendence, remain at the human level. In other words, divinity has not yet emerged within consciousness. The final realm of full transcendence, the realm of the unrestricted desire for knowledge and love is the realm in which knowledge and love of Holy Mystery enters awareness. The language of this realm is essentially prayer and prayerful silence.

Being able to shift between these different realms requires learning, time, and humility. Up to recent times, people managed with the support of commonsense wisdom and/or through the endorsing of certain theories or dogmas. Today, such supports can prove insufficient. More precise use of the transcendental precepts combined with self-appropriation gives us the ability to articulate what is going on in our deepest self as we live within the setting of our own story and the story of world history. If we are unable to be in touch with and take a stand on what lies deep within us, and especially the values we hold important, and simply rely on common sense or theory, we will be incapable of treating complex and ultimate issues in a reasonable and loving manner. Before articulation must obviously come the experience itself. Karl Rahner says in this context "The Christian of the future will either be a mystic, one who has experienced something, or will cease to be anything at all."[14] It is this "experiencing of something" and trusting and developing these experiences rather than largely living off the convictions of others that makes possible and sustains authentic human living.

Finally, it needs to be noted that while relationships, a sense of one's embodied self, culture, and places can profoundly influence human experience, none of these factors are *conscious* innate capacities.[15] Lonergan's concern in elaborating on the nineteen conscious operations was to show the potential they offer when exercised in a patterned way in the journey to becoming fully human. We all operate on the different levels of consciousness with varying degrees of intensity and in accordance with our capacities.[16] No one could constantly operate at the heightened level of all the operations in ordinary living. A more realistic goal would be to heighten our consciousness around whatever activity we are presently doing. For example, our experience is enriched when attention is fully focused on listening to a particular piece of music and, at times, on oneself as the hearer and the capacity for depth experiencing that this subjectively offers. Widening the range of the operations, when it is appropriate to do so, also expands experience.

In summary, we experience greater surety and richness when we notice more accurately what our senses, imaginings, and feelings present to us, when we struggle to understand whatever issues emerge, when we gather and evaluate that evidence, and when we finally make decisions in accordance with our core values and then translate all of this into concrete human living—by their fruits you shall know them (see Matt 12:33).

2

The Religious Dimension of Human Experience

With an understanding of human experience in place, this second chapter explores the religious dimension of that experience. While the phrase *religious experience* is acceptable and commonly used, an alternative and preferred option is *faith experience*.[1] In this chapter both phrases are used interchangeably. The ineffable dimension of religious experience always means that attempts to describe it are problematic and limited. Hopefully a thread of logic is discerned in this book's attempt to gather a variety of understandings, a factor that has led to some degree of overlap of thought.

Discovering the Divine through the Transcendental Precepts

The subjective experiencing of the four transcendental precepts, as described in chapter 1, opens up the "God question." For example, at the first level, the question of how we account for the presence of good and evil in the world arises. At the level of inquiry, questions about the possibility of an intelligible universe and the source of that intelligibility can surface. At the judgment level of questioning, Is this probably so? a connection with the possible existence of a reality that transcends our present knowledge of the real can enter awareness. Finally, at the fourth level, discerning choices around value can evoke the vexed question as to what criteria we use when evaluating and making actual choices. In particular, this leads to *the* challenging question: Is there a source beyond individual conscience and, if there is, what is that source?[2]

When we authentically question ourselves, especially through the use of the transcendental process, we can be led to the question of an ultimate transcendent—the God question. The question that questions questioning itself is something inherent within the human spirit and this ability to reach beyond our present level of knowing, loving, and choosing always remains unrestricted. The human heart and mind forever desires the "more" of truth, the "more" of love, and it is precisely within this activity of reaching, rather than arriving—which is never possible—that the space for the Divine lies. A person at this level of questioning has moved to the fourth unrestricted realm of full transcendence—the domain of faith experience.

While God lies beyond all human experiencing, the divine presence is also immanent and therefore can and does consciously enter human experience. This happens within human activities and especially when we yearn for the more of truth and love, when we open ourselves to appreciate beauty, or when we witness or attempt to carry out the good deed. An apprehension or intuition of the mystery element in these activities can beckon us toward intimations of ultimate mystery. This becomes possible through our innate capacity for reaching for what lies beyond strictly human capacities, namely, toward further graced[3] forms of knowing and loving. When these activities are graced they become transformed in the sense that values and especially the core value—authentic human love—are transvalued. When such activities are graced, they still remain human activities but are now filled with the divine presence.

Part of this moving beyond includes moving away from a form of thinking that is aware of either an overly transcendent or overly immanent presence of God. We need a sense of a God who is other, holy, and before whom we feel inadequate and stand in awe of, as well as needing a sense of a God who is one with us. God's immanence becomes intimately close when the Godself becomes present within personal activities, for example, when sensing, feeling, knowing, or loving. This activity may remain at the unconscious level or, alternatively, may either gradually or dramatically emerge into consciousness. Faith experience occurs through awareness of this profound reality that lies beyond the self.

Views of Selected Authors on Religious Experience

The initiator of the vast range of literature that has subsequently appeared on this topic over the past century was William James.[4] His

Varieties of Religious Experience gave interest and new insight into the need for examining experience as a fundamental element in all religions. As a result the term *experience* is today seen as more fundamental than the word *religion* in determining what the phrase *religious experience* means. His interest was in personal rather than institutional religion. Today James's work has its critics but there are also those who view the present-day emphasis on experience within the phrase religious experience as stemming from James. It is significant today that interfaith dialogue is very much focusing on whether this core element within religious experience is common to all religions.

However one attempts to describe religious experience, it is within ordinary human experiencing that God, the Sacred One, is to be found. Nicholas Lash elaborates on this point when he says that there is no absolute need to set aside special "Sunday-places" in order to find the Divine.[5] He draws attention to the fact that the primitive faith of early Hindu religion—the Vedic people—had no temples, priesthood, or ceremonials, yet each felt they had open access to their maker. He subsequently makes the observation that the more educated Hindu, Jew, or Christian of today is tending to leave aside the external religious trappings in an effort to perceive "everything that is" in relation to its source—the Mystery of God. Grasping this fact means for Lash that "it is God's love which sets in order all those other loves by which, if we love well, God is thereby loved."[6]

Experiences of the Divine should not be equated only with intense experiences. Normally such experiences tend to lie beneath and beyond whatever we are experiencing giving them life and significance. The presence of Holy Mystery in all our experiencing is real and enters conscious experiences as part known and in part not known. Abraham Maslow warns against overly seeking "peak" experiences through drugs, the exotic, or the unusual, which are always transient and which turn one away from the world.[7] Instead he advocates "plateau" experiences that emerge from holistic attitudes and integrated living, which result in more contemplative, calm, and joyous forms of experiencing. He does not actually say that peak or plateau experiences are necessarily religious in nature but he does indicate that it is the fruits of such experiences that insinuate that they could be religious.

Antoine Vergote mentions prereligious experience, which he describes as experiences that open up a depth or intensity dimension that can lead toward religious experience.[8] These could be experiences of power and the need for peace and guidance. He senses that modern science's opening up to the vastness of the universe could provide the basis for a cosmic type of prereligious experience.

Religious experience is described by Dermot Lane as an ordinary experience that at the same time is an experience of *something else.*[9] He suggests that "God is co-experienced and co-known" through our varying forms of human experiencing. Our experience is a mediated experience rather than an immediate one.[10] This mediated experience of God comes to us through a myriad of mediations such as creation, history, the incarnation, incidents of everyday life, and our own thinking and loving. For instance, this experience may arise from or result in feelings of intense joy or profound darkness, or it may lie somewhere in between this range of feelings. It can disturb us, make demands, offer surprises.

The mediating factor for faith experience is personal human experiences, a point that is reiterated many times in this book. Experiences of God are experiences that sustain, deepen, and surpass other human experiences. For example, when we have an experience of the wonders of creation and that experience includes within it some awareness of the Divine then we are having a religious experience. Paul endorses this form of experiencing: "Ever since the creation of the world his eternal power and divine nature, invisible though they are, have been understood and seen through the things he has made" (Rom 1:20).

A key issue is not so much how God becomes present to us but rather how we experientially make ourselves present to the Divine, who is always and everywhere present. Experiencing God is not merely an experience of something perceived in the world *out there*, but rather it is an experience of the ground of all our seeing, knowing, loving, experiencing and as the ultimate source of all meaningfulness. God cannot but be coactive, copresent in all things otherwise that thing would fail to exist. "In him we live and move and have our being" (Acts 17:28).

Wayne Teasdale articulates religious experience as follows: "to experience God...is to experience 'that which is'"; it generates "a *tast-*

ing knowledge of God."[11] The intimacy of this God experience is made possible since God's gift of self to us constitutes our very being and thereby is contained within every movement of our hearts and minds.

The truthfulness of an experience, for Arthur Deikman, is judged by its sense of realness.[12] This quality of realness changes as we become less attached to exterior reality and more to our own interiority. Living the self-transcendent precepts facilitates this shift to a profound sense of realness coming from within our own experiencing—and in the present context within our own religious experiencing.

Religious/Faith Experience—An Experience of Falling in Love/Being in Love

Being in love from a Lonerganian perspective occurs within the fourth transcendental precept—*be responsible*—since this level includes the activity of loving.[13] The religious experience of being in love while analogous to the intimate love between people, is also distinct from it. All the precepts reveal our capacity for self-transcendence and the capacity for religious love becomes most fully realized at the fourth level of consciousness through the experience of falling in love. This stage can proceed to the state of being in love, a state that colors, energizes, and, above all, transforms desires, attitudes, feelings, choice of values, and decisions.

Love, and especially intimate love, is experienced and expressed differently within varying sets of relationships such as between spouses/partners, parents and children, among friends. Ultimately, there is the intimacy of a loving relationship with the Divine offered to each member of the human family. Paul describes this love as "God's love flooding our hearts through the Holy Spirit given to us" (Rom 5:5). It is an experience of being loved without qualifications or conditions. The presence of the Spirit is made known through an experience of deep joy and peace. This does not exclude God's loving presence being experienced in situations of turmoil and deep suffering. In fact, that love may become more keenly awakened and known through pain-filled experiences.

Religious experience is conscious but not known in the ordinary understanding of this term and is therefore *an experience of mystery*. More accurately it is "an experience of love focused on mystery."[14]

God, the term chosen for millennia to indicate the ultimate Other, is transposed by Lonergan to "transcendent mystery." Mystery, while remaining unknown, is not nothing at all but rather is the to-be-known for those who become aware of the fuller transcendent element within human existence and particularly within human loving. "[This] mystery is not merely attractive but fascinating; to it one belongs; by it one is possessed;...inasmuch as it is conscious without being known, the gift of God's love is an experience of the holy."[15]

Religious experience brings with it a horizon that is utterly new and contains within it the realization that personal knowing, loving, and choosing are transformed by God's love. This is all possible through consciousness itself having undergone a conversion due to the gift of God's love occupying the ground and root of the fourth and highest level of human consciousness. When the falling in love stage moves to the state of being in love, an individual not only establishes a relationship with God but this relationship dictates their way of being and living in the world; it forms their worldview.

A core characteristic of this love from the human side of the divine-human encounter is self-surrender. This love does not result from personal knowing or choosing, it happens, it becomes reality, through the free acceptance of a gift. The gift is God's love and since "God is love" (1 John 4:8) the gift given is the gift of the Godself. The act of saying yes to the gift of the Godself is the act of faith. This gift always remains gift. God's gift of Godself is never conditioned by any thing and that includes human knowing. Grace is operative in all stages of the process including the dynamic state of being in love that is continuously supported by operative grace. Our initial response is brought about by religious conversion as is our ongoing response of saying yes. Both responses to the gift of the Godself are made possible through cooperative grace.[16] Authentic religious experiences lead to seeking further knowledge of the Godself. This is a step that follows on from the primary experience of love.

God's gift of Godself always precedes our knowledge of God and included in that gift is given an orientation to an unknown that contains within it a seeking of further knowledge of God. This knowledge of God is a "knowledge born of religious love"[17] and being a loving knowledge it seeks ever-deeper union with Holy Mystery. This happens as a person allows oneself to be grasped by this mystery of love. The phrase *unitive love* is an apt way of describing what inter-personally lies at the heart of the divine-human relationship. It is also appropriate in describing the fruit of this unifying relationship—a fruit that leads to engagement and a seeking of oneness with human-ity and the universe. This service of unity is characterized by its inclu-sive form of love and helps embody in some mysterious way the prayer of Jesus "that they may all be one" (John 17:21).

The Being-in-Love Experience from the Perspective of Other Authors

Erich Fromm saw the religious form of love arising out of the human need to overcome separateness and its desire to achieve union.[18] The maturity of an individual's human love of God tends to flow from one's fundamental concept of God and one's image of God is linked with levels of adult faith. Fromm writes "The love of God is neither the knowledge of God in thought, nor the thought of one's love of God, but the act of experiencing oneness with God."[19] Another author, C. S. Lewis,[20] distinguishes four types of love: affection, friendship, eros, and charity. Grace can transform all human loving into its deep-est form—charity. A difficulty arises, however, first in our impover-ished ability to receive this charity/agape. A second difficulty arises in how we express it. Charity/agape is most chiefly manifested in show-ing love to other people.

The West's understanding of *true love* almost solely in romantic terms is documented by Robert Johnson.[21] He suggests that this form of love has supplanted religion and has become a mass phenomenon. The psychological state of being in love is based on the belief that through this state one has discovered ultimate meaning to life. This state, especially in its earlier stages, offers an experience of being complete/whole and is accompanied by feelings of intensity and maybe even ecstasy. However, romantic love does not satisfy due to its erroneous expectation of the other person continuously supplying intense positive feelings. A consequence of the unfulfilled expecta-tions that ensue turn to feelings of loneliness, alienation, and frus-tration. Only Western society makes romance the basis of loving relationships, and Johnson suggests that it is only by breaking through its false assumptions and expectations that a new awareness of oneself and one's intimate relationships are discovered. Romantic love is an overwhelming experience and only when one learns to manage the power, potential, and beauty of this love and let go of its illusions will this problem in society become a rich opportunity.

The foundation of Gerald May's thought on religious love is based on the view that "God" is never "other."[22] By making God into an object, we separate ourselves from God. This results in us feeling apart from, rather than part of God (and indeed of all of God's creation). This coparticipation that exists between God and ourselves may remain hidden from consciousness. For those gifted with this faith knowledge, the phrase "God in me and I in God" describes more accurately, even if incompletely, the intimacy of this union rather than the more misleading terminology of "God and me." It is through contemplative love that we become aware of and realize the intimacy of this union. This love, founded on contemplative faith, is a faith that is distinguishable from beliefs. Faith, for May, is a way of being, a way that is open and empty to all specifics—it "is like a continual fire of goodness, warming and illuminating every breath." Contemplative love is similar to faith in that it is not a love of some *thing* or a love that leads to the exclusion of others. Like faith, love is "a way of being that we become part of: a flowing energy of willingness, an eternal yes resounding with every heart beat."[23] While speaking about contemplative love, he says such an experience, if one can even call it an experience, lies beyond words and understanding.

Louis Roy uses the phrase *mystical consciousness* as a way of describing religious experience that is pervasive and permanent, in contrast to the transitory nature of other transcendent experiences.[24] He suggests mystical consciousness is a different kind of knowing to normal knowledge and that this word *different* conveys that there is not *unknowing* but rather knowledge of a different kind. He points out that if mystical experience were not a conscious event, no one would ever have been able to talk about it. Roy also describes a difference between the ordinary believer and the one who is gifted with a mystical consciousness, in that the latter takes this mystical consciousness dimension of human experiencing more seriously and is open to a more radical self-surrendering.

A final contribution is from Bede Griffiths.[25] He lived for years in India as a Christian while living close to those of Hindu faith.

While respectful and appreciative of both faiths he remained aware of their essential differences. He says that love lies at the heart of Christian mysticism whereas in both Hinduism and Buddhism the central focus is on transformation of consciousness.

Distinguishing between Faith and Belief

An important issue that surrounds the question of faith is being able to distinguish between what is meant by the terms *faith*, *belief*, and *religious belief*, while at the same time noting that these are not separate entities. This fact is manifest in the close intertwining of faith and belief that occurs within normal religious experiencing.

Faith

The gift of faith is a loving knowledge that is born of God's love flooding our hearts (see Rom 5:5). The act of faith is our (gifted) responding to the reception of this gift. While always a gift, faith is essentially an affective choice as opposed to an intellectual assent— a saying yes to the gift of a God who is love.

Faith, traditionally described as *lumen fidei*, brings enlightenment, since the orientation it gives toward the mystery of love enables us to discern God's revelation of the Godself. Faith can be imagined as a light, a light that primarily acts on the will (at the same time leaving the will its freedom), thereby changing its orientation and inclinations. It plucks at our hearts of stone and changes them into hearts of flesh (see Ezek 36:26). This choice of responding in love to the God of love, leads to attempts to articulate this experience. This is done in the usual way through the processes of understanding, judging, and deciding; however, these cognitional processes are now illuminated by faith's light, which, in the Christian tradition, brings about the decision to believe the word of God.

The experience of faith—an experience of a loving knowing— while always remaining an experience of mystery, also has a quality of certainty about it. This certainty can be deepened when faith seeks further understanding that can result in our faith life maturing toward a deepened loving knowing. In summary, faith can be understood as a threefold reality: the gift of faith itself, the response of receiving that gift, and the living out of that response in daily life.

Belief

The major portion of what we know, be it scientific or common-sense knowledge, is not personally generated but comes through belief in the words and experiences of others. Coming to know something is largely therefore a group enterprise. No one can be constantly reinventing the wheel; so it is mainly through belief that our understanding of truth is enlarged. Beliefs and belief systems change over time as new meanings emerge. A modern phenomenon has been a devaluing of belief, including religious belief. Today it is necessary to restore belief in belief by showing the necessity for belief in order that confusion, disillusionment, and a return to primitivism is counteracted. Individuals and communities need belief systems for both survival and development and this requires a constant discarding of beliefs that may over time have become distorted because of false misinterpretation or because of the availability of new knowledge.

Religious Belief

Faith is the reality that grounds religious belief, or, said in reverse, religious belief flows from faith.[26] It is faith that discerns the value not only of believing but also of believing the word of religion. Faith, however, is not something solitary but is also a gift that is to be shared with others; it is from this common communion with God that a religious community comes into being and religious beliefs emerge. People recognize in the faith of others a commonality of values, goals, ways of living, and ways of feeling about issues. It is this communion in faith that initiates varying forms of religious expression. This outward expression is what forms particular religious beliefs and in turn it is from these beliefs that traditions emerge. These traditions are gifts of God, yet at the same time these traditions are constantly in need of purification.

Up to recent times the norm has been that the "knowledge born of religious love"—that is, faith—has been discovered through the beliefs of a particular religious tradition. Today, however, many people in the West, while discarding certain beliefs or belief systems, may not necessarily be relinquishing their gift of faith. A further emerging factor is that alternative routes to coming to faith are opening up, for instance, from within the scientific world as well as through personal depth experiences. As a consequence there is a need to view this phenomenon through an understanding that discerns this difference between faith and religious belief.

An overidentification of faith with beliefs can lead to problems. The main difficulty has been the identification of faith with the acceptance of propositions through an act of intellectual assent.[27] This distortion is heightened when particular beliefs become associated with mere opinion or even with what is doubtful. So faith is not necessarily going bankrupt despite church attendance figures dropping. Largely empty churches play a powerful role in the popular perception that religion is no more. However from this fact alone we cannot say that faith is absent in people.

Manifestations of Religious Experience

Since religious/faith experience normally occurs on the fourth level of consciousness, the experience is not initially accompanied by acts of the senses, nor does it include acts of inquiry or reflection. Being a fourth level reality the experience becomes manifest in a concern about values, particularly the value of the good. These values are freely and responsibly chosen and are motivated by love. God's love is now the ground of personal deliberations and it is through these activities that God's love is experienced.

We can receive intimations of God's love without initially being able to name the experience. The knowledge born of love is a human experience that fits into the "infrastructure that is consciousness."[28] By heightening consciousness through adverting to the varying activities of consciousness, we can register or experience that infrastructure. The normal commonsense form of knowing is made available to us through the superstructure level of outer experience, whereas the inner form of knowing, where religious experience occurs, is an infrastructure type of conscious experience. This experience may be heard as a leading, middle, or low voice that can present itself as dominant, recurrent, intermittent, or fading. It may fit harmoniously with the rest of consciousness or alternatively may be heard in a dissonant fashion. These varying forms of experience could lead to greater depth or, alternatively, if not noted and fostered, may vanish altogether.[29]

At the same time our experiencing of a God who is love is earthed. Speaking from a Christian perspective, this means we are in contact with Christ; though always present, we encounter him in a sacramental manner.[30] It is through our communion with one another and especially with the poor, as well as our communion through the sacraments that Christ's presence is manifested.

Another important manifestation of religious experience is prayer. In a significant article, "The Mediation of Christ in Prayer," Lonergan points out that each person is immediate to themselves, and that this immediacy is known through our spontaneity, our living, and our loving, as opposed to our thinking about such things.[31] This immediate core of who we are is gifted with a reality that does not belong to human nature. That gift is Christ, who came to share the divine life and love with humanity and in an immediate way. This new reality enters conscious living through prayer but is present, in an unconscious way, if we remain in a state of grace, avoid sin, and do good deeds. For Lonergan, prayer is a habitual form of conscious living, which does not mean thinking about this new reality all the time, but is a reality that is present as something that we can easily turn to. It is a reality that can develop, and growth in prayer is revealed when immediacy of this graced self transforms our ways of conscious, spontaneous, and deliberate living. This life touches into every thought, word, and deed. So when our basic orientation in life is turned toward Holy Mystery, truth, beauty, love, and goodness, then all our human activity and, more explicitly, our prayers are referred to Christ.

No one apprehends God, Christ, the Spirit, as someone else does, be they apostle, saint, or anyone else. Rather, we apprehend God with our own unique apprehension. "It is as it were, putting on, acquiring our own view of him...in accord with our own capacities and individuality, in response to our own needs and failings. It has its foundation in tradition and revelation, but it arises from what is immediate in the subject."[32] It is this immediacy to oneself as revealed in living through acts such as reaching out to others, through activating as well as being touched by beauty, truth, goodness, and love that

Holy Mystery/the Sacred is discernible. This happens sometimes in an explicit way and other times in a more hidden manner.

Through the process of religious conversion, God's gift of love becomes "real to me from within."[33] An overflow of that love is the realization of the intelligibility, truth, and goodness of that love. That love draws us to pay attention to it in prayer and this prayer overflows into loving all that God loves. Finally, there is a movement of longing for closer union with the Divine. "An experience of love focused on mystery"[34] is the closest Lonergan gets to describing such a happening, and that other writers would term *mysticism*.

Writers on the mystical life, such as Karl Rahner, view it as one and the same thing as living our ordinary religious tradition. If "the Mystery we call God" is the focus of all religious experience then the mystical element must form an essential component to a study on the religious dimension of human experience. Others say that the mystical life means the ordinary life but with the additional note of living this life in a more committed way. Religious experience is available to everyone. There is no hierarchical order; hence, religious experience can occur within the commonsense level of experiencing as well as within the realm of interiority. Margaret Smith's perception of mysticism—as the vital element in all true religions—is extended by Richard Wood's words: "the greater mystics are those whose identification with their fellow human beings is more profoundly human." Wood's line of approach offers the clearest way of validating the authenticity of a religious experience.[35]

A manifestation of growth in religious experiencing is also shown in the movement from a predominantly active mode of living to a more receptive mode—a mode of self-surrender. Moving to greater receptivity is, for instance, essential for experiencing deeper love since love can only be received in receptive mode. Religious experience, which is brought about by receiving the gift of God's love, makes the receptive mode imperative. As the human-divine relationship grows the receptive mode becomes uppermost. A core human experience of receptive mode is sexual intercourse. Satisfying sexual experience is related to an individual's ability to relinquish control. A similarity with such letting go is called for in the reception of God's love/self being poured into the human heart. Receptive mode is not the desirable approach in every human situation so both active and receptive modes are required according to the demands of particular situations.

Ultimately it is always the fruitfulness of personal living—a living that clearly and consistently manifests a loving respect of oneself, others, and the universe—that is the clearest indicator of the genuineness of religious experiencing. This genuineness and how this has been understood and lived over two thousand years is offered to us within the Christian tradition.

Religious Experience as Understood within the Christian Tradition

First-Century Christianity

The initial question for early Christians was how contact with the Divine, as manifested in Jesus, was to be found and fostered. Their earliest answer was that Jesus' presence was found within the community to which one gained entrance through baptism (see Acts 2:37–47). Baptism led believers to proclaim Jesus as Lord and to adopt a wholly new form of living whose purpose was to become united with the risen Jesus (see Rom 6:1–4; 1:3–5).

The New Testament writings, set down between 50 and 100 CE, became the sources of knowledge and inspiration that fostered the faith of local communities. The emergence of Christian scriptures was a natural evolution that grew from the early disciples' familiarity with reading, interpreting, and being nourished by the Hebrew Bible. The early church members continued reading the Old Testament but from a christological perspective and the Christian scriptures became of utmost importance. A consciousness of the Divine presence took place within the exercise of reading, meditating, preaching, and teaching the biblical text. The distinctive elements that formed the core of early Christianity were its community setting, scripture, and sacramental practice (especially baptism and Eucharist).

Some passages from Paul and John are pertinent on the question of union with God. Paul stressed the centrality of love and knowledge in the realizing of this union, as the following texts illustrate. "I want to *know* Christ" (Phil 3:10); "*God's love has been poured into our hearts* through the Holy Spirit that has been given to us" (Rom 5:5).

At the time Paul writes (51 CE), the Christian community already had its own theological language that placed the word *agape*, with its specialized and rich meaning, at the center of the new religion. In the text on love (Rom 5:5 above) God's *agape* is shown to live in the heart of believers. The word *ekcheo* (meaning "to pour forth" or "flood"), used in Romans 5:5, suggests lavish giving or fullness. God's love is now the source of all love. This pouring implies the gift of a continuous relationship between the giver and the gift. Once given in baptism, the flow never stops. The metaphor of *being poured into* suggests the continuous nature of the pouring—so accepting God is not to accept God as a giver, or even as a gift, but rather as a giving.

Twenty to thirty years later, the writers of John's gospel and letters moved to a deeper understanding of the meaning of a life of union with God through Christ. Jesus is presented as the enlightener who brings knowledge of God to humanity, for instance: "I am the way, and the truth, and the life" (John 14:6); "If you know me, you know my Father also" (John 14:7). The heart of the knowing that Jesus brings is love, as is found in the foundational statement "God is love" (1 John 4:8).

The Johannine writers often used metaphors to describe Jesus' loving union with his Father and to indicate the intimate union that is available to disciples. Jesus' closeness to his Father is portrayed in the prologue's metaphor of his being "close to the Father's heart" (John 1:18). The uniqueness of Jesus' union with his Father is manifest in the statement "the Father and I are one" (John 10:30) and when Jesus addresses his Father "[you] are in me and I am in you" (John 17:21). That intimacy of indwelling, abiding, remaining, has moved from Paul's "in Christ" to John's "in me." This union is open to everyone: "I am in my Father, and you in me and I in you" (John 14:20). A metaphor describing this intimate sharing of life is "I am the vine, you are the branches" (John 15:5). To highlight the fact that the union in question is based on love are Jesus' words "As the Father has loved me, so I have loved you; abide in my love" (John 15:9).

This unitive love contains a self-sacrificing energy that leads to an emptying of the love received for the sake of others. The source of this self-emptying movement is the Father: "God so loved the world that *he gave* his only Son" (John 3:16). Jesus likewise loved the world so much that he *emptied himself* (see Phil 2:7). Before his death, he concretely showed how "having loved his own...he loved them to the end" (John 13:1) by washing the disciples' feet and in and through his death he "*gave up* his spirit" (John 19:30). The promise of the Spirit, "I will pour out my Spirit on all flesh" (Acts 2:17; Joel 3:1) from that moment became realized and, in a more personally intimate way, is "*poured into* our hearts" (Rom 5:5). Louis Dupré elaborates similarly: "To accept God is not to accept a 'giver' but a 'Giving.'"[36] The epitome of Jesus' love is manifest in his desire to share his Father's unique love for himself with others: "so that the love with which you loved me may be in them, and I in them" (John 17:26).

Ceslaus Spicq sees the opening verse to the scene of the washing of the feet as a solemn preface to the last part of the gospel.[37] Jesus' statement about loving the disciples "to the end" (John 13:1) is completed in his final words—"it is finished" (John 19:30). Spicq also parallels the washing of the feet preface with the earlier "God so loved the world" (John 3:16) and adds "all love of agape is active and gives itself, perfect agape inspires total sacrifice." The dynamic nature of this self-giving quality of love is on offer to all who wish to accept the demands of full Christian living. The initial call of a disciple is to be with Jesus (see Mark 6:7). Inherent in that call comes the knowledge that one is "sent out" (Luke 9:1) to proclaim the good news to "all nations" (Matt 28:19).

A further expression of this unitive love is the union that leads to communion—a communion of sharing love and life with others. The model of communion is the Trinity where each of the divine persons gives their self away to let the other be.[38] The final desire of Jesus that we share in the actual inner trinitarian life of loving communion is expressed in his prayer "that they may all be one. As you Father are in me and I am in you..." (John 17:21). Peter's words about becoming "participants of the divine nature" (2 Pet 1:4) endorse this truth.

Christian Tradition from the Second to the Twentieth Century

It is noteworthy that all three monotheistic religions started with the personal *experiences* of their founders. It is also true that religions only retain their vitality when their members retain some *expe-*

rience of the transcendent and in a way that has some affinity with the believer's founder. This *experience*, whether of high or low intensity, belongs to the essence of religion. It is in this sense that religion contains a mystical core.

The New Testament and sacramental life have formed the two central bases through which Christian tradition has been handed down. Teaching and preaching were important ways of handing on the faith, but, in addition, tradition unfolded through the recorded experiences of people, principally the saints and, from the medieval period on, through the lives and writings of mystics.

A two-pronged approach to describing Christian tradition from the second century to contemporary times is being used. The first is to describe in some detail the two fundamental paths out of which religious experiences came into being throughout this period. The second gives a broad outline of the historical periods and their varying points of emphasis in relation to religious experience.

THE TWO APPROACHES OR WAYS TO GOD
WITHIN THE CHRISTIAN TRADITION

The two approaches that have been manifested throughout Christianity, especially since the fourth century, are the apophatic and cataphatic forms of religious experience. *Apophatic* is taken from the Greek *apophanai*, "to speak out," "to deny," and *cataphatic* comes from the Greek *kataphasis*, "to speak positively, or in an affirmative manner." These terms emerged due to the development of exaggerated claims concerning rational speech about God.

The *apophatic* approach, stressed by some of the Greek fathers of the church and particularly Gregory of Nyssa, focused on an experiential knowledge of God that goes beyond the mere power of human beings. The apophatic way refuses to identify God by human concepts since God transcends all that can be known of him. This approach, while not irrational, sees that God is best reached through forgetting and unknowing and through an emptiness of mind that is no longer supported by concepts, images, and symbols. Those gifted with this type of experience describe it in words like silence, simplicity, oneness, absence, void, emptiness, darkness—a darkness that can for some be filled with light as well as delight. An apophatic form of prayer lays emphasis on meditation.[39]

Thomas Merton offers a helpful modern analysis of the apophatic way.[40] He had a rich understanding of the primordial religious experience and particularly how it was lived within the apophatic Christian tradition. This later proved helpful in his interfaith dialogues. After his dialoguing with Eastern mystics, Merton saw a radical shift occurring within modern Christian consciousness. The shift was a movement from an experience of stability, comfort, and security, which had been prevalent for centuries, toward something more radical. A Christian today experiences him- or herself as a modern Christian man or woman and, therefore, in a way that is dissimilar to early Christian experiencing. History affects levels of human experiencing due to changed perceptions. The radically changed perceptions of the last fifty years have affected religious thinking and experiencing. Merton views the ongoing discussions on this new Christian self-understanding as resulting from Vatican II's renewed theology.

He notes that the present-day emphasis on human consciousness can lead to the danger of the ego-self becoming imprisoned in its own consciousness. When this occurs the ego-self becomes the arbiter of all personal thinking and willing. Merton suggests that focusing on the centrality of the self inevitably led to the "death of God." A further reason for this "death" was making God into an object, an object that was then maintained by the wills of individuals. Letting go of this "God-object," in favor of God as subject, as the ground of all being, is closer to the truth. This divine ground underlies and is the source of consciousness. When consciousness is gifted in personal experience with an intuition of its own ground—the divine—a transformed self emerges. The new self-awareness that ensues from this transformed self moves toward self-giving, letting go,[41] and becomes aware that it functions from God and for others. The *for others* arises out of the realization that this divine ground is everywhere and that it is through and in this ground that everything else is encountered. The transformed self intuits the divine ground as a ground of openness, generosity, goodness, and love, which diffuses itself as gift. Everyone has received this gift, but not all come to consciously acknowledge this reality. This divine ground is not experienced as either divine immanence or transcendence, but rather as grace or presence. This presence is neither out there, nor within, as some *thing*, but rather is experienced wherever love and freedom are present. Such an experience requires an inner illumination. Everything, and that includes the self, becomes most real when seen in relation to its source or ground.

For a Christian, this experience of transformation is a kenotic transformation due to the self-emptying of the contents of our ego-consciousness. The void this creates enables God's light and love to become manifest. The transformed person experiences loving as a co-loving with God's love, or alternatively, as being loved by God's love mediated through the love of others or through mediating factors in our inner or outer environment. The transformed individual remains distinct from one's ground/God. Yet the individual does not focus on self as separate, since there can also be an experience of being "in Christ" or of the Holy Spirit being within the self. This experience of oneness with Christ, which includes a sense of oneness with the whole body of Christ, is described by Paul as: "It is no longer I who live, but it is Christ who lives in me" (Gal 2:20). This self-emptying or kenotic path is the opposite of the self-fulfillment route and offers a preeminent way of attaining one's true self.

Merton concretizes all of the above when he refers to the modern person's need to be liberated from "his inordinate self-consciousness." How that is done, he suggests, is simply by being who one is, accepting things as they are, and working with them as best one can. The best help to carrying this out is to turn to "the simple lessons of the Gospel."[42] These remarks show Merton's effort in his later years to reconcile the apophatic and cataphatic traditions. He criticized those who focused exclusively on the apophatic way, despite his own writings mainly emphasizing this tradition.

An interest has opened up over recent decades in regard to the expansion of human consciousness. Meditation is seen as a key way that leads to this exploration. People endorse the practice of meditation for a multiplicity of reasons, such as for health, relaxation, personal integration, and some for religious purposes. Self-transcendence is an essential element in all forms of meditation. Some meditators, however, appear closed to the possibility of anything beyond self-transcendence while others claim a transcendent power.[43] Christians acknowledge a personal Transcendent Other. Also some meditators' emphasis is on personal effort, with little acknowledgment given to the gift dimension that is considered essential within Christian theology. However, real benefit is available through a serious practice of meditation and is advocated by practitioners who come from different faiths or from none. A committed Christian teacher of psychosynthesis echoes Assagioli: "it [psychosynthesis and its meditative practices] brings you to the threshold."[44] For this commentator, meditative practices were seen as a prelude to Christian prayer.

Transpersonal psychologists and spiritual directors are conscious of possible dangers when prolonged forms of meditation are practiced. Nontranspersonal psychologists' assumptions are based on the fact that there is only the natural world and, therefore, the dimension of the Transcendent Other is not available to them when their meditator clients come looking for help in this area. The need for spiritual guidance has been recognized for centuries within Christianity, because of the danger of illusions and delusions. As meditation deepens, a letting go of one's ego is required. If this is embarked on before someone has reached some level of integration, psychological harm can occur. Even those whose integration levels are adequate can experience an acute sense of being lost. The experience of the loss of one's ego is not a question of a loss of self. Warning, support, or encouragement, whichever are appropriate, may be necessary in this experience of "lostness."

The second approach, the *cataphatic* or affirmative way, is where religious experience primarily occurs within the happenings of ordinary human living. One could describe this route as the ordinary route of most believers. This approach is no less mystical, in that the goal of those who follow this path is always union with Holy Mystery, the Sacred. The heart of this way is in finding God within the ordinary circumstances of personal living. In order to understand this way, certain key qualities that assist the cataphatic approach have been selected.

A central quality in understanding the cataphatic dimension is *transparency*. Coming to an awareness of a transparent, rather than an opaque, view of reality facilitates the surfacing of an orientation toward the mystery element within life, and hence the discovery of the presence of mystery in the ordinary happenings of living. Entering mystery comes about in many ways; a significant way for some occurs through crises and difficulties. Paradoxically, knowledge itself can become a way to mystery, since the more knowledge gained and solutions to problems discovered, the more the mystery element may emerge as questions begin to outweigh answers. In Christianity, one of the features of mystery is its extraordinary identification with the mundane. This is not surprising because of the wondrous humility of the incarnation, where the mystery of ultimate reality becomes incarnate in a particular person: Jesus. In this event the mystery we call God became human and so limited by factors such as time, geography, and culture.

We can shrink from the mystery present in the ordinary by domesticating it, or we can accept it lovingly in faith. The ordinary includes not just natural realities but also the new technological world that forms part of modern existence. This cataphatic way is understood more clearly when faith is perceived as a perspective that focuses not so much on what we see or don't see, but rather on the way we see reality. For a Christian, faith looks at reality in a *trust-filled* manner—a way that gives ultimate meaning to everything, despite the times when doubt and suffering prevail. It is this faith that leads to the recognition of the divine ground as the source and sustainer of all that exists and, as a consequence, to responding in respect and appreciation to the whole of creation. Pierre Teilhard de Chardin was gifted with a mystical view of matter and the whole evolutionary process. His outer vision as a scientist formed a harmonious unity with his inner vision.[45] The latter was surely inspired by Ignatius of Loyola, whose emphasis on finding God in all things became central to the Jesuit tradition.

Another key notion in relation to the cataphatic path is *transformation* since it is through this process of finding God in all things that a fuller self-transformation becomes possible. The transformed self is in turn the validation as well as the fruit of living an authentic cataphatic way of life. Personal transformation is the fundamental sign in discerning the authenticity of an individual's union with God in both the apophatic and cataphatic traditions. Transformation is a more appropriate category to describe an individual's union with God than attending to the perceived attributes of the religious experience itself. A result of this transformation is developing an attitude of detached involvement. This allows a Christian to challenge the world, without denying or trying to escape from it. In Christlike terms, this means engaging fully in the world while at the same time neither renouncing nor getting lost in it. It is about enjoying things, while not using them for personal gain that requires preventing things becoming ends in themselves. Ultimately, its concern is learning to love the world the way God loves the world, namely, in a non-possessive way, and doing so out of gratitude.

The ordinariness of the cataphatic approach makes it difficult to speak about it. The experience itself is sometimes more easily explained in terms of a *journey*—a further key word in describing this approach. When genuine, this path is ethical and apostolic as well as mystical. From a Christian perspective it is the way of discipleship and as such it is a love affair. If the background of this journey is real life, as it must be, then this means it is also political. All authentic forms of mysticism lead to intense forms of engagement with the world, a relationship Jürgen Moltmann terms "political discipleship."[46] Because mystics have found their true self, they are more enabled to give that self to others. In general, mystical living that sees the Divine in all things has a greater capacity to experience each moment more intensely. This way of living is demanding and entails the suffering of many little deaths. However, the transformation that results from such experiences leads to the enlivening experiences of many little resurrections, especially experiences of love. According to Moltmann, the mysticism of everyday life is the deepest mysticism of all.

Gerald May, already referred to, combines the apophatic and cataphatic approaches. He also chooses the idea of *journey* as a legitimate approach to religious experiencing, since it avoids focusing too much on core experience moments where people can tend to give up when the emotional element wanes. The journey approach can sustain long dry spells, whereas an overly affective approach can be too subjective and tends to assume that individuals can bring about their religious experiences. For May, the essence of religious experience is "an uncluttered appreciation of existence, a state of mind or a condition of the soul that is simultaneously wide-awake and free from all preoccupation, preconception and interpretation. It is a wonder-filled yet utterly simple experience."[47] The journey is primarily about appreciation rather than comprehension, and what one appreciates is the encounter with mystery that lies at the heart of existence. Openness and courage are needed to surrender oneself to this mystery.

Self-surrender is another quality, and one that is central to May's thought.[48] Human experiencing, he suggests, is largely of two kinds: the self-defining kind or the self-surrender kind. It is the latter that leads to unitive experience. When a unitive experience occurs spontaneously we feel swept up, caught, wide awake, and alert, and time seems to stand still. All worries and desires evaporate, leaving everything perfect just as it is. As the experience comes to a close, awe, wonder, or other feelings arise, including a sense of rightness, of having been "at one." From his experience with patients and directees, May believes such experiences are common, frequent, and universal and occur in children as well as in those with mild intellectual disability. The ordinary happenings of life, like walking to the shops, meeting a friend, or taking a shower, can be the locus of unitive experiences. He has the impression that brief unitive experiences happen numerous times each day. The impact of these experiences varies; often they are simply forgotten.

An experience of unitive love flows from recognizing the divine ground of our own existence and the ground of all creation as a loving ground. Awareness of this love, knowing it,[49] is gift. Divine love is available to all, but because it involves surrender of one's importance and control, this love is not always let to flourish. Connectedness with life, with reality in all its forms, calls forth the mystery of love. "The ecstasy of agapic love is characterized by an awesome joining *with* the rest of the world, becoming a part of it. In an erotic 'high' the world disappears in love. In the spiritual 'high' the world appears in love" and one is drawn to becoming "a servant *of* humanity."[50]

Like Merton on the apophatic approach, Karl Rahner has been chosen as someone who had keen insight when describing the cataphatic tradition. Not only did Rahner write about mystery and mysticism but he is recognized publicly as a mystic. Harvey Egan describes Rahner as the most significant mystical theologian of the twentieth century. "*Mystery*" and the "*Mystery we call God*" lie at the center of Rahner's vast range of writings. Particularly striking are his writings on the mysticism of daily life. What lies behind all forms of mystical experiencing is, for him, the experience of God as the mystery "who haunts every human heart."[51]

A collection of Rahner's thoughts from his encyclopedia articles provides background to his understanding of the mysticism of daily life.[52] God, the incomprehensible one, comes as mystery and remains always mystery. God cannot communicate the Godself as something finite but always as mystery, even in eternity. While never being able to speak adequately about mystery, mystery can and does become real and known through grace. Mystical experience is nothing different from the ordinary life of grace and it is the experiencing of this mystery that is the essence of transcendence. While the ground of human existence is the mystery of God, who gives himself in love, everything that exists has its ground in this mystery of love including the mysterious nature of original sin. For the Christian, through the mystery of the incarnation, even secularity itself has been assumed by Christ's humanity. The Christ event led to a transfiguration of all reality.

Accepting Loving Mystery as the undertow of human existence is the primordial mystical experience. Surrendering to the depths of one's humanity is where one encounters this mystery of love. All expressions of that humanity in work or play, prayer or laughter, eating, sleeping or lovemaking, are vehicles through which Loving Mystery is present in a hidden manner. Rahner distinguishes between self-mysticism, nature mysticism, and God mysticism. God mysticism is an experience of Loving Mystery that can and does occur within the humdrum daily happenings, whether they are connected with nature, self, or other. Most profoundly one is led into Loving Mystery through acts of faith, hope, and love. Experiences of mystery include the following: an awareness of being addressed by what no longer has a name; the feeling of being protected by mystery; a realization that within this mystery lies the source of forgiveness, salvation, and an eternal home.

Rahner claims that natural altered states of consciousness are simply that: "*only* natural." For such acts to be authentically mystical they need to be radicalized by God's grace, which is always on offer but needs to be accepted. This gift of grace can be refused. Graced mystical experiences are not distinguished from the experiences of ordinary Christian existence. Neither are these experiences to be seen in an elitist way in the sense of being a higher stage of the Christian life in grace. Intense experiences of the Spirit may be an indicator of a Christian's acceptance of God's self-communication through grace. This is as far as Rahner goes in relation to altered states of consciousness, as well as certain psychological or paranormal phenomena that may accompany intense experiences.

Experiencing Loving Mystery is similar to the expression "experiencing the Spirit" since the Spirit is the Mystery of God's loving communication. All Christians are gifted with an experience of the Spirit in the midst of everyday experience, but this reality is commonly hidden or overlooked. How one experiences the Spirit is outlined in the following dense passage:

> In this unnamed and unsignposted expanse of our consciousness there dwells that which we call God. The mystery pure and simple that we call God is not a special, particularly unusual piece of objective reality, something to be added to and included in the other realities of our naming and classifying experience. He is the comprehensive though never comprehended ground and presupposition of our experience and of the objects of that experience. He is experienced in this strange experience of transcendence.[53]

The experience of expansiveness is manifest in our activities of knowing and willing. It is the experiencing of these activities that allows, makes possible, the experience of their ground—which is the experience of the Spirit. This experience largely remains unreflected, yet is always there. It is akin to the light of the sun that cannot always be seen yet is always there. At times chinks of light appear through manifestations of goodness, beauty, and love as well as darkness and suffering, which alert an individual to the presence of the Spirit. All actual life experiences are experiences of the Spirit, whether this is known reflectively or not, since the ultimate depth of human experiencing is the Spirit. In Ignatian language, Rahner summarizes the mysticism of everyday life as the discovering of God in all things. This is facilitated by regarding no one way to God as being *the* way but rather to seek him in all ways. In homely terms, he invites one to let oneself go in this experience of the Spirit, to savor this vivifying experience, to make sure life in the Spirit is drunk pure and not merely tasted as mere seasoning and garnish. The hour of grace comes when this spirit is recognized as the Holy Spirit and especially when one learns to taste fullness in emptiness.

To end this section on Rahner, a summary of two of his remarks is pertinent. First, look for such experiences, and second, seek specific experiences in which something like that can happen.

As has been shown, the cataphatic and apophatic ways are not totally separate paths; rather, both paths interweave with some people appearing to live lives that blend both traditions. Neither of these ways is superior to the other, they are simply different. A helpful quotation is the following: "What positive theology affirms about God is not false, but it is inadequate. Negative theology tells us that God excels in everything. While the apophatic way alone, without the cataphatic, may lead anywhere, cataphatic theology without an apophatic dimension, may build a system of concepts without an underlying experience of God."[54]

This closing section on the two basic approaches to mysticism turns to Louis Dupré, who gives a helpful analysis of some of today's difficulties.[55] He notes that while intensive religious experiences continue to exist, they are less likely to be supported because of the surrounding culture of materialism and individualism. While the quest for ultimate intelligibility persists, it is deflected by the more immediate need of remaining in control. He senses that the way to begin or revitalize the spiritual journey is to start from within. He suggests that believers and unbelievers need to confront the atheism, or feeling of absence, they find within the self as well as without. Discoveries can be made through experiencing a genuine sense of emptiness that could lead to finding meaning to this absence. Experiencing dissatisfaction, sensing something missing from life, even if it is not yet named, can be an opener to the transcendent. "The very godlessness of the world is invested with religious meaning, and a transcendent dimension opens up in this encounter with a world that has lost its divine presence."[56] This religious consciousness of absence has its roots in Christian tradition. It is the call to move beyond the familiar in order to explore further horizons. When the desert of modern atheism is confronted, it provides the space in which religious significance can be found. It is a process that allows reality to reveal itself. This presupposes an attitude of openness to the real. It requires a faith that can leap beyond present levels of experiencing. It is not a blind faith but one that partially emerges from within the very shallowness and dissatisfactions of present experience. The new religious consciousness will regard existence as both worldly and self-sufficient, as well as having a depth dimension. It will be a consciousness of world affirmation that discovers transcendence through engagement with a world and a human community that is perceived as both autonomous and dependent.

I will mention two phenomena that are noticeable in recent times before I close this section. First, there are certain elitist trends that sometimes appear around prayer and lifestyles that can lead to people's perceptions being limited with regard to the possibility of discovering God within life's ordinary experiences. Second, a lack of knowledge of what revelation (as transmitted through scripture, tradition, and Christian theology) has to say about authentic religious experience/faith experience is also apparent.

An Outline of Historical Periods within the Christian Tradition

The *first period*[57]—the time of the patristic theologians; the martyrs, ascetics, and monks; the councils of Chalcedon and Ephesus—lasted four hundred years. It concluded with Augustine. Bernard McGinn considers this period a time of foundations. The Greek influence in the second-century churches was strong and developed into the Eastern Orthodox Church's understanding that authentic Christianity is potentially mystical. The earlier Christian mystics of both East and West tended not to use their own personal experience of God as part of their teaching, in the way Teresa Avila and others did later.

The *second period*, 500–1200 CE, commences with Gregory the Great. Less significant happenings occurred during this time. Key figures included Benedict, who was responsible for the origins of Western Monasticism, and, later, Bernard and the Cistercian form of life.

The *third period*, 1200–1350 CE, was a time when classical mysticism flowered. Europe had become more integrated and new forms of religious life appeared. Such forms included the two mendicant orders, the Franciscans and Dominicans, whose members included

Bonaventure and Meister Eckhart, respectively. During this period, women mystics such as Hildegard of Bingen (German) and Mechtilde (Flemish) lived. Possibly because they had little access to reading scripture, women mystics tended to resort to imagery and visions as a way of describing or giving expression or interpretation to their experiences of union with God. While such developments were taking place, Christian faith in general came to be experienced more statically as opposed to dynamically. This occurred due to a shift in emphasis over the centuries on adherence to dogmas and rules rather than on the Christ event as an ongoing happening, a relationship. According to Thomas Merton, this was the result of grace being experienced more as "God's nature shared" rather than as "God's act."[58] This understanding continued up to Vatican II.

In the *fourth period* from the second half of the fourteenth to the sixteenth century lived the English mystics Julian of Norwich and the author of the *Cloud of Unknowing*, as well as the Italian mystic, Catherine of Siena. Later in the century the continued search for union with God flowered in Spain. Ignatius of Loyola founded a new form of religious life, the Jesuits. His great contribution, and one that is relied on today, is his *Spiritual Exercises*. The entire aim of the *Exercises* was "finding God in all things." These exercises redressed a certain imbalance in the transcendence of God taking priority over God's immanence, by centering on "how God dwells in creatures." Teresa of Avila and John of the Cross and their work of reforming their Carmelite contemplative tradition took place just decades after Ignatius.

The *fifth period*, the seventeenth to nineteenth centuries continued the spirit of Ignatius. This was visible, for example, in the person of Marie of the Incarnation, a wife, mother, and widow who spent the second half of her life as an Ursuline sister and became the first woman missionary to the new world in Quebec where she worked in education. The Enlightenment commenced in the eighteenth century. Its belief in reason and human progress allied to a questioning of tradition and authority led to religion taking a less eminent place in the thinking and value systems of people in the West. It was a time when God ceased to be a vital concern. During this period, however, and especially during the nineteenth century many new apostolic religious congregations were founded to serve in the areas of education, social work, and health care.

The *sixth period*, the twentieth and into the twenty-first century, the effects of the Enlightenment have continued leading to further declines in awareness of the religious dimension of human living. Vatican II, however, with its stress on the contribution of lay people and its insistence that the call to holiness is for everyone,[59] combined with recent examples of saintly living, shows the presence of an alive faith amid the complexities of the modern era. Selected examples of holy people in this period are the following: two Carmelites, Thérèse of Lisieux, who became patroness of missioners, and Edith Stein, a convert from Judaism who died in a concentration camp; Archbishop Romero, who was martyred for his preaching on justice issues in South America; Dorothy Day, who worked for the homeless in the United States; Matt Talbot, a recovered Irish alcoholic who devoted his life to prayer. They and many others have kept the Christian tradition alive and alert to the new changes called for and, above all, faithful to the centrality of the mission of Jesus. With the present movement toward inculturation, various spiritualities associated with, for example, the Franciscan, Dominican, or Jesuit ways of life are tending less toward living out their spirit in a uniform manner. Instead, while endeavoring to retain the original inspiration of their founders, their spiritual practices are becoming more based in local cultural forms.

A problem throughout history is that each person's experience of God is limited by its expression and, when referring to the past, this means its written expression. Added to this difficulty is the fact that most writings that exist come in Latin, French, and at times in their old language forms, and hence are unrecognizable to present-day readers, which means they were and still are only accessible to most people through translations. Such translations are a second or even third interpretive step away from an individual's original and ineffable experience of the Divine. From the twelfth century onward, the appearance of secondary phenomena such as visions and voices became more noticeable in the lives of some persons, usually women, associated with their experiencing of God. These also call for interpretation.

Little is known about the inner life experiences of the ordinary Christian down through the centuries. These were and are most likely to be described in common religious terminology as an awareness of God's presence. Inevitably, the number and the names of those whose experience of union with God contained that hidden quality remain an unknown entity. Meister Eckhart's words show his awareness of Christian experiencing as lived within the ordinary happenings of everyday: "When people think that they are acquiring more of God in inwardness, in devotion, in sweetness and in various approaches than they do by the fireside or in the stable, you are acting just as if you took God and muffled his head up in a cloak and pushed him under a bench. Whoever is seeking God by ways is finding ways and losing God, who in ways is hidden."[60]

Christian missionary output throughout the ages and the Christian ethos of often being at the forefront of social, educational, and health-care projects suggest a strong and committed faith in "the God of Jesus Christ."[61] This commitment, lasting over two millennia, gave the thrust and sustaining power for these activities.[62] If it is by their fruits they will be known, Evelyn Underhill says, "it is the peculiarity of the unitive life that it is often lived, in its highest and most perfect form, in the world." She offers a list of possible fruits an individual might demonstrate: "a pioneer of humanity, a sharply intuitive and painfully practical person: an artist, a discoverer, a religious or social reformer, a national hero."[63]

3

Religious Experience:
An Experience of the Sacred

This chapter focuses on the referent/ground of religious experience, Holy Mystery, by examining the holiness/sacredness part of that title. The Sacred/Holy One is perceived in several religions as either a personal divinity or the Great Spirit. Expressions of holiness in relation to a person, or sacredness in relation to objects, places, or happenings, are derived in some way from their connectedness with Holy Mystery. Awakening a sense of the sacred in ordinary human living, or actually encountering the Holy One are core elements in faith experiencing. Hence clarifying what is meant by *the Sacred*, *sacredness*, and other related terms, like *profane*, *secular*, and *worldly*, is necessary.

It is difficult to articulate what is meant by the concept of *sacred*. The word is defined in *Chambers* dictionary in its adjectival form with a lowercase *s* and describes what *sacred* positively pertains to, namely, something "consecrated: devoted: set apart or dedicated, esp. to God: holy: proceeding from God." Dictionaries and common parlance indicate that *sacred* and *holy* are largely synonymous, and in practice, both words are often used interchangeably. Examples of this interchangeable element are seen in relation to recognized sacred/holy places (churches, cemeteries, wells); things (liturgical vessels, books—especially the scriptures); times (liturgical feasts and seasons); and religious and human happenings (such as weddings, births, deaths). Everything listed can be referred to as either sacred or holy. In relation to persons, holy, as opposed to sacred, is considered the more applicable term.

When used as a noun, with a capital letter and the article *the* placed before it—the Holy One—is taken to refer to God. Synonymously, though less frequently, the phrase *the Sacred* is used as a term for God/Ultimate Other. The ultimate and the sacred are closely aligned concepts. Often *sacred* like *holy* is used in its adjectival form, usually in the sense of pertaining to or proceeding from the Sacred. The sacred is something conferred on a place, thing, or event when these are acknowledged as related to the Divine in some way. Something becomes religious/sacred when it is expressly invested with sacred character. Every incident in life has the potential to be a carrier that manifests the sacred, hence no individual, such as guru or priest, has an exclusive hotline to the sacred. Neither is the sacred normally found in exotic, strange, or unusual happenings but rather is discovered within the ordinary and only occasionally in the extraordinary.

The word *sacred* is sometimes used in opposition to the words *profane, secular,* or *worldly.* When *sacred* is used in conjunction with any of these three words it is likely to be understood today in a less divisive manner than the view that prevailed throughout Christianity from postbiblical times until the twentieth century. Many dictionaries define *profane* solely in terms of its opposition to the sacred, namely, as "not sacred, secular." The word *secular* is often seen as a synonym for *profane,* a term that is also defined in a negative way, namely, as "pertaining to things not spiritual." A remark of Hans-Georg Gadamer is pertinent here. He says "there is no such thing as profaneness in itself" and that the concepts *profane* and *profanation* always presuppose the sacred.[1]

Numinous is a term that describes a specific quality inherent within religious experiencing.[2] A numinous experience is one that flows from the realization of having been, or continuously being, gifted with a connectedness with the Sacred. This experience elicits a consciousness of one's littleness when compared to the ineffable—the Unnameable Other—by whom one has been awakened in some interpersonal way.

Every experience of the Sacred is a mediated experience. To expound on what this means the glossary plus further thoughts from Lonergan are helpful.[3] He had a threefold view of mediation. First, operations are "immediate" when their objects are present. This occurs at the first empirical level. This world of immediate experience is the world of the infant. Second, by moving through the transcendental precepts to the larger world, what he calls "the real world," we operate immediately with respect to images, words, or symbols and mediately in regard to the reality that is meant, signified, or represented by these objects. This world mediated by meaning is the world of the adult. Third, there is the world of lovers and mystics where the world mediated by meaning is dropped and returns to a new mediated immediacy as we reach for the beloved or God. From a human/divine relational perspective, Christ is the mediator between us and the Father with the Holy Spirit mediating between us and Christ. The church's essential role is also a mediating one, namely, to mediate not primarily its teaching but the Risen Jesus.

All faith traditions rely on metaphors as vehicles that mediate to us experiences of the Sacred. The language of faith is always attempting to speak of a reality that lies beyond literal language. As a consequence, metaphorical language is used throughout scripture and this fact requires understanding—otherwise, biblical texts will be interpreted in an overly literal and fundamentalist manner. Jesus constantly relied on metaphors, for example, his parables. Lonergan uses the term *metaphor* only once in *Method* and again once in *Insight* saying "nearly all we say is metaphor." This taking-for-granted mention of metaphor is endorsed by Sallie McFague: "we are not usually conscious of the metaphorical character of our thought, of seeing 'this' in terms of 'that,' of finding the thread of similarity amid dissimilars, but it is the only way a child's world can be constructed or our worlds expanded or transformed."[4]

Culture and the Sacred

Despite present-day culture militating against experiences of sacredness, the Western world is often fascinated with the sacred. Those who have been exposed in their early years, as well as maybe in subsequent years, to a sense of the religious dimension within human living are gifted with a certain facility of having known this reality, even if this capacity is presently nonactive. Previous experiences affect present experiencing as indicated by the following analogy: we require a degree of musical sensitivity to appreciate truly a symphony, so similarly a degree of religious sensibility/familiarity facilitates a fuller appreciation of religious experience. It is also true that God's ways are not our ways (see Isa 55:9), so nothing in life can ever prevent a sense of the sacred from emerging within human experience.

A numinous experience of Holy Mystery crosses all cultural boundaries. In the Western world, dominated by materialism and individualism, intimating or possessing a sense of the sacred can help restore a sense of balance to the human spirit to counter its constant exposure to merely empirical reality. *Is Nothing Sacred?* an interesting work comprising fourteen essays by agnostics or atheists, is the outcome of a conference organized around the theme of the sacred by the British Humanist Association. The editor, Ben Rogers, states that while these authors can get on without believing in the godhead, or even the existence of transcendent realms, most of them found it difficult to abandon the concept of the sacred. He says that even Richard Dawkins admits "there are some things he can't but feel are sacred."[5] The reasoning offered is that everything cannot be viewed as uniformly secular, since at the heart of human nature is an ethical sense of a hierarchy of values. A concern expressed in some essays was about the value or worth that certain realities have intrinsically and not merely instrumentally. Rogers refers to the quasireligious language of *sacred, sacrosanct,* and *inviolable* used by the various authors in their attempts to make this distinction of worth that is essential to being human. Even the notion of *sacrifice* forms part of this language when an individual forgoes some good in order to benefit someone else. The fact that atheists rely on this category of sacredness to describe realities that are strongly valued, or of supreme value such as life itself, is significant.

One of the authors, Piers Benn, struggled with what was meant by the idea of the sacred, since he considered that most of the essays used the word in too loose a manner. While defining himself as an agnostic, he sees the best way of approaching the sacred as from within a religious context, since certain religions make "the idea of the sacred intelligible, by offering...an approach to life which speaks to the human condition in a way nothing else can." He emphasized that a sense of the sacred is something good to have and something perilous to lose. He warns against taking the wrong things as sacred, and notes that the sacred must somehow speak authentically to our condition as well as elicit feelings of awe or reverence, and not just belief. He alerts his fellow humanists to the consequences of having too much confidence in human power and wisdom. To counteract this fact, he speaks of the need to be conscious of human limitations and fragility, as well as allowing a sense of the sacred to "act as a brake on [this form of] hubris."[6]

While numinous experiences of the sacred were denied by these atheists and agnostics, the usage they give to this word—as the recognized expression of ultimate worth and value—could be a way in which intimations of the ultimate worthwhile Other who lies at the heart of all that is, are discovered. An example of this sense of the sacred is seen in the way people describe as sacrilegious the destruction of certain realities such as art, special buildings, or occasions, thereby indicating that their consciousness is acquainted with the idea of profanation.

Following the death of John Paul II an Israeli journalist writing from another perspective says:

> The return to God happens because the secular messianic ideals have been terribly disappointed. In the name of science, nationalism and communism terrible injustices have also been committed—in many ways worse than what preceded them. Moreover, even when secular life provides great benefits as it does for the upper classes in the West, there is one value that only religion can provide—*the sense of sanctity*.[7]

Opening up people to the possibility of the existence of the sacred by naming it, by alerting them to signs for recognizing its presence, and by fostering awareness of such happenings is an aim of this book. In simple terms, I suggest that the category of the sacred—rather than the categories of religion or spirituality—could prove a helpful way of glimpsing or even connecting with the Divine.

The Human Experience of the Sacred

When personal awareness is graced with openness to the in-breaking into consciousness of the Sacred/Holy One, a numinous encounter comes into being. Such happenings can be described as sacred moments, and the carrier of this awakening, for example, a particular place or person, can take on a sacred or holy quality. The wide range of triggers, such as personal experiences, places, moments, people, can all be avenues through which a sense of the sacred enters human consciousness. Such an experience manifests itself in the lives of people of all religious traditions as well as those with other systems of meaning. Ultimate issues or crisis experiences can unexpectedly be filled with an awareness of the Sacred. An example of a crisis moment could be a confrontation with our own atheism. Such an event could have a positive dimension through what Dupré terms a "sacred 'sense of absence.'"[8]

Ordinary day-to-day experiences can also be infused with an awareness of the Sacred. For instance, experiences of loving or being loved, routine happenings such as a walk in the local park or standing at the kitchen sink, as well as visiting recognized sacred places and happenings, such as a climb up Croagh Patrick or attending a liturgical celebration, offer the possibility of becoming personal sacred happenings through which the Divine is encountered. These happenings can be more truly described as sacred when qualities of the numinous are present within that experience. The possibility of the presence of the Sacred within human experience has existed from primitive to modern times.

Experiences of the Sacred can remain almost imperceptible unless caught and then reflected on. Glimpses of the Sacred can be subtly present in the wow moments of life, hidden in comments such as the sincerely said "it was out of this world," or in a silent inner recognition at some intuition that arises within the self, yet vaguely knowing that the source lies beyond oneself. Discernment is needed to nuance the difference between moments that are special and those that contain a numinous quality. The sacred character of such moments is indicated by being touched by or connected with a divine power that lies beyond ourselves and is accompanied by a sense of creaturehood. Such experiences contain a sense of personal significance—a significance that is invested with sacred character.

Personal holiness, usually discerned by others rather than the person him- or herself, is the result of God's gift of the Godself being accepted and incarnated into personal living. Holiness becomes an intrinsic reality—it is something a person is—and it manifests itself as coming from within a person. The outward expression of holiness is particularly perceived through goodness as revealed in an individual's thinking, attitudes, and activities. A conscious experience of connectedness with the Sacred can lead to a sense of oneself as empowered by a power that is both transcendent and immanent. An authentic realization of this giftedness is always accompanied by humility—a virtue that is inherent within genuine appearances of holiness.

Authentic religious experience manifests itself in a sense of respect that flows from an awareness of the sacredness of all that is created, be it the universe, history, people, ordinary life happenings. The opposing attitude is violence—an attitude that refuses to show respect for created reality. Holy-making possibilities become more likely when we are open to the ultimate otherness of the Holy One and also when we are open to the otherness of all created reality— from the most minute, such as an atom or insect, to the vast, the sun or the whale.

The Sacred in Old and New Testaments

While the phrase *Sacred Scripture* is common, the word *sacred* is rarely found in English translations of Old and New Testaments. Possibly as a consequence, this is why the word *sacred* is not mentioned in biblical dictionaries or concordances. *Holy* and *holiness* are the normal translation for the inspired Hebrew word *qadosh* and Greek word *hagios*. This is not surprising since the referent in scripture is clearly Yahweh, and within Jewish tradition, as a mark of respect for God's holiness, the name of God is never spoken or written.

God alone is the Holy One and the source of all other manifestations of holiness. From a Christian perspective the unique mystery is that the supreme communication of the Sacred became manifest within human history in the person of Jesus. "The Word became flesh and lived among us" (John 1:14). This Word's presence is continued in Jesus' resurrected presence, a presence that remains with humankind through his spirit: "I am with you always, to the end of the age" (Matt 28:20). As a consequence, all authentic encounters with Jesus, the Father, or the Spirit are sacred happenings. Such encounters can occur within the ordinary events of life as well as within those that are considered more specifically religious, such as the sacraments, during prayer, or pondering the scriptures. A special way of encountering the Sacred is given to us by Jesus himself: "Just as you did it to one of the least of these who are members of my family, you did it to me" (Matt 25:40).

Holiness associated with people is a derived holiness by the gift of the Holy Spirit. The Spirit in both Old and New Testaments is the principal agent of sanctification, an activity that reflects the holiness of God. The degree of holiness depends on the closeness of the bond with the Divine. The sanctification of all people is strongly endorsed by Vatican II in one of its core documents—*Dogmatic Constitution on the Church*—whose second chapter is titled, "The Universal Call to Holiness."

Holiness in the Old Testament

The root of the Semitic word *qodes*, according to Leon Dufour, means "to cut off," "separate." Such notions point toward the idea of separation from the profane. Dufour, however, expands its meaning: "far from being reduced to separation or transcendence, the divine holiness includes all the riches and life, power and goodness that God possesses. It is more than just one divine attribute among others: *it characterizes God Himself.* From that time on His name is holy (See Ps 33:21; Amos 2:7; cf. Exod 3:14)." Enda McDonagh, referring to the word *qadosh,* describes it as meaning "other," and when applied to God, the Ultimate Other, it "is translated as 'holy.'" He continues: "without the differentiation or otherness from the Creator there is no distinctive creation."[9]

David Wright states that the Hebrew *qds*, "'to be holy'; 'sanctify' appear[s] as a verb, noun, and adjective over 850 times [in the Old Testament]."[10] Holiness, as Wright points out, is not inherent in created beings; it comes as God's gift. It is God alone who sanctifies. As a consequence the people's responsibility, in particular the priests and prophets, was to acknowledge God's holiness by honoring him and obeying his commandments. Holiness may also include the ideas of consecration to God and purity from what is evil or improper.

A central passage on holiness is contained in Isaiah's vision on the occasion of his call to become a prophet. The scene describes the majesty of God seated on a throne surrounded by seraphs who cry out "Holy, holy, holy is the Lord of hosts" (Isa 6:3). Frederick Moriarity states, "By the triple repetition, the superlative is expressed; God is the all-holy. Holiness is the essential quality of God; its vast range of meaning indicates his otherness, utter transcendence, complete apartness from anything sinful or merely finite. God's glory is the radiation of this holiness upon the world."[11] This overpowering encounter with God led Isaiah to an overwhelming sense of his own unworthiness (6:5).

Of special interest to this book is the sanctification of place. In the Old Testament, cult places, such as shrines and sanctuaries, became known as holy places. The most holy place was the tabernacle that contained the Ark. In Israel's early history this was enshrined in a tent that moved from place to place. Eventually the Temple was built. Its center housed the holy of holies, which at the time of the First Temple contained the Ark of the Covenant. After the Temple's destruction the Ark disappeared. The rebuilt Second Temple left the interior of the space of the innermost sanctuary empty. God's holiness was perceived to be so extensive that there would be no space available for any other object. Yahweh's presence filled the sanctuary. This vacant space was a symbol of this truth.

Locations where theophanies[12] occurred were also seen as holy places. These included mountains, particularly Mount Sinai (see Exod 3:5; 19:9–5; 24:16–17), and also the Garden of Eden. Sometimes pillars or altars were set up as a result of a particular manifestation of Yahweh's presence. Jerusalem was specifically seen as a holy city (see Isa 48:2; 52:1; Ps 46:5).

Three incidents from early biblical history involving Abraham, Jacob, and Moses are significant from the aspect of the personal response of each one to their encounter with Yahweh. In all three, it is a creature-feeling of awe and fear that indicate a sense of the numinous that had been aroused in these people.

The first is Abraham's dialogue with God where he intercedes on behalf of the people of Sodom. From the outset, Abraham appears to be aware of whom he is speaking to: "The men left there and went to Sodom while Abraham remained standing before Yahweh. Approaching him he said, 'Will you indeed sweep away the righteous with the wicked?'" (Gen 18:23). The conversation continues with Abraham's bargaining skills reaching, as it turns out, their halfway mark. When the number reaches fifty his awareness of his own creaturehood appears more acute. He cries out from his awareness of the utterly dependent nature of who he actually is: "Let me take it upon myself to speak to the Lord, *I who am but dust and ashes*" (Gen 18:27). His experience is a combination of two opposites—an awareness of the holiness of God combined with a sense of his own creatureliness. This is a hallmark of all divine-human encounters. This moment of truth, however, does not cower him into a false humility but rather gives further energy for the bargaining to continue.

Jacob's and Moses's encounters with Yahweh arouse a sense of the holiness of place, even the ground itself, as a result of a manifestation of the presence of God in a particular spot. Jacob has his dream of the ladder reaching from earth to heaven (see Gen 28:10–22). Yahweh was standing over him, saying, "I am the Lord, the God of Abraham your father and the God of Isaac....Know that I am with you" (vv. 13, 15). On awakening, Jacob exclaims: "'Surely the Lord is in this place?—and I did not know it!' And he was afraid and said, 'How awesome is this place! This is none other than the house of God, and this is the gate of heaven.' So Jacob rose early in the morning and he took the stone that he had put under his head and set it up for a pillar and poured oil over the top of it. He called that place Bethel; but the name of the city was Luz at first" (vv. 16–19). Jacob marks the sacredness of the place by two consecratory actions, namely, the use of anointing with oil and the renaming of the place. Anointing and renaming are symbolic activities that have continued within the Christian tradition.

In the Moses incident, "There the angel of the Lord appeared to him in a flame of fire out of a bush; he looked, and the bush was blazing, yet it was not consumed. Then Moses said 'I must turn aside and look at this great sight, and see why the bush is not burned up.' When the Lord saw that he had turned aside to see, God called out to him out of the bush 'Moses, Moses!' And he said 'Here I am!' Then he said 'Come no closer! Remove the sandals from your feet, for *the place on which you are standing is holy ground*'" (Exod 3:2–5). An interesting point in this story is the fact that God names the ground as holy—holy because of the manifestation of his intimate presence to Moses, his special servant. The story ends: "at this Moses covered his face, afraid to look at God" (v. 6). The inability to see the face of God, the gesture of taking off one's shoes, and keeping a certain distance are gestures that indicate being in the presence of the Holy One and of the creature's unworthiness when moving toward greater closeness to God.

Holiness in the New Testament

The New Testament word for *holiness* is the Greek *hagios*. The focus in the Gospels is on Jesus as the supremely Holy One, due to his divine Sonship. From the moment of his conception, scripture says he "will be holy; he will be called Son of God" (Luke 1:35). Revelations of his holiness are manifest in the several texts. For example, holiness is inherent in Jesus' relationship with his Father: he addresses God in prayer as "Holy Father" (John 17:11) and teaches his disciples to pray in similar fashion, "hallowed be your name" (Luke 11:2). Jesus himself is recognized as holy, for instance, by the man possessed with an unclean spirit: "I know who you are, the Holy One of God" (Mark 1:25) and in the conversation that follows the miracle of the loaves and fishes. "We have come to believe and know that you are the Holy One of God" (John 6:69). The climax in Mark's Gospel is reached in the words of the centurion following the death of Jesus: "Truly this man was God's Son!" (Mark 15:39).

The numinous element with religious experience acquires a startlingly new element within Christianity. It seems likely that it was Jesus' holiness that attracted the crowds, who on many occasions "gathered around him," "followed him," shared table fellowship with him; it was why individuals sought his company or felt drawn by his invitation to come to him—to be with, to sit with, to eat with, to walk along the road with, to follow him in a more committed way. Diverse groups of people were drawn to him: apostles, disciples, groups of women, children, sinners; sick people, their relatives; named people like Zacchaeus, Nicodemus, Martha, and Mary, the centurion, the Samaritan woman. Possibly Herod's curiosity of wanting to know more about Jesus was due to this fascination. Jesus' holiness radiated in a way that magnetically drew people toward him for healing and teaching. Even to be in his presence appears to have elicited something special in the hearts of those open to that presence. At a crisis point in his public ministry there are the evocative words of those who chose to remain in his company—"Lord, to whom can we go?…We have come to believe and know that you are the Holy One of God" (John 6:68, 69). The appearances of the resurrected Jesus have a more intense quality about them. This is well illustrated by the comment made by the two disciples on their return from Emmaus, "were not our hearts burning within us while he was talking to us on the road?" (Luke 24:32).

The role of the spirit in the Old Testament was to guide the prophets and other special servants of God. In Acts and the Pauline letters, the prominence of the Spirit of God in a sense takes over. Following the death and resurrection of Jesus, there is a universal outpouring of the Spirit: "I will pour out my spirit upon all flesh" (Acts 2:17). Peter states with authority that this prophecy of Joel is now realized and that the kairos era of the Spirit of God has begun. The Spirit's primary mission is the ongoing implementation of God's plan as established by Jesus (see Eph 1:13–14). As the Spirit of Jesus, the Spirit's essential activity is primarily the sanctifying of people but also the sanctification of time, places, and the entire cosmos.

In reference to Christians, Paul states: "Your body is a temple of the Holy Spirit within you, which you have from God." "You were washed, you were sanctified, you were justified in the name of the Lord Jesus Christ and in the Spirit of our God" (1 Cor 6:19, 11). The same letter continues a similar theme—both individuals and communities are considered temples of God due to the presence of the indwelling Spirit (see 1 Cor 3:16, 17). The Spirit's essential role both within the Trinity as well as throughout the universe is that of love, a love that sanctifies, unifies, and creates communion.

Several of the Pauline letters begin and end by addressing the members of the various Christian communities as holy. Membership in the church through baptism (see Rom 6:1–11) endows a state of sainthood and this state remains unless serious sin alters this status.

The Sacred from the Perspective of Rudolf Otto

Rudolf Otto's *The Idea of the Holy*, is considered particularly relevant in furthering our understanding of holiness/sacredness.[13] This work has become a classic and classics are recognized as having an ability to challenge horizons and disclose new meanings and possibilities. His unpacking of the word *numinous* contributed greatly to understanding the core element in religious experiencing, namely, sacredness. His elaboration focuses on the three words of his constantly repeated phrase: "mysterium tremendum fascinans." In this work he moves to what he terms the "non-rational" or "suprarational" yet at the same time states that this was not a move toward "irrationalism" but that this new direction necessitated a rootedness in the rational. He particularly realizes the need to reintroduce feelings into theology as well as the distinctive category of the holy or sacred. He becomes aware that Christianity and the science of comparative religion were presenting an overly rationalist interpretation to the idea of God.

The Numinous

The holy, Otto stated, had for too long been understood solely in moral terms, namely, as moral goodness. The equation between being holy and being morally good he saw as inaccurate due to its inadequacy. While goodness is included in holiness there has been an "overplus" of meaning that is left out. This surplus of meaning was present in Hebrew language (*qadosh*), Greek (*hagios*), and Latin (*sanctus*). He believed this missing something is what lies at the core of all religious experience as found within all faiths. He speaks of "*a unique original feeling-response*" that is ethically neutral. The added meaning to the term *holy* is enriched by his use of the term *numinous*. This numinous category of value or "state of mind which is always found when this category is applied" is "irreducible" to any other category or mind state. As such it is incapable of definition and therefore of being known through the rational route. One can only come to know about the numinous by analogy. Experientially one knows its presence through an awakening or a surrendering to the Spirit from whom this gift ultimately comes.[14]

For Otto, this sense of the numinous exists at the heart of all true religious experiencing. Feelings such as gratitude, love, rapture, uplift, and wonder are analogous feelings to the feelings evoked by the numinous. An experience of the numinous, however, is uniquely and not merely qualitatively different to all other feelingful experiences; it is both similar yet unlike. The feeling closest to describing the feeling aroused by the numinous is *dependence*. This feeling of dependence aroused by the numinous is distinguishable from all other feelings of dependence. The most apt analogous feeling he terms a "*creature-feeling*"—"it is the emotion of a creature, submerged and overwhelmed by its own nothingness in contrast to that which is supreme above all creatures."[15] Emotional states can be experienced in a weak or intense manner and the same is true of this feeling of creaturehood. The experience might be a mild intuitive sensing of something unnameable or an awareness of a gentle touch of the ineffable. Such experiences can be so fleeting that they are barely perceptible or, in rare examples, so powerful as to bowl someone over either physically, emotionally, or intellectually.

In the context of the sacred, personal feelings can suggest and indirectly point toward "something." This something is made known at the level of experience and is known as a reality that lies beyond the self. This something is termed the Unnameable One, the wholly Other, God. No one can bring about this experience by personal volition. It is utterly gift when an awareness of Holy Mystery enters personal consciousness. The only adequate response is surrender to this presence. Otto cites a quotation from William James's *Varieties of Religious Experience*, as offering a thought close to his own: "It is as if there were in the human consciousness, a *sense of reality*, a *feeling of objective presence*, a *perception* of what we may call *something there*."[16]

Otto dives deeper in his reflections on the numinous by adding another phrase "*mysterium tremendum.*" The numinous is suggested to us through feelings that stir the human mind and heart. This religious emotion or state is, he feels, appropriately expressed as mysterium tremendum.

> The feeling of it may at times come sweeping like a gentle tide, pervading the mind with a tranquil mood of deepest worship. It may pass over into a more set and lasting attitude of the soul, continuing, as it were, thrilling vibrant and resonant, until at last it dies away....It may become the hushed, trembling and speechless humility of the creature in the presence of—whom or what? In the presence of that which is a *mystery* inexpressible and above all creatures.[17]

While mysterium could be deemed a negative reality, for Otto it refers to an experience that arouses intensely positive feelings. He attempts to unravel the elements that make up these feelings: fear in the sense of awe, religious dread, a feeling of something uncanny, eerie, or shuddering, are all possible ingredients. The experience is not so much one of craziness or bewilderment but rather of the ineffable—"it has become a mystical awe."[18]

Whereas numinous consciousness may only arouse a stirring of feeling, inherent in mysterium are feelings of incredible wonder and astonishment. "This feeling or consciousness of the 'wholly other' will attach itself to, or sometimes be indirectly aroused by means of objects which are already puzzling upon the 'natural' plane, or are of a surprising or astounding character." He warns, "here once more we are dealing with a case of association between things specifically different— the 'numinous' and the 'natural' moments of consciousness—and not merely with the gradual enhancement of one of them, 'the natural,' till it becomes the other."[19]

Otto refers to what he calls St. Augustine's "benumbing element of the 'wholly other'" when he quotes from Augustine's *Confessions*: "I am both a-shudder and a-glow. A-shudder, in so far as I am unlike it, a-glow as far as I am like it."[20] Otto had just described mysterium in similar fashion as the "mysterious" that lies beyond one's comprehension, being "wholly other" and "incommensurable," "and before which we therefore recoil in a wonder."

The second element, the *tremendum*, arouses a feeling of overpoweringness due to an awareness of a sense of majesty. It is this experience that elicits creature consciousness. "In contrast to the 'overpowering' of which we are conscious as an object over against the self, there is the feelings of one's own submergence, of being but 'dust and ashes' and nothingness. And this forms the numinous raw material for the feeling of religious humility."[21]

Otto distinguishes between a consciousness of createdness and a consciousness of creaturehood. The first is a knowing that one is created and preserved in existence by God's creative act, whereas a sense of creaturehood makes an individual conscious of their littleness, or nothingness, as some mystics would say. An awareness of "the transcendent as the sole and entire reality" or "plenitude of being," makes possible the experiencing of a profound sense of creaturehood. A further quotation of James used by Otto elucidates the above experience: "The perfect stillness of the night was thrilled by a more solemn silence. The darkness held a presence that was all the more felt because it was not seen. I could not any more have doubted that *He* was there than that I was. Indeed, I felt myself to be, if possible, the less real of the two."[22]

Otto mentions energy as a third element in relation to mysterium tremendum. This energy he says "clothes itself in symbolic expressions—vitality, passion, emotional temper, will, force, movement, excitement, activity, impetus....a force which is urgent, completing and alive."[23] The authenticity of sacred experiences is shown by their fruitfulness. Such fruit is marked by this energy, an energy that propels toward engagement with global concerns as opposed to a flight from personal, local or world issues.

The third word in the trilogy *mysterium tremendum fascinans*, is *fascination*. Another aspect of the numinous experience is its uniquely attractive and fascinating quality. The daunting and the fascinating combine within the phenomena Otto calls "numinous consciousness" and he continues: "The 'mystery' is for him [the creature] not merely something to be wondered at but *something that entrances him*; and beside that in it which bewilders and confounds, he feels *a something that captivates and transports him with a strange ravishment*."[24]

The awakening of numinous/religious consciousness may commence with bringing the daunting aspect of the numinous to the fore. Later, yet as part of the one moment of a more complete experience, the individual is drawn toward the "wonderfulness and rapture" aspect by a process of greater self-surrender. The numinous always remains the object of our searching. We never fully arrive. Neither can we explain how this movement occurs other than by grace. It is known in experience through its effects, such as an all-pervasive and all-penetrating glow, as well as a peace that surpasses all understanding. "It can be firmly grasped, thoroughly understood, profoundly appreciated, purely in, with and from the feeling itself."[25] The fascination aroused could be perceived in intimation, or, more fully, within present experiences.

Otto sees an affinity between the category of the beautiful and that of the numinous especially in relation to the sublime. Aesthetic and religious experiences resemble each other in that both terms are inexplicable and mysterious and that each experience can be daunting and attracting, humbling and exalting, fearing and rejoicing as well as sharing an element of extending beyond the self.

The importance of respect in one's encounter with the Sacred as well as in all aspects of human living, can be deepened from Otto's views. An example of respect in liturgical settings is particularly marked in Eastern rite liturgies where an experience of the ineffable seems more palpable. The Eastern rite way of worshiping as expressed in music, use of many icons and candles, reverent gestures (particularly that of bowing), facilitate a response of awesomeness to the presence of the Sacred, and particularly in eucharistic celebrations. Roman rite liturgies on the other hand, while gaining much through Vatican II's liturgical reforms, seem, in the West, to elicit a sense of the Sacred in a less obvious manner.

Respect is needed in relating to everything created by God—persons, places, objects of all kinds. A question today is the following: Is today's phenomenon of lack of respect for people (no matter what their position in life), for property, for objects, and even for nature itself due to an erosion of a sense of the sacred in human living? A glaring example of irreverence is the claim of ownership that is allowed by some countries in the legal patenting of plants. This is surely an example of a modern sacrilegious act. Otto's notion of awe and the subsequent creaturelike feeling that authentic awe evokes deserves comment. This sense of our creaturehood is totally different from the belittling sense of worthlessness that some people experience today. The first leads to positive feelings of humility and gratitude, whereas the second is a negative experience that can lead to depression and even to suicide.

A Contemporary Understanding of the Sacred-Secular Distinction

Secularization comes from the Latin *saecularis*, meaning "worldly" or "temporal." The word *secularization* was introduced as a legal term, entering Canon Law in the eighteenth century. It dealt with the confiscation of church property for secular use. In the nineteenth century the secularization process widened with attempts to deprive the church of its influence in cultural matters and particularly in the area of education. In summary, it is a term that denotes a shift from church to civil authority. Elements in the secularization movement have become hostile to the church, but on the other hand, the church itself has, since its infancy, shown a wariness toward the *worldly*. St. Paul found reason to warn the young church to separate itself from a profane society. Since then, there have always been dilemmas surrounding the relationship between church and the world.

Since the last quarter of the twentieth century, however, the perception of *sacred* set in strict opposition to *secular/profane/worldly* has diminished. This has led to divergent results. On the positive side, this can foster a healthy tension between both the sacred and the secular dimensions of human life, where each reality is seen as having a contribution to make to the other. A second consequence, however, can lead, and to an extent has already led, to an overly pronounced blurring between sacred and secular. Maintaining a distinction, while being cautious about total separateness, is closer to the truth. This means moving away from a common assumption, that *this* or *that* are perceived as mutually incompatible. While distinctions are helpful to aid clarity of thought, dichotomous thinking becomes a problem when the things distinguished are seen as unrelated to each other.

Rigid separation is nonbiblical and neither is it true to modern human experiencing. The sacred can break through any created reality even if it is labelled *secular, natural,* or *worldly.* A new shift in thinking is emerging where the world of the secular is being seen in a more positive light. Secular is not in itself something ungodly or desacralized, and neither has the sacred to be shunned out of sight within ordinary human experiencing. Scan MacReamoinn, relates secularization with Christianity in a positive and healthy way: "Secularization is that process by which human life in both personal and social aspects is liberated from the detailed control of religion, while still remaining lit and guided by faith."[26]

Many people today, including Christians, use the term *secular* in a nonhostile manner. Alongside this fact, culture in Western societies tends to appear more a-religious or religionless, which is a modern phenomenon. This has led to secularization—meaning that the varying elements of human living, such as opinions, customs, social happenings, are often no longer determined by religious values. Secularization, a secular viewpoint or way of life, has always been a reality from primitive times. Secularism, namely, when secularization itself becomes an ideology, is something new.

Rahner's approach is by way of offering a corrective to those who perceive a-religious living as alien to the sacred. "Whenever *sec-*

ular life is lived with *unreserved honesty* there *ipso facto* an essential element in religious life is already present because God loves the world in itself, endows it with grace in itself and in no sense regards it as a rival to himself as though he were envious of it." God created all that is and "saw that it was good" (Gen l:10, 12, 18, 21, 25) and saw "everything that he had made and indeed it was very good" (Gen 1:31). Rahner continues "That in man which is really of value and fundamentally alive is already summoned to receive the grace of Christ even before it is explicitly 'baptised.'"[27]

There have been stages in the trend toward secularization. The first is perceived in the New Testament, where it is shown that the religious and secular spheres are seen as different, yet neither sphere dominates, excludes, or is hostile to the other. The second stage, from patristic to modern times, is a period when the religious realm largely dominated the secular. One consequence of this situation was the placing of value on detachment from the world. The third stage, the modern era, has swung the second stage in reverse. Since the period of the Enlightenment, rationalism, democracy, advances in science, technology, and more recently the electronic revolution, have resulted in a more empirical worldview. The move from modernity to postmodernity has, for instance, led to a dismantling of certainties, pluralism, and a desire for greater freedom. A consequence of this has been the perception of some that religion is superfluous. A further view sees religion's competence accorded solely to the inner life, and even this sphere is regarded as being hijacked by depth psychology. Since the 1990s, while God may remain dead for some, a sense of the sacred has demanded attention.

A return to an understanding of religion that does not view the holy as a special realm apart from the profane is required. There is no need for rivalry between worldly and religious activities since the sacred can be found in the profane and the religious task will call for its expression in the world. This changed orientation connects with some contemporary questions that require pondering: Why does religion appear inadequate or even meaningless? Has Christianity been largely reactive rather than proactive to this reality? What underlying misunderstandings have allowed this situation to develop? Is secularization entirely negative or is it something to be tolerated, even embraced? On the other hand, is the blurring between the sacred and the secular becoming too pronounced? Where does the doctrine of the goodness of creation and, most of all, the Christian understanding of a God who "so loved the world that he gave his only Son" (John 3:16) fit? Is respect and tolerance for all expressions of otherness being disregarded?

In the biblical literature we find such difficulties as well as discover some answers. The Hebrew Scriptures stressed the divide between pure and impure, holy and profane, and named in precise fashion what was considered unclean. For instance, an individual became unclean by ordinary human happenings such as eating forbidden foods, menstruating, or touching a dead body. Impurity led to exclusion from all that was considered sacred, like sacred places or sacred events such as worship, and even at times led to expulsion from the community. Rectification of this state was achieved by cleansing rituals and acts of repentance.

A salutary experience for the Israelites was their period in exile. They are told in a letter from Jeremiah to intermingle, and in a sense, to lay aside their strict codes of the sacred/secular divide. "Build houses and live in them; plant gardens and eat what they produce. Take wives and have sons and daughters...seek the welfare of the city where I have sent you into exile, and pray to the Lord on its behalf, for in its welfare you will find your welfare" (Jer 29:5–7). Jeremiah's text clearly encourages the Israelites to live in harmony among those with whom they find themselves.

The emphasis of Jesus was and is striking. He taught that profanity and immorality came not from without, but rather from within, the human heart. "The good person out of the good treasure of the heart produces good, and the evil person out of evil treasure produces evil" (Luke 6:45). Central to Jesus' teaching and way of life was his focus on relationships. Love, especially manifested in the form of respect and care, became a special avenue for encountering the sacred. This relational dimension was threefold: with God, with other people, and with the universe. What hides the presence of the sacred is when distortion enters any of these relationships, namely, when love is absent. Jesus clearly expressed his love for his Father. He also expressed his love for humanity in his acts of humble service and supremely by his death for others on a cross. His love of people was unique for its total inclusiveness—to the extent that no one is considered beyond redemption—its preference for those marginalized or outcast, and its quality of forgiveness. His love of nature is palpable in his parables and other teachings.

Jesus relativized aspects of the sacred in Old Testament religion that were perceived as absolute. In regard to laws, Jesus said: "In vain do they worship me, teaching human precepts as doctrines" (Matt 15:9). A further instance, when the hungry disciples ate ears of corn on the Sabbath, led to Jesus reminding the disapproving Pharisees of how David took the sacred bread from the Temple to feed his hungry followers (see Matt 12:1–4). In other words, no thing is so absolutely sacred that it cannot be used when human need dictates such a necessity.

A significant moment in the early church was Peter's vision at Jaffa about the question of food. The vision concludes with God's thrice repeated words: "What God has made clean, you must not call profane" (Acts 10:15). The implications of this vision were dramatic for any Jewish person. It was a conversion moment for Peter. He responded affirmatively: "God has shown me that I should not call anyone profane or unclean" (Acts 10:28). Gradually the newness of the vision's truth altered the church's understanding of the sacred-profane distinction. For instance, Paul states: "nothing is unclean in itself" (Rom 14:14).

Since Vatican II, secularization is now seen to have a positive role to play on behalf of religion even to the extent of helping the church, to understand its tasks better. In one sense, Christianizing the world means to secularize it; therefore, the secular order needs to be seen as an ingredient of Christian faith and practice. Ignatius of Loyola hinted at something similar when he took as the motto for his order "to find God in all things." He also spoke of the need for employing all human means with as much prudence and energy as if success depended on oneself while at the same time relying utterly on God. At the heart of all reality is mystery, but, although this mystery is not totally incomprehensible, neither religion nor science can ever fully explain it. However, religion and science when acting together can further humanity's ongoing search for truth and meaning when each offers views/findings from its own field of exploration.

Humanity necessarily relates to God in both secular and sacred ways. While the sacred should be distinguished from the purely human, there exists a unity between these two essential dimensions of human living. This unity can be interfered with by either humanist or religious forms of fundamentalism. The sacred-secular task requires seeing afresh the interconnections between both activities and by valuing their distinctions as well as their interconnectedness. Truth needs to be valued from whatever source it comes and, as McDonagh states, "it will be a priestly people [who] recognise and protect the divine spark that illuminates all things seen, the sacred intrinsic to the secular, the transcendent in the immanent."[28] He views the priestly role as one that recognizes holiness in its diverse manifestations. While the diverse combinations of sacred and secular will vary, even among Christians, each dimension needs the other. The role of the secular is one of providing contrast and context. McDonagh gives examples of how God's word needs the human word, the sacraments require the secular realities of bread, wine, water, oil—items that in turn necessitate the secular services of the baker, the wine maker, the hydrologist, the farmer. Alternatively, "the secular needs the sacred to safeguard its very secularity"[29] since the sacred offers the secular an enduring base of values that allows its projects to endure.

When a greater mutual respect, trust, and appreciation between the secular and religious interpretation of reality exist, the sacred-secular divide, in the negative form that prevailed for millennia, is diminished. When struggling with the issues of our time in both religious and secular spheres, the childishly held ideas and images of God, where God is domesticated as a gap stopper or fixer, are likely to alter. Whatever these images might be, they must inevitably contain a quality of sacredness in order to be authentic, since their referent, the whom to which they point, is the Holy One.

John Wilkins, in his retirement address after twenty-one years as editor of the *Tablet*, spoke about wrestling with the issues of our age. He recalled his first editorial, written in 1982: "Our concern is with the world as much as with the Church: with everything human. We shall seek to inform and interpret as well as to comment. We shall seek to entertain. Above all, we shall hope that in the future as in the past, readers may find in our pages that message without which the world perishes."[30] Concern for "everything human" is surely the point where the sacred and secular meet and where divisiveness and exclusivity diminish.

For a Christian, holiness is not about rejecting the world but rather is concerned with holy action in the world. The sanctifier—the Holy Spirit—makes this work possible. The world is totally changed through the incarnation to the extent that the sacred and profane character of the world are part of the one reality from a Christian perspective.

Holiness is not confined to Christianity. Everything in creation, all human concerns, has the potential of being a vehicle for disclosing Holy Mystery. Created reality is not merely neutral—it is good in itself. When one allows goodness to show itself in whatever form it is encountered, letting it be itself as opposed to becoming something to be used, the sacred is reflected in and through that goodness. Holiness is not identical to goodness but pervades it. Holiness is totally of God. No one becomes holy in the sense that a person can become good. An individual is holy inasmuch as they point beyond themselves toward Holy Mystery.

Jürgen Moltmann's and Lynda Sexson's Views on the Sacred/Secular Distinction

Jürgen Moltmann

Moltmann's theology of creation is particularly significant to the sacred/secular conversation.[31] The very title of his work *God in Creation* says a great deal. Fundamentally, he sees a false view of the world arising from a distorted understanding of God; and so, a new way of thinking about God is now vital. The center of this thinking is no longer the distinction between God and the world but rather the recognition of the presence of God *in* the world and the presence of the world *in* God. This notion forms the core of his thought. He notes that early Old Testament theology grew out of an environment of pantheism and animistic religions and therefore it stressed the *difference* between God and the world. It portrayed a monotheistic God who was increasingly stripped of connection with the world, and the world was increasingly secularized. A consequence of this understanding was that God was perceived as Lord and owner of the world. A further consequence was that humanity's role was to be similar because it was created in God's likeness. Separateness, difference, and confrontation with the world became realities as a result of such thinking.

The true way to perceive God is as triune—a unity of intricate relationships of Father, Son, and Spirit, a "relationship of community— many-layered, many-faceted, and at many levels."[32] Understanding the inner life of God in a relational way calls for a different way of thinking not only about God but also about how we think and act in all spheres of human living.

If objects are to be understood in relation to their environment, a more integrated and less analytical form of thought is required. Integrated thinking is less of the isolationist and splitting-up type of knowing. This way of knowing diminishes the drawing of hard-line distinctions between subjects and objects. While an analytical approach to knowledge is essential to the exact sciences, it can be limiting in other general modes of thought. Richer perceptions are discovered in relational thinking, where the goal is "inclusiveness that is many-sided, and ultimately fully comprehensive."[33] The fruit of such relational knowing is participation, not domination.

God's immanence, as understood by the *Shekina*[34] in the Old Testament and the incarnation in the New Testament, points to "the marvel that the infinite God himself should dwell in his finite creation making it his own environment."[35] God dwells in his creation, yet it is equally true that all created reality dwells in God. These two indwellings are, however, distinguishable: "God and the world are related to one another through the relationship of their mutual indwelling and participation: *God's indwelling in the world is divine in kind; the world's indwelling in God is worldly in kind.*"[36] For Moltmann, God's environment is his creation. The world is part of this environment and, as such, is filled with God's presence. Everyone is destined to participate in this environment not statically but in ever-fuller ways as they also participate in God's relating to his environment, the world.

How God's environment fits in relation to the Mystery of Divine Being is offered in the following quotation:

The created world does not exist in "the absolute space" of divine Being; it exists in the space God yielded up for it through his creative resolve. The world does not exist in itself. It exists in "the ceded space" of God's world-presence. It is not the eternal God himself who is the boundary of the worlds, as Newton seems to think. It is God the Creator. In the doctrine about the world as God's creation we therefore distinguish between three things: first the essential omnipresence of God, or *absolute space*; second, *the space of creation* in the world-presence of God conceded to it; and third, *relative places*, relationships and movements in the created world. The space of the world corresponds to God's world-presence, which initiates this space, limits it and interpenetrates it.[37]

The reason for God's creation is summed up in one word: *love*. Moltmann explicates this thought: "God goes out of himself and makes a creation, a reality, which is there as he is there, and is yet different from himself....The overflowing love from which everything comes that is from God, is also the implicit ground for God's readiness to endure the contradictions of the beings he has created."[38] The "contradictions" Moltmann refers to could be the distortions of created reality, yet such distortions firmly exist within and never separate from God's presence. For example, "The evolutions and catastrophes of the universe are also the movements and experiences of the Spirit of creation."[39] He views evolution and creation as complementing rather than opposing each other—"we have to see the concept of evolution as a basic concept of the self-movement of the divine Spirit of creation."[40]

John Polkinghorne expands Moltmann's thoughts on evolution: "The God of love has given to creation the gift of being allowed to be itself....By bringing into existence an evolving world in which life slowly developed and complexified, God had made a world *that could make itself*." Polkinghorne sees an evolving creation as a greater good than a ready-made creation would be. Evolution itself necessitates death—where one generation gives way to the next. He accepts, with other scientists, that there will be cosmic death, which can take either of two forms, namely, where "cosmic expansion beats gravity or gravity beats expansion....It is either freeze or fry, as far as the universe's future is concerned."[41] He continues by saying that creation matters to its creator and therefore it will not be abandoned to futility but will have a destiny beyond death. He adds that God is present in the world in a veiled manner so that creatures are not overwhelmed by the power and majesty of "the divine reality."

Lynda Sexson

Aligned to Moltmann's thought and in similar mode to the cataphatic form of religious living, Sexson perceives the sacred within the ordinary happenings of life. Religious consciousness is about sacralizing human experience—apprehending the divine through "utilizing the stuff of the ordinary." There is nothing, she notes, that lies outside, or is separable from "ordinary life" and speaks of "the religion of picking up the pieces, improvising, making up and making do."[42] Elements of the ordinary can be marked out, imagined, remembered, and thus become extraordinary; the extraordinary comes into being through the celebration of the ordinary.

The stated aim of her work is to illuminate the sacred quality of experiences that on the surface level might appear mundane or secular. No object, event, or thought is inherently sacred; it is special contexts that make them so. While culture or religious traditions may agree something has a sacred content, there are universal experiences that are "common yet set apart...mundane yet sacred." For Sexson, "Religion is not a discrete category within human experience; it is rather a quality that pervades all of experience."[43] She argues convincingly that labelling things *mundane, profane,* or *secular* can devalue and deprive them of the quality of the sacred. This view arises from dualistic thinking and particularly the dualism that divides reality into matter and spirit. "*All* reality must be—or is potentially—sacred (consecrated)."[44] Holiness ensues when a person or experience, no matter how mundane or secular it may be, is consecrated. This occurs through one's way of perceiving and knowing. Since anything, and that includes the mundane, can mediate the sacred, sacred happenings can occur anywhere. Unlikely places can become associated with the sacred when there is recognition of sacredness within particular contexts. Essentially such occurrences are experiences of relatedness.

Sexson's understanding goes further when she says that the sphere of the ordinary is "saturated" with the sacred, since the ordinary is always either holy or potentially holy. A favorite phrase of mine is that everything can be a "container" of the sacred—it is a question of perception. The Ark of the Covenant is a powerful symbol of such a container, but everything from temples, chalices, ceremonies, memories, words, or places, can "become agents of the divine"; "envelop the shock and become associated with the sacred."[45] She does suggest, however, that there is need for preparation before one can "gaze upon the mysteries" that are contained within the ordinary. She remarks that the collective term *religion* does not refer to a special category that imposes artificial barriers between sacred and profane, but rather is the way one perceives and integrates all of reality. For this to happen, she suggests a need for unfolding stages within religious experiencing:

> One must be able to *look*: something attracts us ("Let me turn aside and see this great sight"); something causes us to reflect upon our own nature in relation to the transpersonal ("Take off your shoes"); and changes reality ("For you are on Holy Ground"); and reveals the transcendent ("I am I..."); and demands the transformation (Go,...").[46]

Concluding Comments

The relevance of viewing the human-divine encounter through the terminology of the sacred rather than that of religion or spirituality has been illustrated in this chapter. While a certain sense of desacralization prevails today, what Cardinal Hume referred to as "a loss of the numinous," an area through which a sense of the sacred appears to be breaking into people's experience, is through core events associated with life. These would include key moments such as birth and death, events that threaten or alternately enhance life, as well as significant happenings in the arena of personal relationships. Personal relating, the area of human living that is critical to achieving a sense of wholeness, can be an experience akin to that of holiness.

This question of sacredness being experienced within human relating can be particularly manifested through experiences of intimacy, such as between spouses, partners, friends, and parents and children. The experience of loving and being loved, as discovered in the falling in love experience, the deepening and multifaceted experiences of love that grows over time, and finally the ever-maturing experiences of love in the older years, are all vehicles through which the sacred can be manifested. Encounters with strangers can also offer profound experiences of sacredness.

For those gifted with religious faith a profound sense of the Sacred contains within it the knowing that one is intimately loved by Love itself and the awareness of this intimacy can become something intensely real. For the Christian the in-breaking of God is described beautifully in the liturgy: "In him [Jesus] we see our God made visible and so are caught up in the love of the God we cannot see."[47]

While the everyday life events of family, work, and leisure activities can evoke the sacred, other specific happenings can have the potential to specifically elicit such an experience. Examples would include outstanding personal or community achievements in areas such as art, sport, science, or other fields of human endeavor; acts of heroism; gestures of kindness, especially acts of self-sacrificing love; exposure to beauty/the sublime; giving birth or being in the presence of a newborn child; personally experiencing or companioning someone on a healing journey; accompanying a dying person's slip toward death's mystery. Encounters with nature, healing events—whether brought about through the services of medicine, the Alcoholics Anonymous twelve-step program, or other ways—are also paths through which the sacred can be potently awakened. An experience of suffering and the journey of dying when lived through with courage and compassion can become especially sacred moments. A new way of experiencing the sacred is through cyberspace. The Web site Sacred Space has literally reached more than ten million people in five years, with thousands of respondents saying how the Sacred became alive for them through this form of mediation.[48]

4

The Aesthetic Dimension of Human Experience

This chapter attempts to enhance further an understanding of the depth quality of human experience by viewing its aesthetic dimension. While the heart of religious experience is the experience of holiness, the core of aesthetic experience is largely the experience of the beautiful/the sublime.[1] Experiences of beauty or sublimity are also found within the experience of the holy thereby indicating the close links that exist between aesthetical and religious experience.

Aesthetic experience draws on all aspects of the human person— body, mind, and spirit. Particular components of aesthetic experiencing include intuition, imagination, affectivity, creativity, the senses, the cognitional processes required to express meaning and significance, perception and particularly the perception of beauty, truth, love, and freedom. Aesthetics commonly associated with art, but nature, events, and most of all people, their relationships and in particular the human-divine relationship, enter the domain of aesthetical experience through the human desire for beauty, truth, and goodness. Beauty plays its part in discovering not only itself but also the beauty of truth. In relation to the good, beauty appears as the accessible aspect of the good since goodness itself is not visible. The sublime aspect of beauty can, for instance, be experienced through nature's awesomeness, such as the majesty of mountain peaks and the power of crashing waves, as well as in tender self-sacrificing expressions of interpersonal love.

Aesthetics as Found in Scripture and the Christian Tradition

The term *beauty* is nonexistent in the vocabulary of biblical Hebrew. The word comes from the Greek word *aisthesis*, which means "perception." Translations alter the meaning of words and in English translations of the Old Testament the use of the words *beauty* or *beautiful* are largely used interchangeably with terms such as marvel, magnificence, splendor, radiance, glory. All of these terms attempt to convey the concept that today is summed up in the words *beauty* or *sublime*. Aesthetical descriptions are frequently used in connection with Yahweh and in relation to particular events often described as the "Mirabilia Dei," thus illustrating that a keen aesthetical consciousness was present in the writers of the Old Testament. The Wisdom literature, in particular the Psalms, wax lyrical about the beauty of God and God's creation. Paul makes specific reference to the human person as "God's work of art" (Eph 2:10; *Jerusalem Bible* translation, 1966 ed.).

There have always been references to beauty within the Christian tradition. The early fathers of the church such as Origen and Irenaeus wrote specifically about the aesthetic aspect of the Christian faith, and theology of the first five centuries had a distinct "glow" about it. Augustine in particular had a great sense of beauty, especially noticeable throughout his *Confessions*. A classic example is his well-known exclamation "Late have I loved you, Beauty so ancient and so new, late have I loved you!"[2] Later Thomas Aquinas's words "what is received is received according to the mode of the receiver"[3] have become famous in an interpretive form: "beauty lies in the eye of the beholder." At the end of his life, Aquinas spoke of moving from a sitting to a kneeling theology, namely, to a theology of wonder at the mystery of a God who is love.

Theology, in Anselm's phrase "faith seeking understanding," has over centuries led to theology being perceived as an academic discipline. This omission of the beautiful within the heart of Christian living as well as in its theology has led to impoverishment and distortions. Most significantly it has affected central issues such as people's image of God, and as a consequence, the way people relate to God. When perception about God and God's creation is no longer permeated by the beautiful, the sense of being captivated by, attracted toward Loving Mystery can suffer. The understanding of revelation and grace, post–Vatican II, points to the wondrous happening of simply allowing ourselves to be grasped by God's loving outreach to us.[4] The response movement of openness to receiving this gift of Godself, of allowing oneself to become enraptured by the beauty of Holy Mystery, of surrendering, is a different approach to attempting by personal effort to win God's favor and thereby earn access to his presence.

This lack of expression of beauty, particularly from the Reformation until modern times, has led to a diminished awareness of beauty as a way of describing an individual's experiencing of Holy Mystery. This is surprising since Christian theology has always recognized the three great transcendentals—truth, goodness, and beauty—as key concepts, symbols, or ways of thinking and talking about God. The three approaches offer different insights: truth is about discerning what is truly real, goodness is about value that is made operative in deeds, beauty focuses on wonder and mystery, with love lying at the heart of this mystery. None of these transcendentals can be divorced from the other. Their intimate interdependence means that if one transcendental is affected either positively or negatively, the remaining two would be affected. For example, if the beautiful is neglected, truth and goodness are impoverished and can become "dull, lifeless, boring, formalistic and cold. It is beauty…which excites and nourishes human feeling, desire, thought and imagination. It is the splendor of beauty that makes the true and the good whole."[5] If, alternatively, truth is diminished, beauty can appear as irrational.

Personal Aesthetical Experiencing

Personal aesthetical experiencing is available to everyone since we are endowed with an aesthetic sense. Aesthetic experience begins at the first level of consciousness, where our senses and imagination are activated. Our senses are naturally attracted to or, alternatively, repelled by the stimuli they are exposed to. For example, the eye is stimulated by form and color, the ear by sound, taste by flavor, smell by odor, touch by texture and temperature. Aesthetics is normally spoken of in relation to two of these senses: sight and hearing. If beauty attracts, alternatively the aesthetic instinct tends to dislike what is ugly, discordant, drab, dirty, colorless, messy, disorderly, coarse. Imagination and memory also play a vital part in aesthetic experience. The importance of developing a keen aesthetic sense is highlighted by Hilary Mooney: "in the absence of the aesthetic much of the versatility and hidden creativity of concrete living would fail to surface: the human person would be presented as less than fully human."[6]

Patrick Sherry views the Holy Spirit's role within human creative activity as communicating God's beauty to the world. All earthly beauty is therefore a way in which the Spirit perfects creation and "those who destroy the beauty of God's creation or who create ugliness may be sinning against the Holy Spirit." Sherry is concerned that natural beauty and art have become merely a luxury element in life. He suggests a "failure to create beauty and a lack of appreciation of it, are signs of an absence of the Holy Spirit" since "the Spirit is the source of all real beauty and aesthetic merit" and can inspire "whomsoever he wills, without much regard to the recipient's moral character or religious orthodoxy."[7] As a consequence, beauty can be discovered within surprising contexts.

Personal aesthetic sense manifests itself in a myriad of ways, from the type of clothes worn and the way homes are decorated, to the more acquired appreciation developed around the beauties of nature, relationships, the events of personal living, and works of art.[8] According to John O'Donohue, "the human soul is hungry for beauty; we seek it everywhere—in landscape, music, art, clothes, furniture, gardening, companionship, love, religion and in ourselves. No one would desire not to be beautiful."[9]

John Paul II, in his 1990 New Year message, referred to aesthetics in relation to creation: "The aesthetic value of creation cannot be overlooked. Our very contact with nature has a deep restorative power; contemplation of its magnificence imparts peace and serenity. The Bible speaks again and again of the goodness and beauty of creation, which is called to glorify God" (see Gen 1:4ff.; Ps 8:22; 104:1ff.; Wis 13:3–5; Sir 30:16; 43:1–9).

Our aesthetic sense is aroused through perceptions. These can be instinctive, surprising, and at times immediate, while at other times the perception may dawn more gradually. Where beauty is present, the perception is one of appreciation. Some people's aesthetic sense appreciates and expresses itself in a stately, orderly, measured manner, whereas other peoples approach might tend toward more ecstatic or charismatic forms. Aesthetic experiences can arouse positive feelings such as delight, joy, wonder, awe. But other reactions are possible, such as horror or even a sense of emptiness. An example of an intensely mixed and disconcerting reaction is elicited when visiting the Children's Memorial in Jerusalem's Yad Vashem's Holocaust Museum. The exquisite beauty of the memorial depicting something so horrific throws one's feelings off balance. The same could be said of Michelangelo's *Pietà*. A supreme example of beauty is found in Jesus' dying on the cross. Gross ugliness, tragedy, betrayal, and enormous suffering are manifested, but the startling truth, the intensity of meaning, the enormity of love hidden in this event is what makes it so exquisitely beautiful.

By personally participating in a sense of beauty we can be lingering close to, or have actually entered, a religious experience. Daivetz Suzuki says that "the appreciation of the beautiful is at bottom religious, for without being religious one cannot detect and enjoy what is genuinely beautiful"[10]

Insight into truth, or involvement in or observing the good deed, can also lead to an awareness of the beautiful. The most profound of these experiences is perceived in loving and being loved, activities that Eric Fromm describes as an art.[11] The clear manifestation of beauty found in human relating moves to a more profound level in human-divine relating and is found most supremely within the inter-trinitarian relationships.

Beauty gives a sense of aliveness. Strictly, it has no *for* attached to it, in the sense that is has no function other than to be delighted in, although it has a secondary function in being a conveyor of meaning. Beauty always comes as gift, is usually a transient experience and often manifests itself in surprising ways and places. T. S. Eliot's dictum, found in *East Coker*, says "Humankind cannot bear very much reality." This is particularly true of beauty. Beauty touches a person but we are able neither to control or to possess it. When we participate in beauty and surrender to its captivating power, it can take us out of ourselves. Like love, every encounter with beauty is different; each experience is new, fresh. Beauty has a dignifying and healing power. It calls us beyond our smallness toward expanding horizons that enlarge our lives. Exposure to beauty can result in a new way of perceiving and being in the world.

As with religious experience, the experience of beauty takes precedence over the understanding of it. Yet understanding enhances that experience and in particular it helps reveal the significance of such experiences. Experiences are unique, but growth in understanding deepens personal aesthetic experiences as well as enables us to partially enter other people's aesthetical experiences.

The Aesthetical Experience of the Artist

The fundamental source of art is the Creator. The more immediate root of art lies in a story, metaphor, or configuration of a shape or sound that calls for attention and development from the artist in his or her search for its expression. This call for attentiveness requires artists to put aside their own eye as the center of the world and to focus more on things as they are. Creative activity, a capacity to see and think innovatively, opens up what was not previously understood, and even when the work is finished it may not be fully understood. The playwright Nigel Ford says, "I don't know what I know until I start to write about it. The very process of writing becomes the process of revelation. I write not *because* I see but *in order* to see." Art's creativity is essentially about discovery as opposed to illustration; it opens up something new. It is never about shrinking back to what is already known or achieved. Similarly in the area of faith, as Rowan Williams points out, God is not interested in repetition. Relationships within the Trinity do not reveal "a process of divine cloning" but rather a "God whose passion is for difference."[12]

Artists, precisely because they reflect on the deeper meaning of life can contribute to other people's lives. They inspire because they express/articulate in fresh, surprising, and at times, shocking ways something that their observers may have only intuited or not previously known. Often artistic works offer more questions than answers. Their work can celebrate coherence, at times bewilderment, and sometimes can awaken an awareness of mystery.

Lonergan's Thought on Aesthetical Experience

Lonergan in his later life gave more attention to the affective dimension of the human person, "feeling gives intentional consciousness its mass, momentum, drive, power. Without feelings our knowing and deciding would be paper thin."[13] This development added greatly to his views on aesthetics. He also hints at an aesthetic consciousness having a predisposing potential toward religious conversion: "There occur experiences commonly named religious. Their emergence into consciousness may be anything from slight and unnoticed to absorbing, fascinating, dominating."[14]

Patterns of organizing experience include an aesthetic pattern of experience (alternatives being biological, intellectual, or dramatic patterns). The aesthetic pattern is an experience that is savored for its own sake and can be accompanied by feelings of pleasure as well as a sense of wonder. It is especially this element of wonder that can facilitate a readiness to being touched by God. Everyone has a capacity for wonder, awe, fascination, adventure, daring, greatness, goodness, and majesty.

Art by its very existence, its being there, attempts to communicate truth and value. The thereness of this truth and value is made available to the judgment of the individual apprehending the work of art. Art does not itself defend truth but offers access to significance since the artist grasps what is or seems significant.

Understanding Lonergan's aesthetics is assisted further by turning to his four realms of meaning: common sense, theory, interiority, and transcendence—to which he adds two more in *Method*, scholarship and art. Of interest here is the added aesthetic realm. Those who live almost entirely within the realm of common sense can remain largely unaware of the realms of interiority, art, and scholarship. Differentiation of consciousness is what enables people to "master more realms" and also helps to understand those who are at home in these realms. Lonergan continues: "artistically differentiated consciousness is a specialist in the realm of beauty. It promptly recognizes and fully responds to beautiful objects. Its higher attainment is creating: it invents commanding forms; works out their implications; conceives and produces their embodiment."[15]

The aesthetic is experienced in a myriad of forms, for example, in people, relationships, nature, art, symbols, and it can be perceived preeminently for Christians in the person of Jesus. Traces of a real presence of the Divine may be revealed within any or all of these aesthetic forms. Within the aesthetic form of art, Lonergan says:

> Artistic meaning is a break from routine meaning. In routine meaning we are the ready-made man in the ready-made

world. The meanings are all settled beforehand, and we take them on and fit into them. The light is red and we stop....The artistic intention is to break that routine, and by the fact that it is broken there emerges a new subject in a new world, with fresh meaning....The artist has to take it [this "fresh meaning"] and sharpen it, bring it to the point, unfold it, develop it, present it, express it effectively.[16]

Lonergan acknowledges being influenced by Susanne Langer. This author writes profoundly about art, for instance, "The criterion of good art is its power to command one's contemplation and reveal a feeling that one recognizes as real, with the same 'click of recognition' with which an artist knows that a form is true."[17] A lengthier passage is particularly insightful:

Art does not affect the viability of life so much as its quality; that, however, it affects profoundly. In this way it is akin to religion, which also, at least in its pristine, vigorous, spontaneous phase, defines and develops human feelings. When religious imagination is the dominant force in society, art is scarcely separable from it; for a great wealth of actual emotion attends religious experience, and unspoiled, unjaded minds wrestle joyfully for its objective expression, and are carried beyond the occasion that launched their efforts, to pursue the furthest possibilities of the expressions they have found. In an age when art is said to serve religion, religion is really feeding art. Whatever is holy to people inspires artistic conception.[18]

Two Specific Characteristics of Aesthetic Experience

The *first* characteristic of aesthetic experience lies in its ability to liberate consciousness. The biological pattern's concern is with survival and hence immediate physical needs; the intellectual pattern, especially if it operates solely at a scientific level, is concerned with proof; and the dramatic level's concern is with self-realization. In pure aesthetic experience, these patterns are largely nonoperative. There is a "coming-into-thereness" of the aesthetic dimension and we are free to move or not move into this dimension. The initial phase of noticing is based on receptivity. Consciousness then moves to understanding what is noticed, and finally to participating in the beauty of that object. A work of art invites participation, a seeing for ourselves, and offers the possibility of living in a richer world. The freedom quality is further enriched when the dynamism of human consciousness is permeated by grace; when the experiencing, understanding, judging, and deciding about aesthetical endeavors become graced activities.

Enda McDonagh explicitly traces this liberating aspect of beauty back to the divine artist: "On Golgotha, in the garden of Gethsemane as in the garden of Genesis, the creative, transforming, liberating 'artist' is God, the Spirit of God."[19] The creative process that leads to liberation often requires struggling with the mysteries of human living, a struggle that lies inherent in all aesthetic work, be it, for example, art or human relating.

The *second* characteristic of aesthetic experience is its transcendent qualities. Beauty arouses wonder but also questioning, a questioning that can point toward ultimate reality—the ultimate reality we call God. As we become more sensitive to beauty and inquiry the closer we move toward Mystery. An aesthetic experience has the potential for heightening an experience of mystery and even of drawing an individual to the actual acceptance of Ultimate Mystery. Just as a pure experience of beauty is a given, so too entering into an experience of Mystery is also a given. Both are true experiences. In a true sense all experiences are givens and as a result need no explanations. Experiences simply are. In regard to aesthetic experience, this especially means we find ourselves in it rather than choosing it, and as such, it is an experience akin to religious experience.

Theological Aesthetics

The term *aesthetics* was introduced into philosophy in the eighteenth century. When later it entered theology, it was mainly used in relation to revelation, creation, grace, and faith. Gesa Thiessen offers the following descriptive definition: "Theological aesthetics is concerned with questions about God and issues in theology in the light of and perceived through sense knowledge (sensation, feeling, imagination), through beauty and the arts."[20] She suggests that the beauty and vision of God are theological aesthetics' central themes. The importance not only of hearing but also of the desire to see God has been paramount within the Christian faith tradition. The revelation of Holy Mystery, as shown to humanity in the person of Jesus, was "what we have heard, what we have seen with our own eyes, what we have looked at and touched with our hands, concerning the word of life—this life was revealed, and we have seen it and testify to it" (1 John 1:2). That physical seeing was short-lived and became transformed, through the power of the resurrection, into a faith-seeing, where the risen Jesus remains for all time "the light of the world."

Theological aesthetics became a separate discipline in the mid-twentieth century. Like religious experience, it emphasizes aesthetics' experiential dimension. This occurs when a connection is made between beauty's origins and its appropriation by the human heart. Aesthetics existed when the first human heart was moved by beauty and theological aesthetics arose when recognition of the sacred within human experiences of beauty was awakened.

Balthasar's Thoughts on Aesthetics

Hans Urs von Balthasar is considered by many to be the preeminent theologian in the field of theological aesthetics. He particularly deals with the suitability of aesthetics when describing Christian revelation. The first volume of his seven-volume work *The Glory of the Lord: A Theological Aesthetics* titled *Seeing the Form* lays the foundations of his aesthetics. The lengthy introduction outlines much of the core of his thinking on aesthetics. He comments that a theology of beauty should be elaborated in a beautiful way, and this summary of his thought begins with his emphasis on the three great transcendentals: truth, goodness, and beauty. He likens them to sisters, saying that neglecting one would have a "devastating" effect on the other two. "[Beauty] 'dances' around its sisters...is the disinterested one...[yet] demands for itself at least as much courage and decision as do truth and goodness."[21] He points out that without beauty, goodness ceases to be attractive and truth loses its cogency.

Balthasar outlines his understanding of beauty as the meeting of two great moments—*form* and *splendor*. These are experienced first in the act of "beholding" or "seeing," and second in the act of "being enraptured." Form must first be "espied...by an eye that recognizes value." "Admittedly," he says, "form would not be beautiful unless it were fundamentally a sign and appearing of a depth and a fullness that in themselves and in an abstract sense remain both beyond our reach and our vision."[22] The question is, how does the form appear as beautiful? He explains:

> The form as it appears to us is beautiful only because the delight that it arouses in us is founded upon the fact that, *in it, the truth and goodness of the depths of reality itself are manifested and bestowed*, and this manifestation and bestowal reveal themselves to us as being something infinitely and inexhaustibly valuable and fascinating.[23]

This sentence contains the core of his understanding of "seeing the form"—a movement that he summarizes in two phrases: "the form which contains the depth" and "the form that transcends itself by pointing beyond to the depths."[24]

This first movement proceeds to the second—*splendor*. "We 'behold' the form; but, if we really behold it, it is not as a detached form, rather in its unity with the depths that make their appearance in it. We see form as the splendour, as the glory of Being. We are 'enraptured' by our contemplation of these depths and are 'transported' to them."[25] In simple terms, one can combine together the meanings of both movements in the following way: one *beholds the form* and becomes *enraptured by the splendor* discovered within that form.

An essential note in Balthasar's aesthetics is the perception of God's self-manifestation, with *glory* as the key characteristic of this revelation. Central to Balthasar's thinking is the relationship between beauty and Christian revelation; and so, the incarnation is the fundamental form since it is the expression of the divine in human form. All created forms are derived from this Jesus-form and find their deepest depth in the light of this form. He strikingly states that being a Christian is itself a form. Hence it is through the form of Christian faith that one perceives all other forms. Alternatively, beholding created forms in their very thereness attunes and sensitizes us to the form of God's self-revelation in Jesus. Both "beholdings"—Jesus and other created forms—are brought about through the category of the beautiful.

All those who have been once affected inwardly by the worldly beauty of either nature, or of a person's life, or of art, will surely not insist that they have no idea of what beauty is. The beautiful brings with it a self-evidence that en-lightens without mediation. This is why, when we approach God's revelation with the category of the beautiful, we quite spontaneously bring this category with us in its this-worldly form.[26]

When beholding the Jesus-form, Balthasar refers to the need of a "new light," a light that empowers us to see Jesus, to see how the divine glory is reflected in the face of Christ, especially in his death and resurrection. This form makes its most extraordinary appearance in the risen Jesus whose presence is a revelation of sublime splendor (*kabod, doxa, gloria*). A key to some level of understanding the profound harmony that lies within the paschal mystery, he suggests, is to let Christian revelation set our standards of beauty.

The mystery of God's love poured out for humanity is perceived most radically when God in Jesus became so lowly, humiliated, rejected, powerless, pain-filled, and even ugly in his dying, that he appears almost without form. "He had no form or majesty that we should look at him, nothing in his appearance that we should desire him"(Isa 53:2). It was only after descending to the depth of death itself that Jesus entered the exalted state of living "close to the Father's heart" (John 1:18). The paradox and yet the harmony that lies within the paschal mystery is almost too great for human psychology to be able to hold together. The only possible comprehension available comes through the light and experience of love.

> "Light" is expressly required which illumines this particular form, a light which at the same time breaks forth from within the form itself. In this way, the "new light" will at the same time make seeing the form possible and be itself seen along with the form. The splendour of the mystery which offers itself in such a way cannot, for this reason, be equated with the other kinds of aesthetic radiance which we encounter in the world...
>
> That we are at all able to speak here of "seeing" shows that, in spite of all concealment, there is nonetheless something to be seen and grasped. It shows therefore, that man is

not merely addressed in a total mystery, as if he were compelled to accept obediently in blind and naked faith something hidden from him, but that something is "offered" to man by God, indeed offered in such a way that man can see it, understand it, make it his own, and live from it in keeping with his human nature.[27]

Essentially for Christians, their encounter with the Godself comprises the element of an initial gift of light that draws one into itself and then follows the graced act of allowing oneself to be seized by the beauty of that light—a light that reveals itself in the person of Jesus. Such an experience *is* the experience of rapture. Through faith, the beholder is given the eyes of perception that allows this wondrous experience of rapture to occur.

Being encountered by the form of God manifested in Jesus and at the same time being touched by the radiance that emerges from within that form is not a one-off event but rather an illumination that grows slowly. Throughout the Christian life our initial illumination can acquire ever-deepening understandings. This will necessitate constant and frequent corrections, clarifications, and focus in regard to the initial, as well as ongoing, illuminations.

Balthasar's aesthetical vision filters through the fifteen volumes of his trilogy. In *Theo-Drama*, in the second section of the trilogy, Balthasar's focus is on the good—the goodness of God as manifested in the deeds of Jesus' life, death, and resurrection. The beauty and goodness of Jesus' revelation are intertwined when perceived in the historical form of Jesus' life. The final part of the trilogy, *Theo-Logic*, links beauty with the truth of God's saving work in Jesus.

Similarities between Religious and Aesthetic Experience

A key link is found in the similar processes within consciousness that allow for the unfolding of aesthetic or religious experiences. When these occur at the fourth level of consciousness the concern is about authentically apprehending values. Religion by its very nature communicates ultimate values. The core value from a Christian perspective is love. Art also communicates values such as truth and beauty and always the values that the artist sees as significant.

Within the aesthetic experience, we are not in control; the work of art encounters us with what David Tracy describes as "surprise, even the shock of reality itself."[28] Through that experience we can come to a fuller knowledge of a truth through the recognition of a work of art. We can be transformed by this truth and return to ordinary life with new sensibilities, a happening that has similarities with religious experience. It is not a subject/object type of experience, but rather an experience where we transcend ordinary self-consciousness through being caught up in our *relationship* with the work of art. It is in Buber's terms an "I-Thou" experience, an experience that establishes the world of relationship, as opposed to an "I-It" experience, which does not. "When *Thou* is spoken there is no thing [no object]."[29]

Stephan van Erp's work shows the close connection between faith and beauty, while at the same time stressing that the beautiful and the religious must not be reduced to each other. For instance, he shows a distinction between beauty and sublimity when he writes, "The beautiful is judged for its form. In contrast the sublime is judged for its formlessness and its boundlessness....The beautiful gives us a pleasurable feeling, whereas the sublime overwhelms us...and fills us with an enormous vitality that enthralls us."[30]

McDonagh demonstrates the link that exists between aesthetic and religious experience by suggesting that artists contribute to both distinguishing and uniting the holy and the beautiful through their creativity. "The beauty-making of the artist and the holy-making of the believer, however inadequately in either case, reflect the creative and sanctifying work of God." Appreciating a work of art involves letting that work of art be. The further letting go of actively surrendering to this thereness leads to a sense that, it could be said, one inhabits a work of art. These events of letting be and letting go "in every sphere of life reach their culmination in letting God."[31]

Various qualities are shared in both religious and aesthetic experiences. First, a *search for meaning* lies at the heart of both experiences. Art, as a powerful carrier of meaning, invites encounter and, by offering a break from other routine carriers of meaning, it affords the possibility of new and fresh meanings, including that of religious meaning. When an art form has symbolic qualities, its impact as a carrier of meaning can be strikingly effective.

Second, authentic religious and aesthetic experiences can have an *expansive effect*. Living in a religiously converted state is the result of a decision made about, as Lonergan says, "one's horizon, one's outlook, one's world view....It is a decision about whom and what you are for, and, again, about whom and what you are against."[32] When a religiously converted person has also been aesthetically converted, or vice versa, the enlarged horizon of one conversion can profoundly affect the other. Someone who exemplifies this is the hermit-mystic and television art critic, Wendy Becket.

Third, *imagination* plays a key role in both experiences. This capacity allows us to receive what comes before us and discover further meaning within what is presented. Images play an important role in religion as well as in art. Apart from a dispute about the use of images—the iconoclast schism, which was quickly settled—images have held a favorable place within Christianity. For example, fine arts are considered by Vatican II to be "the noblest expressions of human genius"[33] and John Paul II urged artists to "bring forth ever new epiphanies of beauty" while warning that beauty cannot be divorced from the good.[34] The term *sacred art* is used when a true and beautiful work evokes and glorifies the mystery of God.[35] Yet as John Ruskin, English poet and art commentator, perceptively states, "All great art is praise."

A fourth quality is *nonattachment*. Authentic art and religion are non-self-centered. This requires letting go of selfish concerns and letting nothing else exist except what is seen. Beauty attracts unselfish attention. Art and religion are teachers and revealers of how to look at, love, and delight in places, things, relationships, and ideas, without the need to personally grasp and use these realities solely for one's own benefit. Nonattachment facilitates experiences where something is savored for its own sake. It fosters a freeing quality that leaves individuals free to enter or reject what is on offer, a coming into thereness, a seeing-for-oneself quality, through an apprehension that lets the other/Other be. Irish Murdoch sees good art as being non-self-centered: "beauty is that which attracts this particular sort of unselfish attention."[36]

Fifth, a sense of *wonder* is central to both religious and aesthetic experiences. When questioning is combined with wonder, the element of mystery can present itself within religious and aesthetic consciousness. McDonagh refers to living in the mysterious region that exists between human wonder and divine attraction and notes how great artists can open one to the attraction of God.[37] The surprise of God can come into awareness more easily through moments of wonder. Such moments come unexpectedly. The poet Patrick Kavanagh speaks of the same reality in reverse: "Through a chink too wide there comes no wonder."[38] The wonder elicited by entering mystery or appreciating art comes about by participating in it. This necessitates surrendering to what is being experienced.

Sixth, an apt notion that contains significance for authentic aesthetic and religious experiences is *recognition*. Recognizing that something has occurred, that one is caught up in the truth that has been disclosed, that this truth is important, real, and not something one can manipulate, that it is not one's own achievement, are all components of both religious and artistic experiencing. Recognition is a central factor within the Christian tradition. Christian faith is based on the first witnesses to the resurrection recognizing the power and implications of that happening. The core recognition was and is that Jesus is now Lord.

Seventh and final, an added contemporary similarity is seen in the increasing *marginalization* of art and religion in society. Both have been largely relegated from the public to the private realm and are mainly seen as a question of personal choice and taste. Rarely are either viewed as resources of truth and beauty that can benefit society. They are perceived by some as an escape from real responsibility. Yet marginality, by offering a different vantage point, can lend itself to forms of creativity that are at the cutting edge of contemporary thinking. A focus of some modern religious art has been on the mysteriousness, unpredictability, and even wildness of God rather than on creeds and laws.[39] When either a religious thinker or artist, for example, a film director, produces some classical expression of the human spirit they move beyond the marginalized status. A modern example of a possible emerging classic is the simple, large, and striking *The Way of Life* sculpture by Jonathan Clarke erected in the medieval Ely Cathedral in 2001.[40] Clarke says of his own work that the simpler the sculpture became the more possibilities it opened up.

"Less is more. Not everything was 'spelt out' and so it affects different people in different ways."[41]

Today some people are turning to the artist for elements of transcendence, seeing art as more uplifting than religion. Others consider that artists have become the spiritual leaders of our age, that they are among the few who take time to reflect on the deeper meaning of life as well as to search for ways to express their turmoil and tentative insights. To regain a healthier balance between art and religion, Gerard Manley Hopkins urged, in relation to poetry, that the language used should be the current language heightened—not an obsolete form. This suggestion could also be followed by visual artists using the language of contemporary forms, symbols, and images.[42]

Despite the above named similarities, however, there remains a distinction. Aesthetic experience can remain solely a human reality, carrying meaning that does not go beyond the realm of interiority, whereas religious experience, and the ongoing transformation of consciousness that such experience continuously offers, brings one into the unrestricted realm of meaning. In this fuller transcendent realm, access to Holy Mystery and to all of reality becoming known and loved in and through divine reality can be realized by those graced with such a gift.

Examples of Aesthetic Experience That Contain Possibilities of Connection with Religious Experience

The Aesthetic Dimension as Experienced through Art

The artist, like the thinker, hero, or saint, is likely to live life in a more intensified and radicalized manner. When, for the artist, this intensity is combined with talent, discipline, and imagination, authentic works of art come into being. While undertaking the journey of intensification, an artist's creativity can be experienced as a gift that comes unawares.

Artists' attempts to express the sublime can, for instance, be achieved through music, with recognized examples of this sublime quality being found in the last movement of Beethoven's *Ninth Symphony* or *In Paradisum* in Faure's *Requiem*. Apart from being beautiful, such works can convey a sense of transcendence or even of the Transcendent. A sculptural example of this is Dublin's Millennium Spire of Light whose artist, Ian Ritchie, specifically stated his desire to give a transcendent dimension to this work. The sublime, the spark of the Divine, can also be found hidden in the ordinary—a hallmark visible in Patrick Kavanagh's and Gerard Manley Hopkins's poetry. In efforts to express a particular truth, especially if it portrays the dark side of human living, artists may choose grotesque or horrific forms, colors, or raw materials. Examples would be Picasso's *Guernica*, the heavy metal sculptures at Yad Vashem.

Motivation is a significant factor in art, and especially for the modern painter Norman Adams, who is distressed that so much art today seems to be about hatred. He does not think that art can be made that way but rather it should be made out of love and firmly believes that it is beauty not hatred that "leads to religion."[43] Alice Ramos questions the intentionality of works of art. Her concern is that some works could have morally harmful effects by the negative impact they can have on morals and beliefs. This fact, she feels, is not taken seriously enough: "We often think of ourselves as being sufficiently grown-up and thus almost invulnerable to such influence. I think, however, that this is naïve." She suggests that certain art forms can be harmful not only to children but also to adults and "particularly to those without sufficient moral and doctrinal formation."[44]

In a different context there can also be a profoundly positive aspect to darkness. Gordon Strachan, writing about Chartres Cathedral, says the building itself produces a spiritual experience that is connected in some way with its interior being so dark. "Chartres embodies the most profound expression of the Dionysian divine darkness that the world has; it has a *jeweled* darkness which comes through countless windows of the most beautiful and priceless stained glass. This light transforms the vast emptiness of the building."[45] O'Donohue offers a further thought: "the more luminous the form, the deeper we are afforded a glimpse into the dark riches of the unknown."[46] Luminous form is the medium that many artists attempt to create as they express themselves in their particular type of art.

The Aesthetic Dimension as Experienced through Personal Knowing

The unknown both fascinates and frightens, and the veil between the two can be slight. Consciousness has the capacity to be open to the unknown, but society and personal fears can dull the desire for such encounters. Also, if something uncomfortable becomes known, it can be let to slip into the unconscious. The task of consciousness is to search for meaning and it can do this in two ways. First is the analytic approach to knowing. This occurs through *description*—an approach to knowledge that is not always appropriate within different life situations. Second, art uses *suggestion* as its way to truth. It helps excavate the unknown by inviting the viewer/hearer to participate in that work of art. A work of art is in a certain sense something alive and calls for participation from its observers. A dynamic art form from a religious perspective is the imagery offered by dance; the supreme expression of this art form being the perichoresis of the inner trinitarian life into which everyone is invited to participate.

The Aesthetic Dimension as Experienced Interpersonally

The most profound aesthetic experiences can be interpersonal. The human person is irresistibly drawn to and thrives on encounters with the beautiful, especially in the area of human relating. The lover who loves and the loved one who receives love offer experiences of beauty, especially when such love is reciprocally expressed with tenderness and received with gratitude. A public expression of this beauty was shown in a television documentary that highlighted the beauty of an older man's love for his wife, who was suffering from Alzheimer's disease. He lovingly caressed his wife's hands while singing to her one of their favorite operatic love songs. The importance of interpersonal relating, in the form of love of neighbor at both local and wider levels, has always been prominent within the Christian tradition. With migration being a major issue of this age, however, an openness and welcome for the stranger is becoming ever more pertinent. The unique contribution of Emmanuel Levinas's metaphor of "the face" as an expression of human communication is especially called upon in relation to the stranger.[47] The stranger challenges the welcomer to risk reaching out, not out of need, but with the generosity of giving the self away to that person. Welcoming the stranger, sharing his/her world, becoming an "infinitizer" (a word Levinas used to describe someone who strives for what is other than oneself) is an outstanding expression of both aesthetics and religion. Levinas terms this activity "authentic altruism." The concern and concrete help that poured out from the citizens and governments of many countries of the world to inhabitants affected by the tsunami disaster of Christmas 2004 was an outstanding global expression of this altruism.

Within all forms of human love, one can receive an inkling of the riches that are possible within the human-divine relationship. Being in love with Holy Mystery is the most wondrous of all human happenings for those who receive glimpses of it and especially for those who live within a state of being in love with Love.

Capacities and Dispositions That Facilitate Awakening the Sacred

This chapter examines the innate capacities and specific disposi-tions that facilitate an individual becoming more open to religious and aesthetic experiences. From the perspective of faith experience, while the core of this experience is always gift, the reception of this gift can be prepared for and fostered by the activation of certain capacities and the acquiring of particular dispositions.

The chapter commences by noting present-day difficulties in coming to religious faith. While philosophies and religions with an Eastern orientation tend to explore the spiritual dimension of human experience through the notion of expanding consciousness, Western societies live increasingly within a culture that imposes an empirical worldview. The strong influence of the West's individualistic and materialistic culture has led to a need in some people for prereligious experiences. In Christian terminology, this could be called a pre-evangelization phase.

Sandra Schneiders lists some of the problems of "contemporary first world western culture" and suggests these are ironically the result of an abundance of wealth, leisure, and freedom. With religion in decline and spirituality in ascendancy, the frequently expressed state-ment "I am a spiritual person but I am not religious," has led to these realities being viewed as "rivals," rather than as "partners in the search for God."[1] A partner approach, according to Schneiders, sees the institutional element in religion as passing on its tradition and the living out of this tradition as its spirituality. A religious tradition that has stood the test of time offers a sharing of belief, a theology, a tested tradition of moral ideals and restraints and the wisdom of great figures within that tradition. Today the element of tradition in faith is disappearing due to the institutional element being abandoned by so many. Without the support of tradition, personal spiritualities can be vague, shapeless, and private and have no recognized ways of being shared with others or embodied in public life.

Another difficulty is that some institutional elements become inauthentic or empty over time, and this has led to disillusionment regarding religious matters. A consequence of this has been a rejection of religion due to a failure to distinguish between the authentic and life-giving religious tradition and an inauthentic institutional form on the other. Postmodernism's emphasis on relativism and immediate satisfaction has also alienated people from a religious tradition. These and other factors have led in recent times to a culture of religious disbelief.

According to Rudolf Siebert, a collapse of meaning "within established religious and cultural systems," offers society three choices in working out its future: first, "the totally administered, bureaucratized, computerized and robotized signal society"; second, "the totally militarized society preparing one war or civil war after the other"; and third, "the reconciled society in which friendly and helpful living together of all people will be possible."[2] The latter choice is achievable when society frees itself from varying forms of alienation and particularly when religious and secular people work together toward this future. The ability for this to happen, from a Christian scholarship perspective, requires not separating faith from reason. For Alice Ramos, only "a faith that is fully received, thought out and lived, will penetrate culture and there is no doubt that present-day culture stands in need of transformation."[3]

Michael Paul Gallagher speaks of a "cultural desolation" and calls for a spiritual or cultural catechumenate. The early church's catechumen was directed toward baptism. Today many are baptized, but perhaps have never made a personal faith decision nor been invited to do so in a way that makes sense to them. He says, "we often need to get in touch with ourselves before we can be ready to hear the surprise of God" and that many people "are nowhere near this threshold."[4] Others may have had a genuine experience of faith, but inadequate faith development has led to personal faith remaining at a child's level of understanding. Faith nourishment has been hindered by individuals' inability to take personal responsibility for a more adult faith and also because of the church's reduced ability to reach out to where people are in their lives. While there have been some creative attempts to do so, these have been limited by recent difficulties within the hierarchical church surrounding sexual abuse, authoritarianism, the impoverished status of women, and other issues. This has resulted in numerous people claiming they no longer believe in, or even need, religion.

"Getting in touch" with oneself means, for Gallagher, exploring "avenues towards depth" and becoming attuned to desires "to dive deeper"; referring to young adults' comments, he says: "in this society it is impossible to be oneself. Superficiality reigns. Appearance is everything."[5] It is a world of images and designer labels, where stepping out of one's peers' line of thinking, attitudes, or behaviors, such as dress code is considered taboo. Coming to an awareness of being comfortable and accepting of oneself plays a central role in the research analysis of this thesis.

The present cultural situation, according to Dupré, has led to the West losing religion's essential element—transcendence. Transcendence allows one to recognize another dimension within ordinary reality. In today's world, he states "the quest for ultimate intelligibility merely detracts from the urgent and immediate task of exercising rational control over the world."[6] With such an approach to life, a transcendent horizon fades. Dupré also notes that there is a tendency today to reduce religion to one experience among others and to do so with little or no awareness or acknowledgment of its transcendent source. He states that in an atheistic culture, especially where the supports of a community of faith are absent, the only place to turn is inward. In that space, a waning believer can, by confronting one's own atheism, come to restore the vitality of one's own religion. What is needed, he feels, is expectant waiting and attentive listening to the possible signs that will allow a new perceptiveness to emerge. The first attraction is more likely to come from discovering the significance of the religious message as personally meaningful. This key insight can reveal itself in an initial awakening of faith that is likely to come from partial insights. This is likely to be the case when early awakenings are accompanied by a dissatisfaction "with the shallowness of a closed, secular world" that leads one to abandon a "conquering grasping attitude for a more receptive one."[7]

The situations just described indicate the need to look at the area of human capacities and dispositions, and the role a conversion of dispositions and enlivening of certain capacities play in facilitating a coming to, or deepening of, faith in today's Western world.

What Is Meant by Innate Capacity

In the first chapter, I gave considerable space to the cognitive processes of experience, understanding, and judgment in coming to know truth. There are, however, two other significant ways that complement and enrich the path to knowledge—these are *imagination* and *intuition*. These two abilities are operative in people in varying ways and degrees and are clearly activated by artists and mystics. The assistance that imagination and intuition give to the cognitional processes already described is less essential for the scientist whose quest is for scientific or empirical knowledge. It is also true, however, that scientists, including Einstein, recognize the importance of intuition when they make a leap forward in their understanding.

Since capacities are innate, everyone has the potential to exercise these functions. This applies particularly to desire—an inner capacity that lies deep within every human heart. By discovering and listening to personal desires, we begin to discern where our desires are drawing us. Some of the discoveries that may be opened up in this process could be seen as a heart way of coming to know.[8] This knowledge does not bypass the cognitional processes since the genuineness of this form of knowing requires verification from one's intelligence and judgment.

Imagination

Imagination is the faculty that forms images in the mind. Its etymology comes from the French and means "to picture to oneself," and contains the notion of representation, likeness, or resemblance. To some, imagination is concerned with mere fantasy, a reproduction of absent or literal meaning, or to a weakened notion of perception where the image evoked is seen as a vague substitute for the real. The *merely* imaginary is for others an illusion that is expressed in the common comment "it's just your imagination."

The Enlightenment led to reason being promoted over the imagination. Examples of this are found in nineteenth-century British education, which required rote learning. Similarly in philosophy, logic held a foundational place in coming to know truth, which led to the relegation of other ways of coming to discern truth. A balance between reason and imagination needs to be restored so that imagination's capacity as a shaper of meaning is reinstated. The Irish poet Brendan Kennelly says that it is through the imagination that we are energized to connect with reality. Imagination has a particular capacity for opening to wonder, and in turn, wonder can be a gateway to mystery. It is through imagination that we are enabled to "cross over" and connect with mystery. The capacity of our imagination to establish a connection between matter and spirit is particularly helpful in forming a sacramental view of life. The importance of the imagination, for Van Erp, is its ability to enable perception to "relate to existing interpretations in a new way. Imagination therefore will play an important role for a new generation that is not brought up within a self-evident context, to relate to the Christian narrative."[9]

"Imagining" is placed in Lonergan's list of operations between inquiring and understanding. He therefore situates it within the intelligent level of experience. It is an activity that is mediated by meaning and can operate in relation to the past, the future, the absent, the possible, the ideal, the normative, the fantastic.[10] The intending of imagination can be creative or representational and when either of these imaginary forms operate alongside the other processes of intelligence, insight can ensue. Imagination used in this manner is an enriching way of coming to know and experience reality.

David Tracy associates imagination with language rather than with perception and sees it as the power that expresses or gives form and meaning to human experience.[11] This notion is supported by Kees Waaijman who says that in the reading process a reader imagines the imaginary world: he "receives" the meaning of the text by "composing" it; by "performing" the text it comes alive.[12]

The *relationship between imagination and faith* is well described by William Lynch.[13] For him, the images formed by the imagination are the way we experience the world. When faith informs and gives shape to those images, faith itself becomes a way of experiencing the world, whether that world be politics, relationships, even personal thinking. The images of faith are embodied in history and as images they have the ability to move between the past, present, and future.

If, from Lynch's viewpoint, faith becomes the primary internal force in our lives then it forms our worldview and affects all levels of experience. As already stated, faith is "the knowledge born of religious love," therefore faith is formed out of something more than evidence. In an empirical understanding of knowledge, faith neither adds to that form of knowing, nor is the result of it. Faith knowledge on the other hand can operate as the energizer and creative force within personal thinking, feeling, and acting.

A role of the imagination is to imagine what is real, and it is through imagining something that one tells oneself how something actually is. An example of the above, from a Christian faith perspective, is faith informing an individual of the truth of Jesus' words: "I am the Way." Faith is not limited to specific images, hence identical ways of experiencing faith realities are not the norm. So the image of Jesus as the Way will be imagined differently by different people. Imagination can become crippled if too narrow or if inflexible approaches to what is imagined are used, or worse still imposed, in an overly suggestive manner. This can be seen in reference to images of God, who throughout both Testaments and over history has been imaged under both helpful and unhelpful guises. For the Christian the truest image of God is revealed in Christ.

Imagination has the capacity to hold what is opposite or contrary together, an ability that bears fruit in wisdom. It is within this context that Lynch speaks of the "ironic imagination" and the "irony of faith."[14] Christian faith is full of this juxtaposition of opposites—humility/greatness, power/weakness, belief/unbelief, good/bad, death/resurrection—and full of lives with the simultaneous presence of these contraries. A function of this form of contrast is that it educates faith by deabsolutizing things—in the sense that often it is a question of holding opposites together rather than an either/or approach that proves most helpful when searching for truth. As faith matures, it also learns to live with the coexistence of the expected and the unexpected. The great unexpected within history is the Christ event. This happening as well as other unfathomable elements in human living, which often surface when the *why* question is elicited, call for faith in the Incomprehensible One—in Holy Mystery. Faith consistently wrestles with this incomprehensible element in life, while at the same time, realistically facing facts, including the fact of death. Authentic faith, however, does not allow the tragic element in life to become victorious because of belief, for the Christian, in resurrection.

An image that Christ manifested by his life, and especially by his death and resurrection, was that of redemption. This reality has to be imagined and received. The West's present experience of powerlessness in the face of terrorism, combined with diminished hope and some having a personal sense of not needing redemption, call for a transformation of our imagination, especially in this area of redemption. For example, Jesus' words, "unless a wheat grain falls on the ground and dies, it only remains a single grain; but if it dies, it yields a rich harvest" (John 12:24), offer an image that helps flesh out our imagining, and therefore understanding, of the mystery of redemption.

Ignatius of Loyola laid great emphasis on the power of imagination in relation to faith.[15] First, it played an important role in his early conversion process (1521 CE). This was initiated, during a convalescent period, by comparing his readings of a life of Christ and of the saints with other "worldly" books. He had the habit of "imagining what he had to do" following his reading. After his religious reading he queried whether the thoughts that occurred in his imagination were from God or from a more worldly source. "After his eyes were opened a little" he began to notice that his ideas about God led to consolation and the latter to desolation.

This attention to imagination was not only central in his life but featured prominently in his *Spiritual Exercises*. He exhorts excitants throughout the four weeks of the exercises to use their imagination. "Make a mental representation of the place" (and often of the specific people in the scene contemplated) is a refrain he used as a prelude to many of his exercises.

Imagination works by association and can evoke imitation. Images are assimilated from our culture, and Western culture today is particularly image laden but largely at an empirical level. Some modern images contain negative components such as violence, a tendency to scapegoat, distortions of various kinds, and all of these could elicit copycat reactions. An unlearning of negative images, coupled with learning more positive ones, is an important factor in predisposing people toward faith. Gallagher terms this unlearning "salvation,"[16] a salvation that is focused not so much on what it is saving one *from*, but rather on what the saving is *for*. This *for* element is concerned with what is life giving. Christianity, a religion that proclaims salvation, teaches a specific form of imagining reality—one that calls for an imitation that works toward being nonviolent, just, and loving. Negative images, such as those that result in acquisitiveness, suspicion, and individualism, require a transformation that turns to other-centeredness.

Attentiveness can cultivate our imaginative capacity and this can enable new ways of seeing reality. Shocking the imagination can be provoked when, for instance, reflecting on a gospel parable that surprises us into defamiliarizing what previously seemed familiar. Noticing loveliness even in the mundane offers a path to recognizing the divine presence within the whole of reality. Gerard Manley Hopkins well describes this recognition: "the world is charged with the grandeur of God."[17]

Although personal images of God play a significant role in life, there is the constant need to remember that all images of God are only images and that every image inevitably remains more unlike than like anything that can be known about God. The ability to allow these images to alter as imagination and insight develop is necessary when culture or other factors impoverish, distort, or even ridicule images of God. Images are like a lens that can bring into focus aspects of reality, while filtering out others. Being disposed to challenge a notion of God, for instance, as a "fixer" of human affairs or as a male figure might lead to new ways of visioning God. Changed images could prove meaningful and helpful in entering into and sustaining a relationship with God in the modern world. Christians are gifted with a particular image of God—Christ—which "is the image of the invisible God" (Col 1:15), an image that reveals a suffering God who walks the road with people rather than changing things for them.

Our image of God affects the way we see the world and especially our own self-image. David Ranson says that, in his experience, he sees the majority of Christians living out of a distorted "monadic understanding of God" and that this has led to patriarchy and its accompanying images of domination, judgment, and exclusion.[18] Yet Christians are gifted with the knowledge of God brought by Jesus. Jesus' revelation is of a relational God, a community of persons, "a mystery of mutuality, reciprocity and dialogue."[19] Made in God's image, the human person is, as a consequence, made for relationships. This means that "the place for the experience of God is not the mystical experience of the self: it is the social experience of the self and the personal experience of sociality....The Trinity is our social programme."[20] Reimagining community and discovering ever-deepening experiences of relationships are where we discover both God and the fullness of one's own humanity.

In summary, I have shown that the imagination is particularly helpful in four areas. First, it helps us to live with paradox due to its greater ability than reason to hold opposites together. Second, imagination is better equipped than reason in fostering hope through its capacity to explore and envision future possibilities. Third, it is in the imagination that human deeds—whether good or evil—originate. Fourth, it is through imagining God, and especially as Trinity, that we discover more truly who God is and also who we are and who we can become, namely, more fully human.

Intuition

Intuition is a philosophic term and refers to a recognized way of knowing within epistemology. Gerald May refers to intuition as "the state of apprehending or appreciation that occurs before any thinking takes place" and suggests it is a more direct, even if more unusual, form of knowing.[21] For him, the goal of contemplative psychology is to expand our innate capacity for intuitive perception.

Intuition is more than a hunch[22] and can exist within a variety of experiences. Examples would include knowing what is going on behind what is unsaid or half said, or having a sense of what is required in a situation without anything being named. Some people seem to have a keener intuitive sense than others, but everyone has the capacity for this sense. Intuition is sometimes called a sixth sense since it does not follow the usual cognitional processes.[23]

The path toward intuitive perception is willing surrender rather than willful mastery. May suggests that intuition's "laboratory is the stillness of the human mind in silence" and indicates that a contemplative realization that we are rooted in God helps develop and deepen intuition. This author likens the state of intuition to the experience of pure consciousness. For him, this experience is a moving into the world just as it is; "everything is there and immediately present, more so than in other states of consciousness."[24] The state of pure knowing contained within the contemplative experience is an intuitive form of knowing. It is a knowing that is quiet, certain, simple, and full of love.

Lonergan warns about a "naive intuitionism,"[25] meaning intuition's capacity for error, which results from a failure to utilize our powers of understanding and judging. May, while not denying the importance of using these powers, stresses the importance of intuitive perceptions and how these dispose one to awakening. Balancing trust in personal intuitions, coupled with a prudent caution by use of the transcendental processes, shows the need for discernment in this area.

Desire

While intuition might in some appear latent, everyone recognizes desire as something inherent in the self. Gerard Hughes writes on desire and shows how desires act as powerful influences in determining decisions, actions, and reactions. Since desire is an innate capacity, we do not create it but rather discover it within ourselves.[26] At a superficial level, desires are easily recognizable; discovering deeper desires is more difficult. Words that describe desire include: wanting, longing, aspiring, aching, anguishing, and yearning, and the object of desire is something or someone that is not in our possession or full possession.

Desires are sources of concentrated energy whose power can be used creatively or destructively. If desires are positive, they can, for example, "lift us from lethargy, energize us, and draw us beyond."[27] Alternatively, desires can be inordinate and lead to destructive attitudes and behaviors toward oneself and others. Paul offers a reminder: "I cannot understand my own behavior. I fail to carry out the things I want to do and I find myself doing the very things I hate" (Rom 7:15). Satisfying one desire can frustrate another, and this can lead to desires being experienced in multiple and, at times, conflicting ways. For example, we might desire to have many friends yet not be prepared to forgo the time that would be lost from a much-desired sporting pursuit. Our understanding of reality tends to be adjusted to serve personal desires, thereby making desires a fundamental element within human living. Prayer begins with desire.[28] This can express itself in reaching out to God, hungering, thirsting for God (see Ps 42:2).

Ignatius, a master of discernment processes, showed that knowing good from bad desires can be learned from reading our moods. Throughout his *Exercises*, he specified in his preludes to most meditations to "ask for what I desire…" and then names specific desires that are appropriate to a particular exercise. He names the overall desire for those who do the *Exercises* in the "First Principle and Foundation" meditation: "Our one desire and choice should be what is more conducive to the end for which we are created."[29] One of Ignatius's greatest insights was that God is found in our deepest desires. In line with this thinking are Blaise Pascal's famous words: "you would not be seeking me if you had not already found me."

Searching is desire's great activity, even if the object of that search may not always be clearly seen. Deep desires are often difficult to name. The positive ones are likely to be experienced as an inner restlessness for the "more" of truth, beauty, love, freedom. Naming and acknowledging our deepest desires can be a key indicator of what we are being drawn to. Sensitively listening to deeper desires can facilitate inklings of inner peace, and in that space the Divine can be discovered. Augustine recognized that the human heart remains restless until it learns to rest in God; it is there alone that desire is satisfied.

Understanding and activating more fully the three capacities of imagination, intuition, and desire foster conditions that can render us more open to the Sacred within ourselves and in others, as well as in the cosmos. These capacities also lay the foundation for and are further enhanced through the acquiring of particular dispositions.

Dispositions

Dispositions, as described by Rahner, are the inner conditions that allow one to move from potency to act, in other words, to change from present "determinations, states and attributes" to the acquiring of different determinations.[30] The lack of a disposition may make the producing of certain acts difficult, maybe even impossible. Applying this to faith, while both the act and the predispositions that prepare for its reception are graced realities, certain dispositions prepare for this event while others can block it. The former would include openness and particularly openness to the possibility of a transcendent reality, while the latter would include prejudices of all kinds and especially those against religion. According to *Chambers'* definition, a *predisposition* is "an 'inclination' towards something" whereas a *disposition* is the possession of a "natural tendency."

Attention in this chapter is devoted to the dispositions that help prepare a fertile ground for the seed of religious faith to take root. Such dispositions can also nourish growth in faith. Examples of some of these are a disposition of openness that can facilitate a readiness for faith. Initial intimations of the Sacred can proceed to the awakened stage through the disposition of wonder. The state of being awakened to the Sacred is ultimately a gift and so requires the disposition of receptivity for its actualization.[31] While the fostering of appropriate dispositions is the focus of this chapter, it needs to be borne in mind that the in-breaking of the Divine into a person's awareness is not bound by any disposition or predisposition. A good biblical example of such an occurrence was Paul's incident on the road to Damascus. The significant fact here is Paul's free yet graced response to this in-breaking of God.

John Henry Newman emphasized the importance of dispositions and particularly "the disposition for faith."[32] He saw his vocation as helping truth find a home and defending the credibility of Christian faith against the skepticism of his day. Suspicious of external proofs for God, his principal concern was with dispositions that prepare or impede coming to personal faith. Newman's unsuccessful attempts to persuade his brother of the truth of Christianity after he had become an atheist are likely to have given Newman the impetus to explore the dispositions of others. He seems to have learned from the experience that rejection of faith arises "from a fault of the heart, not the intellect." While not downplaying the role of reason, he stressed further, "what is *felt* rather than *thought* plays a central role in any truly *religious* idea of the divine." Similarly today, what is particularly significant is not how a person thinks about God, but rather how they feel about God.

Conscience plays a central role in Newman's thought, and for him, the stirrings of conscience "mediate two things at once, conscience itself and a divine presence." One can assume that initial stirrings can arise more easily in those who possess appropriate dispositions. He consistently emphasized that it was *attitudes* that make faith possible and not evidence. In a sermon entitled "Dispositions for Faith," he said, "with good dispositions faith is easy; and without good dispositions, faith is not easy." He ended that sermon by saying that the best argument for faith is careful attention to the heart and to conscience. He also wrote, "most people believe, not because they have examined evidence, but because they are disposed in a certain way" as well as affirmed that faith is born from "a right state of heart": "we believe because we love." He attempted *"to liberate people's dispositions for faith"* from the distortions of certain cultural pressures rather than to blame the culture. In that italicized phrase, he was clearly speaking about a conversion of dispositions, a factor that is particularly relevant today.

Newman's understanding of what he terms "the assent of faith" is offered in his notion of "illative sense."[33] In summary, this could be described as a coming to know something with certitude through probabilities converging sufficiently to allow one to recognize and judge its truth. His clear view is that foolproof evidence is unnecessary for faith—a convergence of probabilities is sufficient. He was a strong voice against a liberalism that reduced religious truth to mere feeling or private opinion, while at the same time being sensitive to the subjective conditions of individuals that could make faith more or less accessible in each person's life.

Gallagher acknowledges being influenced by Newman's understanding of disposition and draws a parallel between Newman's time and today. He notes the upheavals in both periods due to the secularization of society and the marginalization of the church. He feels that help is required today at the level of dispositions, emphasizing that present-day culture has difficulty with the dispositions that surround "the antechambers of faith" rather than with faith itself. He mentions certain qualities that he senses are impoverished—high on his list is a stunted imagination. He also suggests the need for "paying attention to the soil of experience"; developing "a quality of listening and presence"; and visiting with tenderness personal inner depths.[34] Such predispositions can lead to a readiness for wonder. Ultimately, his hope is "to awaken the sleeping beauty of our wonder so that we can be ready for the greater wonder that is Jesus Christ."

Specific Dispositions That Facilitate a Readiness for Faith

The first two dispositions, which are examined together, are *willingness/self-surrender*. This combined disposition is basic, since it establishes a certain stance toward life. Willingness also facilitates the adoption of self-surrender and of other dispositions such as resonance and receptivity. For May, willingness and willfulness are the two underlying attitudes that form our view of life. He describes willingness as "a saying yes to the mystery of being alive in each moment" and, alternatively, willfulness as "the setting of oneself apart from the fundamental essence of life in an attempt to master, direct, control or otherwise manipulate existence...[it] is saying no, or perhaps more commonly, 'yes, but...'"[35] The tensions that arise between these two opposing attitudes are manifested in the struggle between self-determination and self-surrender, mastery and mystery. May associates willfulness with being driven by the will, and says that this attitude is characterized by qualities such as independence, personal freedom, intention, and decision making. Willingness, on the other hand, although ordered by the will, is very much aligned with spirit, and its contrasting qualities are those of energizing, unifying, and loving. Willingness and willfulness are both necessary within human living, each being called for in different situations. At the level of fundamental option, May strongly advocates willingness.

The basic component of willingness is self-surrender, which does not come easily in Western culture. There is the possibility that surrender could be seen in a false form that turns to fatalism and inaction when action is called for. The constructive form of willingness, however, connects with and responds to the needs of others and the world as these needs present themselves. Through willingness, personal agendas and driven forms of living recede. Authentic self-surrender is based on truth that is manifested in choices that engage with life at a deep level. In more concrete terms, willingness involves surrendering our self-separateness as well as entering into, immersing in, life at a deep level. It contains a realization that we are already a part of some ultimate cosmic process and it is a commitment to participation in the process.

Willingness and willfulness are not about specific situations or things but are concerned with dispositions and attitudes. The ability of willingness to elicit wonder and to notice and revere reality is in contrast to willfulness's ability to ignore or even destroy reality. Willfulness attempts to control not only the external environment but also inner movements and feelings. May suggests that mastery needs to yield to mystery. He also notes that fulfillment comes as gift not accomplishment.

Though a psychiatrist himself, May sees a sister discipline, psychology, as largely willful and secular, whereas religion tends toward willingness and the mysterious. Due to human limitation, religion also contains subtle or not so subtle forms of willfulness in some of its outward expressions. Instead of a healthy integration between psychology and religion there is a tendency today for religion to be absorbed into psychology. This is seen in a number of modern psychological mentalities: the *coping mentality*, which falls into either mastery or submissiveness (in the victim sense); the *happiness mentality*, which denies "the negativity of life" and shuns suffering (having fun is highly sought and valued by young adults in the West); the *growth mentality*, where getting and self-assertion are goals, as opposed to letting go and self-surrender.[36] He emphasizes that while all these mentalities offer a great deal that is positive, they are *not adequate* in addressing deep spiritual longings.

The primary expressions of willingness—letting go and self-surrender—are found preeminently in contemplation. This spiritual activity is a wonder-filled yet simple experience that most easily emerges from an "uncluttered appreciation of existence" and from a state of mind that is "wide-awake and free from all preoccupation, preconception and interpretation."[37] Contemplation's primary concern is appreciation rather than comprehension. Because comprehension and apprehension etymologically contain the notion of *grasping*, May prefers the word *appreciate*. The relationship between appreciation and comprehension reflects the difference between willingness, with its root meaning "to value," and willfulness's notion of mastery, which can lead to acts of *depreciation.*[38]

A willing approach to life emerges from and contributes to some of the dispositions already mentioned: openness, readiness, receptivity, a sense of wonder and awe. The ability of willingness to engender self-surrender, openness, and sensitivity to the mystery element that exists within all aspects of living makes awareness of the presence of Mystery more possible. Mystery is something "experienced, sensed, felt, appreciated, even loved, without being understood."[39] It is through willingness that an encounter with Holy Mystery becomes possible.

Discomfort or alienation can be aroused when willfulness meets mystery since the response to mystery calls for simply being with—doing nothing other than responding to its beckoning, being present to or entering its embrace. For those who are at home with willingness, being in the presence of mystery even in small things is likely to evoke awe, vulnerability, and not being in control. In that latter sense it can at times have an orgasmic quality.

Self-surrender, vulnerability, and dependency, according to Sarah Coakley, lie at the heart of Christian kenosis.[40] She takes on the tangled questions of the forced and, what she considers, false choice that exists between dependant vulnerability and liberative power. In her opinion, the subtle response "to the divine allure" makes it possible to meet ambiguous forms of human power "in a new dimension." This new perception assists in discerning different forms of power, thus not becoming enslaved by or dismissive of manifestations of power.

Coakley's special contribution is her analysis of a special form of *"power-in-vulnerability."* The self-effacement that occurs within Christian contemplation offers the clearest example of vulnerability and personal empowerment being held together "precisely by creating the 'space' in which non-coercive divine power manifests itself." After tracing several exegetical views as well as patristic interpretations of Paul's text, she summarizes six possible interpretations and then expands on her own. Fragility, suffering, and self-emptying, she suggests, need to be looked at in terms other than victimhood. Knowledge of the distinction between abusive suffering and other forms of undeserved suffering that become sources of empowerment has also to be borne in mind.

Christian kenosis is "a regular and willed *practice* of ceding and responding to the divine."[41] Through "a self-emptying of the heart," as one waits on God in prayer, making space for God to be God as opposed to setting personal agendas, one is empowered ("in a 'Christic' sense"). This empowerment is, in Coakley's thought, a fruit of the Spirit and can be a discerning factor of one's religious authenticity. It is a fruit that reveals itself in courage and prophecy. Self-emptying is not a belittling or negation of oneself but rather an expansion into God. Jesus underwent a self-emptying, not of his divinity but of his human nature. When Christians similarly become nongrasping in their attitudes toward life, they more clearly "take on the mind of Christ" (Phil 5:5).

A specific form of surrender is acceptance. Accepting the historical happenings of our existence, both expected and the totally unexpected can be difficult. Accepting *unavoidable* unpleasantness and even deep suffering is a profound Christian attitude. Human freedom is subject to superimposed conditions from without, and when these cannot be changed acceptance is called for. Planning ahead is necessary but has to be accompanied by a fundamental trust that ultimately life's unfolding lies within the greater divine plan. This accepting form of surrender to "the graced unfolding"[42] of one's life is closely linked with being a good receiver.

The second two dispositions are *receptivity/resonance*. In order for an awareness of God's presence to become manifest and active there has to be receptivity. The biblical term of the Spirit coming to dwell in the human heart requires the graced human cooperation of receptiveness. Activation of this receptiveness is assisted by the predispositions of *attunement* and *resonance*. These two terms are used by Fraser Watts to express the tuning of the human with the divine will to mutual resonance.[43] The resonance of being attuned to God could be seen in terms of a receiver being attuned to a transmitter. An individual remains free to receive or refuse this continuously offered gift of the Spirit. Personal freedom is an element in all the dispositions that are adopted, and the activation of every positive disposition is a consequence of cooperative grace at work. There are particular occasions throughout life that foster attunement. These can result in new possibilities being opened up that might not otherwise have arisen.

I discussed the necessity of receptivity in the chapter on religious experience (chapter 3). Arthur Deikman's movement from active to receptive modes of operating is a basic disposition in relation to awakening.[44] Even if receptive modes of operating are largely foreign to an individual, receptivity can never be completely alien unless we have never had the experience of being loved. Receptivity's emphasis is on acceptance, taking in, as opposed to controlling, acquiring, acting upon. Deikman considers the receptive mode as a basic orientation and uses the metaphor of the open hand versus the grasping one to illustrate this point.

Deikman refers to two ways in which we can relate to our environment, namely, by acting on the environment thereby remaining separate and disconnected from it or by taking in the environment by receiving it. There are two ways of taking in the environment: the first is when we do so from a stance that is without and the second is from within, when there is an awareness of being intimately part of that environment. These different approaches lead to either self-centered or world-centered forms of awareness. The receptive approach leads to experiences that are "'richer,' 'deeper,' 'mysterious,' and 'meaningful.'"

Having looked at certain dispositions and innate capacities, the question arises as to how we can change some of these to those that facilitate attunement to an awareness of the Sacred within the self and within human living.

Conversion

We are conditioned by the horizons in which we live. Achieving greater personal autonomy occurs when we make choices about shifting or radically altering our bounding circle that limits our present field of vision. Conversion is about breaking through these boundaries. What lies beyond our present horizon of knowledge is unknown at this moment. But when horizons expand toward something new, that new reality either may be embraced instantly or take some time to fit, or, alternatively, may appear too alien and be discarded. "Horizons then are the sweep of our interests and of our knowledge; they are the fertile source of further knowledge and care; but they also are the boundaries that limit our capacities for assimilating more than we already have attained."[45]

Change takes place through choices made within an established horizon. *Conversion* is a more radical form of change since it takes place by adopting a new horizon. Lonergan makes the link between horizon and conversion as follows: "the movement into a new horizon involves an about-face; it comes out of the old by repudiating characteristic features, it begins a new sequence that can keep revealing ever greater depth and breadth and wealth. Such an about-face and new beginning is what is meant by conversion."[46]

Conversion can be described as a radically dynamic inner movement that brings about a transformation of our thinking, feeling, valuing, and believing as well as our dispositions. It is a force that affects every aspect of personal life positively and opens up a transformed world to those who are converted. Conversion in its radical and less radical forms occurs occasionally as a sudden happening. Conversion is normally, however, a process of gradual transformation.

The path to becoming authentically human is brought about through conversion. It is not easy since it means entering a world of changed meanings and greater inner freedom. Radical conversion can dramatically alter attitudes and behaviors and lead to an expanded experience of being human. Authentic conversion is inevitably transformative and affects conscious activity at all four levels: it heightens perception, enriches understanding, guides judgments, and supports decision making. It is within these varying activities that conversion of predispositions and dispositions occur.

When the conversion process affects the realm of the transcendent, it may commence as a conversion from a predisposition to surface living to an experience of wonder. If this wonder is nourished, this transcendent experience may lead to an apprehension of the presence of the transcendent within created reality. Intimations aroused and enhanced through newly found dispositions that allow for a widening of horizons can open an individual up to a readiness for the Divine being made known in some way. The continued process of altering dispositions may pave the way to acceptance; to saying yes to the Transcendent Other in one's own existence, others' existence, and the universe.

Being awakened to the Sacred could occur as a casual encounter with the Divine, meaning an encounter that is overlooked and forgotten. Or, it could develop into a more serious and permanent form of relating. The *serious* as opposed to the *casual* encounter could be described as entering the awakened state or, in gospel terminology, as "staying awake" (see Matt 24:42). The converted or awakened state is a reality that never remains static; growth and, alternatively, decline are its two possible directions.

The Impact of Western Culture on Human Experience

Because all human experiencing, whether aesthetical, religious, or other, is set within and colored by the cultural background of the society in which individuals and communities live, our cultural background affects the way we think, feel, and behave. Understanding our contemporary cultural ethos[1] and its influences is particularly relevant to attempting to see the relationship between our inner experience and outer environment. By *environment* I mean not merely the strictly physical world but also all that affects us from without, such as relationships, situations, and happenings.

An example of the impact of modern culture is shown in the surveys done by many Western countries regarding religious practice. Each has shown a drop in numbers attending churches. A question that arises from these findings is where do those who say they believe in God, yet do not go to church, nourish their belief? This question is pertinent in discerning whether within present-day culture a sense of the sacred can be awakened in places that are not church buildings or other officially designated or recognized sacred places.[2]

History's Impact on Culture

Developing what Bernard Lonergan terms "historical mindedness," enables us to understand the world and our life within it, including our own self-understanding: "Nature is given man at birth. Historicity is what man makes of man."[3] When history is taken into account, it is easier to comprehend how past and present viewpoints have been shaped by it. The past is the capital on which we live and from which we learn. Without this resource there would be the need to constantly begin afresh. Because of history's ongoing process, each individual or group's historical context keeps enlarging since everything happens within history, everything is affected by it, and in turn it affects everything.

A historian's task is to explore not only what meanings were prevalent in particular times and places but also what progress as well as decline are going forward. A radical interest for Lonergan was in what was being propelled forward. For him this was primarily the need for social and cultural change. He held firm on the unchangeable nature of God's self-revelation—the core content of Christianity—but saw the necessity of adjusting the forms and structures of theology and religion. "If theology has to operate within a different context; *it will have to operate differently; but it will not therefore be a different theology.*"[4] The gift of Godself to humanity cannot change, but the predisposing factors that lead to religious experience and the forms in which that religious experience is expressed and lived out will alter as culture changes.

Knowledge itself is historically conditioned; an alteration in knowledge can change the meanings, perceptions, values, and goals within society and personal living. Due to our social nature, personal meanings are particularly influenced by the meanings and values of the people we associate with. An awareness of our interdependence on one another is required not merely to survive but to flourish. This realization has come strongly to the fore over the past century. The establishment of the United Nations and, in particular, its "Universal Declaration of Human Rights" are evidence of this. Vatican II in *Lumen Gentium* gives an understanding of church as the "People of God," and *Gaudium et Spes*, especially in its chapter "The Community of Mankind," outlines the social aspect of Christian anthropology. These documents as well as some of the great social encyclicals covering the last one hundred years give clear indications of the importance of humanity's social reality and the need to attend to this reality.[5]

Another potent influence today comes through the power and pervasiveness of the media. The media can be an insidious or a positive shaper of the way we experience ourselves. Any source that acts as a shaper of meaning can, for example, lead to words changing their meaning; to taste (in the sense of fashion or architecture) altering; to perceptions and our hierarchy of values shifting. Change happens over periods of history as well as within an individual's lifetime. A positive illustration of a recent change is a keener realization of the interrelatedness of all things, be it people, the earth, or our particular moment in history.

A growing historical consciousness, one that includes local as well as global perspectives, leads to the realization that particular present understandings may not be in tune with contemporary life. Even views that were held in a sacrosanct manner might need to be changed, prioritized differently, or expressed in a way that fits appropriately with people's experience of themselves and the world in which they live.

Newer forms of knowledge, such as those offered by the relatively new disciplines of psychology and sociology, as well as ongoing efforts to eliminate bias assist in developing more realistic perspectives. Inevitably, over time misunderstandings develop and irrelevancies emerge. These require critiquing so that behaviors and practices that are devoid of meaning can be either altered or dropped. The church is not exempt from this critique. Lonergan saw the need for healing and suggested that the agent of healing should be dialogue. According to Karl Rahner, "The church is relatively out of gear with the historical situation and with the needs of the hour."[6] A keen historical consciousness calls for a "millennial paradigm shift" that is concerned not just with restructuring or rethinking old questions but rather rebuilding from foundations.

Thomas Kuhn describes a paradigm as "an accepted model or pattern" (in relation to both thought and practice). His primary approach is to give paradigms priority over laws, rules, and theories, and he suggests that "substituting paradigms for rules should make the diversity of scientific [religious?] fields easier to understand."[7] He focuses largely on the emergence of paradigms that affect groups involved in a particular field such as professional groupings. The success of a particular paradigm is shown by its reception by the group. This is likely to occur when problems are solved in ways "that its members could scarcely have imagined and would never have undertaken without commitment to the paradigm."[8] Paradigms can also gradually disappear as new paradigms arise. When speaking about "paradigm applications," Kuhn gives the example of the paradigm of quantum mechanics, which, although accepted by many, is not necessarily explicated by them.

A Modern Understanding of Culture

History and culture are closely intertwined. Culture is a difficult reality to perceive, describe, or interpret. One analogy is found in Anthony de Mello's story of "The Little Fish" that was unaware of its water environment as it searched for the ocean.[9] Alternatively, culture can be likened to the air we breathe; it is all around us and within us. Like the air, culture is hardly noticeable because of our immersion within it. The changing atmospheres we unconsciously inhale and exhale, such as faith/church, secular/religious experiences, political/socioeconomic realities, remain largely unnoticed until there is either a clearing of the air or a marked pollution problem. This immersion phenomenon makes it difficult to observe our culture from a neutral stance. Every culture is selective, and such selectivity can lessen sensitivity and clarity of vision regarding the bigger picture, even regarding the culture in which we live.

The classical notion of culture as universal, permanent, static, conservative, traditional, and an ideal to which one aspires, flourished for over two thousand years. Today's empirical notion differs—culture is perceived as liberal and historical. "Classicist culture was stable, taking its stand on what ought to be."[10] Modern culture is, in contrast, culture on the move. "The past is just the springboard to the future....The future will belong to those who think about it, who grasp real possibilities."[11]

"The set of meanings and values that informs a way of life" is the closest Lonergan gets to defining his understanding of culture.[12] This meaning component is not fixed but "shifting, developing, going astray, capable of redemption."[13] The transition from a static classicist notion is not easy since the differences are great. For example, "they [the classical notion and today's empirical notion] differ on their apprehension of man, and in their account of the good....There are differences in horizon, in total mentality. For either side to really understand the other is a major achievement."[14]

In one sense, *society* and *culture* are indistinguishable, yet in another sense, there are distinguishable elements. *Society* refers more to the externals of togetherness such as structures and organizations, whereas *culture* refers to more intangible realities such as ideas, attitudes, beliefs, and ideals. These intangibles become visible when expressed in behaviors.

A significant element in culture today is its diversity/pluralism. Pluralism entails allowing all cultures not merely to exist but to be embraced. For this to happen there can be no dominant culture. Instead an *uber-*[15] or *meta-*culture is required. Vatican II specifically acknowledges pluralism in the respect that it has shown for other world religions. Benedict XVI, following in the footsteps of John Paul II, mentioned in his first address his desire to foster interfaith dialogue. The relevance of religious pluralism has been endorsed by writers such Jacques Dupuis.[16] He acknowledges that Jesus is the universal savior of all of humanity, even if that is difficult to explain. The Asian Synod of Bishops stresses this central christological question, saying that there should be "no arrogance in the proclamation of Jesus who emptied himself."[17]

From a Jewish faith perspective, Jonathan Sacks also defends "a plural society—what I call a 'community of communities.'" His vision is of not a conversion of nations but a world of "co-existence and peace," which flows from the fact that "He [God] is the author of all being in its irreducible diversity. A plural society tests to the limit our ability to see God in religious forms which are not our own." He argues strongly against the view that a plural society must mean a secular society where religion is banished from the public domain, a view that, he indicates, is based on the false premise that religions cannot tolerate diversity. While Judaism is based on a covenantal relationship with God, this he says, "does not negate the possibility of other covenants with other peoples" and adds "we have tended to believe that pluralism, freedom and the right to dissent are secular ideas. It is not so. The absolute dignity of otherness is a spiritual proposition. Religious commitment may yet prove to be its best defence."[18]

Even if cultural pluralism is considered desirable, clashes of values can and do occur within or between modern cultures. A present tension, for instance, is the prevailing emphasis on empirical or scientific truth. This has led to a downgrading of transcendental truth and values. Yet George Ellis, a Templeton Prize winner, refers "to this important stage in history" when, "as we gaze with amazement and appreciation at the incredible progress of science in the last century, we can also start to see clearly some of the limits to what science can achieve. Science cannot and will never be able to handle issues of aesthetics, ethics, metaphysics or meaning."[19]

Clashes can be particularly disturbing for religious people, especially if the clash is centered on central issues of our religious faith. This clash can be apparent or real. If real, a sense of alienation from our culture could ensue. This is more likely to occur when the dark side of culture emerges. There is also the possibility of a clash in reverse if aberrations within religious belief systems are too rigidly adhered to.

This book is written from living within in a Western, European, Irish, and largely middle-class culture. Within Irish culture, there are other diversities, such as youth culture, traveler's culture, pop culture, and the beginnings of an emerging older person's culture. Awareness of the great variety of cultures that exist within a particular society calls for respect for one's own culture as well as the cultural traditions of others. Appreciation of a multiplicity of cultures is realized when no culture perceives itself as superior.

An example of the difficulties of living in a multicultural age is the following: Antjie Krog spoke about black African culture's notion of forgiveness and how this is misunderstood by Westerners, particularly by their journalists who perceive forgiveness as a sign of weakness.[20] This led to a further difficulty in understanding South Africa's Truth and Reconciliation Commission. Another difference arose around the role of political opposition parties—for the Westerner, this role is perceived as confrontational; whereas the African way is to work toward consensus. The latter approach arises from Africans' sense of sharing a common humanity, for example, if an individual hurts another person, one is in some way harming oneself.

If "modern culture is culture on the move,"[21] cultures can develop, which takes time, or decline, which is usually rapid. The slow process of growth involves new understandings, new meanings, and the acceptance of higher values. Development is assisted by an awareness of the tension that exists between tradition-oriented and future-oriented cultures, and at a practical level, by turning from being dominated by the past to being open to the future. Adjusting to this newer dynamic can be difficult unless one acquires a historical perspective. Some, for instance, may too quickly discard inherited belief systems (religious or other) when these no longer seem to fit into one's peer culture and may opt instead for unbelief and possibly skepticism of previous systems. This can happen when little thought is given to the fact that individuals and communities need belief systems for survival and development. A task today is to restore belief in belief. The remedy for irrelevancies, errors, bias, oversights, "is not the rejection of belief and so a return to primitivism, but the critical and selfless stance that, in this as in other matters, promotes progress and offsets decline."[22]

Concrete Examples of Contemporary Culture

Modern culture, largely perceived as a cluster of assumptions, penetrates all areas of human living such as value systems, lifestyle, the arts, and human rights and raises central questions such as what does it mean to be human, to be caring, to be religious? The abundance of interpretations concerning these basic questions causes problems. Due to the discarding of traditional certainties and having no arbiter to take their place, whatever truth lies in a particular view has led to different sets of answers. This has resulted in new questions arising in relation to everything including fundamental human issues.

Culture can humanize or dehumanize people. While everyone is embedded in a culture, individuals are free to act counterculturally. An appropriate time for acting in this way is when truth points in a different direction to what our culture presents. Such instances might be about issues such as concerns for justice and peace since contemporary culture is particularly characterized by its tendency toward individualism. Individualism, however, is multifaceted in its challenges and is not entirely a negative reality.[23]

Enculturation is a frequently used term in Christian circles and denotes "the presentation and re-expression of the Gospel in forms and terms proper to a culture. This necessitates a reinterpretation of both faith and culture without being unfaithful to either." This definition by Aylward Shorter shows that enculturation has nothing to do with syncretism.[24] The Judeo-Christian tradition has always seen

God speaking to people within the culture of their age. Jesus immersed himself in the particular culture of his time, place, and specific ethnic and religious affiliation. He exemplifies a similar way for his followers. This challenges Christians to be open to all cultures and to not be tied to any particular cultural form. Shorter offers a reminder that enculturation is a task that is never fully realized; it continually calls for an ongoing cultural conversion.

Since modernist times, the split between religion and culture has accentuated. While Vatican I focused on the relationship between faith and reason, Vatican II centered on faith and culture. In the latter case, emphasis was placed on attempts to bridge the gap between the two. The fruit of this emphasis was particularly noticeable in Paul VI's reference to the need to transpose the gospel into a language that is "anthropological and cultural."[25] The good news needs to be brought alive within each new cultural shift and not merely to be seen as alongside or, worse still, against culture. The way to narrow the rift is through dialogue that extends to all religions as well as those with other systems of meaning. Fruitful dialogue is a process of mutual understanding that attempts to unveil undetected differences that could lead to "a dialogue of the deaf" and thus prevent movement toward solidarity and communion.

If culture touches everything in human living, then it also affects our aesthetic and religious consciousness and sensibilities. Gallagher notes that "to grasp its [culture's] significance involves a series of surprises and awakenings."[26] Part of that awakening is the realization that culture is a nonneutral reality. The word *culture* itself comes from *colere*—"to till" or "to cultivate." Culture is created, cultivated by human thought and endeavors and is, therefore, the opposite of natural.

People today can suffer from isolation and a lack of connectedness. "One of the surprises of post-modernity seems to stem from their loneliness and shows itself in openness to spiritual searching....Permanent hungers of the heart come to expression with new honesty and the quest for liberation and authenticity takes on a new humility."[27] It is because of this situation that Gallagher senses a return of interest in religious experience after such a possibility was despised and described as illusory during modernity.

Gerald O'Collins describes Western culture's main features as capitalist and competitive with "success as *the* preoccupation and health the great dream."[28] Reconnection with the depth of our being, while living within a particular cultural milieu, helps alleviate the consequent inner restlessness that can ensue from such preoccupations. In the midst of busyness each human heart has the capacity for wonder, receptivity, listening, searching, and especially for love, out of which faith can come. No cultural shift can obliterate such a happening.

Today, culture is particularly marked by its technologically driven nature. According to Jim Corkery, this technology is largely dominated by what is bigger and better, faster and finer, and has as its main goal profit. As a consequence, people are seen as consumers of products or users of services. Aesthetic and religious values are lower on the totem pole, as are ordinary human activities such as parenting, worshiping, or celebrating a meal. "In the final analysis it is the *doing* that defines us—not 'who are you?' but 'what do you do?'"[29] Further negative components include culture's emphasis on know-how, efficiency, production, getting things done, and achieving results. A prevailing mentality that tends to divide the world unhealthily into us and them (for example, oppressors and victims), plus a sense of apathy, desolation, and being trapped at surface living, could be added to the negative list. These "McDonaldized" or "Mac" cultural factors can close people off from humanity's inherent transcendent dimension by turning human desire for the infinite toward finite "satisfiables."

While antitranscendent elements in culture prevail, there are also factors that foster human growth and allow for the possibility of the presence of the Divine. Corkery points out some of the present positive signs: a hunger for a spiritual dimension to life, the search for different forms of community, conversations with the non-like-minded, greater tolerance especially when allowing the unvoiced to be heard, and a general movement "away from the harshness of the 'modern' to the greater openness and pluralism of the 'postmodern.'"[30] The Christian message of self-emptying love and the possibilities this love offers to "this troubled, yet salvageable, technological age"[31] provide an impetus to move away from managing and processing people to appreciating, listening, and loving them. Communicating religious faith requires listening to and respectfully entering into people's cultures.

The negative aspects of modern culture require healing. Imagination, openness, and exposure to beauty can facilitate this healing process. Beauty in the form of nature and the arts can facilitate the movement from negativity toward joy, inner peace, and intimations of Holy Mystery beckoning. The positives sometimes hidden in the negatives are worthy of attention. For instance, despite modern cultural changes, a hunger for depth and connectedness remains prevalent. Also noteworthy is the fact that there are today many shapers of meaning. Certain religious meanings have become out of gear with present-day needs, and so new understandings are required, including understanding what is meant by religious experience. The *Where is God* question was, for instance, raised loudly in lectures, letters to papers, television and radio interviews, and within ordinary conversation following the 2004 tsunami disaster. The search for some meaningful answer was revealing and showed that religious faith is still perceived by many as a shaper of meaning and value within society. A thoughtful leading newspaper article suggests that modern global trends point "to one general and unavoidable truth: human beings are religious creatures....The secular belief in progress, in the future, which was intended to supplant religion, has failed."[32]

An answer to this wrestling to find meaning in life and especially in its tragedies is offered in Paul Tillich's phrase "The God above God."[33] By this he means not a "Super-God" but rather a God who "is not only the God of those who are able to pray to him—but he is also the God of those who are separated from him." He suggests that atheists, especially those who are concerned about ultimate questions, separate themselves from the God of theists, particularly if that God is perceived as an object among other objects, yet they do not necessarily reject the "God above God." God is not bound by the sphere of the holy, according to Tillich, but is also present in the secular sphere with neither sphere having an exclusive claim on God. He summarizes cryptically the meaning of "God above God" as "the God who is above the God of theists as well as the non-gods of the atheists."[34]

This notion of "God above God" and its interpretation by Tillich, combined with the present-day cultural changes that have been outlined, necessitate a reexamining of the forms, situations, and places in which religious experiences are expressed and lived.

The Impact of Place on Human Experience

Contexts greatly influence human experiencing.[1] The specific contexts of culture and history have been explored—now the focus is on the context of place. *Space* and *place* are often used interchangeably, a factor that is noticeable when the quality of sacredness is applied to either of these words. Each term, however, has its own specific meaning. *Space* is difficult to define. It can mean regions beyond the earth's atmosphere, an interval between two objects or moments, or an open or empty place. *Place* is defined as a portion of something (surface, building, ground), a position within some arrangement (getting second place in a competition), or a specific area of space. Space, considered as unspecified place, has neutral connotations, whereas a space that contains memory and meaning becomes a place. Place, seen as a specific area of space, can be termed *location* or *territory* and such terms are usually associated with a people or individuals either because that place is or was occupied by them or because it has some human significance.

Place holds a central position within the Hebrew-Christian tradition. The *land* is of paramount importance within the theology of the Old Testament, and the entire *cosmos* is contained within the Christian understanding of the mystery of the incarnation. Places within the Christian tradition have frequently played a significant role when particular spots were or are still considered to have a special predisposing ability that allows for the in-breaking of the Sacred.

All human living is enmeshed in a variety of contexts. Insight into the importance of this fact led Philip Sheldrake to view context as an essential component within contemporary theology.[2] Belden Lane particularly focuses on the context of place and "the need for a theology of place."[3] Walter Brueggemann, in his major work on land in the Old Testament, emphasizes that place helps establish personal identity.[4] People often identify themselves as coming from or belonging to a particular place.

Two Contemporary Usages of the Term *Space*

The first use of the term *space* refers to *metaphorical space*. Commonly heard is the exclamation "I need more space," meaning not only physical space but also interior space, particularly when the clutter and complexity of personal living become burdensome. The word *sacred* when connected with space often refers to the space that lies deep within the human heart, a space that can be termed *sacred*.[5] That depth dimension is given a sacred quality precisely because it is the space where one meets God—the Sacred One.

The second use of the term *space* refers to the virtual reality of *cyberspace*—awareness of this is becoming one of today's major phenomena. Alan McGuckian, the originator of the successful Web site Sacred Space, spoke in an interview about "the communal potential of cyberspace."[6] Since the launching of this Web site in 1999, people have consistently responded on their feedback page about their isolation from the faith community and how praying at Sacred Space led them to feeling united with their brothers and sisters all over the world. McGuckian sees this as the work of the Spirit since "people do sense God touches them when using Sacred Space. They come back again and again to it." In this cyberspace prayer meeting the focus is on God's presence, present and active. The emphasis is on the Holy One and on divine activity by the Web site attempting to bring precisely the Godself to the forefront of consciousness. This focus on the Sacred differs from the category of *spirituality*, where the emphasis tends to be placed on the individual's own activity.

Place as a Fundamental Category of Human Experience

Place, considered as a specific area of space, is not something that is added to or subtracted from human experience but rather is the element within which all experiences takes their form or expression. At the most fundamental level, Martin Heidegger's concept of "dwelling" is "place as the house of being."[7] This notion of being housed in being flows from his concept of person as *Dasein*, or *being there*. Owning this "being at home in oneself" is basic to good psychological health. Also, since the human person is embodied, we are always in a particular place, a somewhere. Healthily experiencing the home of oneself, coupled with a sense of belonging to the physical home where we reside, work, or play, is a further extension of experiencing belonging to our environment—both local and global. All these factors help establish personal and communal identity as well as personal and communal good health.

Being *somewhere* involves being committed to a place and not being a mere observer. The power of one's *landscape*, be it inner city or countryside, and especially the foundational landscapes of one's childhood but also later adopted ones, can have great significance because of the events that happened in certain places. People often remember the localized setting of an event more vividly than the time or precise content of that event.

Environments, whether natural or built, are normally considered an external reality, yet place is largely interpreted and therefore becomes internal. It is also through interpretation that the quality of sacredness is given to a place. The power of place arises out of this interpretation. The landscapes of our early years can have a special poignancy that can influence us for the rest of our lives. The fact that places can unlock memories just as memories can deepen our sense of place makes varying places significant realities in all our lives.

Places are set apart for a multiplicity of purposes, for instance, housing, worship, leisure, sport, work, or for their historical, cultural, or religious significance. Landscapes and seascapes, especially those of great beauty, can become significant places, as sadly do places with negative reminders—war-torn places, places associated with tragic happenings,[8] or places of ecological degradation. The most significant place of all is possibly the place one calls home, where one has, or had, a sense of rootedness and belonging (despite this being a painful experience for some in early years), particularly when it is possessed, "owned." Having a sense of being at home is enriched when it extends to feeling at home in the universe. This sense of being at home is the opposite experience of feeling homeless or marooned in the universe, on a city street, even within one's actual dwelling place, or more poignantly still, within one's own self.

The idea of *place* has many forms. Extravagant forms include *elysium*—a place of great delight; *paradise*—a place of bliss; and the nonexistent place of *utopia*. Similar to the term *space*, *place* can also be used metaphorically. For example, one speaks of "knowing one's place," "having a sense of place," feeling "out of place." A further usage of *place* is in relation to offering refuge, for example, a repository for safe keeping or a sanctuary that provides safety.

The term *nonplace* suggests a new reality today. It is a negative consequence of globalization, which can dissolve a human sense of place. The new freedoms and possibilities for travel and the proliferation of nonplaces such as airports, motorways, and supermarkets, that tend to have a quality of sameness, make them strange places that could be both anywhere or nowhere. Enclosed shopping malls that contain international stores with identical features can result in a feeling of being hermetically sealed from the landscape and weather outside. An example of this hermetic effect was seen during a power outage in San Francisco—outside the shopping mall everything was in darkness yet those inside were oblivious to this happening. Some chain hotels whose design, decor, and furnishing styles rarely alter can also be disconcerting in the sense that while one is in the hotel, the hotel could be anyplace. Nonplace, in contradistinction to the concreteness of place, interferes with meaningful forms of social living and fails the human person in three ways: by not engaging with identity, relationships, or history. Media, and especially the Internet and e-mail, although offering vast means for communication and thereby the establishment of a network of relationships operate without belonging's component of connection to specific places.

This phenomenon of nonplace can lead to a diminished sense of place. Contemporary culture has glamorized mobility and anonymity with their promises of endless choices, little commitment, and unlimited freedom. This unrooted way of living has led to a sense of being lost, displaced, and homeless. There is a human hunger, not always met, to belong somewhere, to have a home, to be safe. Those today that are denied the gift of land/place are called *dispossessed* and this is often accompanied by the denial of power and a voice. Refugees suffer from an acute form of displacement by being excluded from their country of origin. This leads to an experience of placelessness. Being forced out, kept out, left out of one's place, whether as a refugee, through homelessness that leads to street living, or in other ways, is a painful human experience. A sign of being settled is when a sense of belonging is restored. At the opposite end of the spectrum are those who choose to exclude themselves from their place within the local environment by setting up private dwellings such as gated communities or other high-security measures that deliberately isolate people from their locality. Modern symbols of exclusion such as fences, walls, and gates are used deliberately to keep people out of places (e.g., nuclear sites, Israeli settlements in Palestinian territory, or even Palestinians from their own towns and villages). Alternatively, barriers can be used to keep people in, such as refugee camps, prisons, and other exclusionary situations. Such exclusivity and marking of boundaries raise issues for Christian faith, Christian community, and Christian morality, where the law of charity is the supreme norm. I will return to this issue later.

The Role of Place in the Old Testament and the New Testament

The Old Testament—Erets

Erets is a Hebrew term that permeates the entire Old Testament and contains a variety of meanings—"earth," "ground," "underworld," and "land." It is often difficult to determine whether, for instance, "earth" or "land" is correct in a given instance. Each text's context, aided by biblical scholars' opinions, suggests which meaning is generally preferred. *Earth* is largely viewed in its antithesis to heaven. From a theological perspective, Yahweh is seen from the outset as creator of both heaven and earth (see Gen 24:3). *Ground* refers to the constitution of the earth and its produce, which can be either fruitful or barren. *Underworld*, known as the *netherworld*, is located in the depths of the earth or under the earth.

Land is a more concrete use of the term *erets* and denotes a circumscribed territory. In Genesis, that land's extent was described as between the river of Egypt and the Euphrates (see Gen 15:18) but in other passages as "the land of Canaanites, the Hittites, the Perrizites and the Jebusites" (Exod 3:17). Yahweh was seen as God of the land and disobeying Yahweh's laws was considered to be violating the sacred character of the land (see Jer 2:7). Hence, the land, the people, and God belonged together. This land, described metaphorically as flowing with milk and honey (see Num 13:7), was perceived as gift and not the result of human conquest.

Adamah, a similar word to *erets*, refers to soil, dust, or clay. Genesis (1:26) uses *adam* to describe humanity—men and women. In the creation account in Genesis 2, the center of interest, the first object of divine activity, is man (*adam*, in a collective sense), who has a relationship to the earth (*adamah*). The earth is destined for humans' use and they will return to it (see 3:19).

Old Testament Land Issues

WALTER BRUEGGEMANN'S VIEWS

The theme of land, of being displaced and yearning for a place, is central to Walter Brueggemann's views. The land is considered as *actual earthy turf*, where people can be safe and secure, where meaning and well-being are enjoyed without pressure or coercion. The land is also used symbolically as an expression of joy, prosperity, security, and freedom.

Biblical faith's relationship with the land has a twofold origin. Genesis begins with a history of the land that begins with Adam living in the land and then being expelled from it. It is a story that presumes the land is his and then he loses it. From Genesis 12 onward is the story of Abraham, who lives in expectancy on a land that is to be given to him and his successors. Brueggemann suggests that human life, then and today, is a living between land-expelling history and land-anticipating history, between losing and expecting, between being uprooted and re-rooted, and that "the remainder of biblical faith is the history of those who have broken off the old life of expulsion and have walked the risky way of anticipation."[9]

Biblically understood, land is not unclaimed space but "*a place with Yahweh*, a place filled with memories of life with him and promise from him and vows to him."[10] The land always reminds Israel of the historical dimension of its faith. Despite that fact, its history often showed that the Israelites were without their own place, while at the same time they retained a sense of being on the way to a promised place.

Old Testament history highlights three experiences of placelessness. The first was the Abrahamic period, when Abraham, on leaving his land, went as a *sojourner* to another place where he did not belong and did not settle in but lived with the promise of doing so. After a period of slavery in Egypt, the Israelites were led to become *wanderers* in the precariousness of a desert. This experience of landlessness was one of survival. Centuries later, the Israelites experienced a third form of placelessness—*exile*. In exile, the Jews experienced displacement, resulting in alienation from their way of life and from the forms that gave expression to their faith. This profound experience of emptiness and homelessness led them to a deeper trust in Yahweh, the land giver and land promiser, even when they had no land and to an increased awareness of Yahweh's intimate presence with and to his people.

Israel's faith "is essentially about journeying in and out of land."[11] There were extensive periods of settled living in their land—celebrating it, managing it, but at times exploiting it. Having land became nearly as big a problem as not having it. The land was given to Israel as gift and not as the result of achievement or force. Realization of this giftedness was expressed through care of the land. When memory of their responsibility for caring for and sharing the land with others—especially the poor and the stranger—became dim, however, this led to exploitation.

Prophets, especially Jeremiah, continuously remind the people to cherish the giftedness of the land. He leads Israel through and out of the land-loss period of the exile. When they have no Israel, no king, no temple, when Israel is homeless and forsaken, comes the realization that the reliable *hesed*—Yahweh's loving kindness—continues. Jeremiah announces that Yahweh's love is everlasting and that a new history is about to begin.

Ezekiel also writes of this period in more radical terms, suggesting it is the end of land history (Ezek 7:2–7) and that Yahweh himself is in exile, present alongside his people. Through repentance, however, the gift of a "new heart" and a "new spirit" is offered (Ezek 36:24), and the resurrection motif of the dry bones parable (Ezek 37) is to become a reality. The covenant and with it the land are restored but with a new dimension—aliens are to be included and given an inheritance (Ezek 44:9). The rehabilitated space of Israel is now reclaimed by "the space occupying God."

Throughout the exile, second Isaiah comforts the people with his message of transformation and homecoming through the use of imagery of a new creation that is to displace chaos and exile. On their return, however, in their desire for security, understandable after displacement, an element of exclusivity creeps in as they begin to institutionalize their "new covenant" (Jer 31:31). The community divides into ordinary citizens and an elite bureaucracy. The latter group imposes heavy taxes on the produce of the land, which leads to disregard for the poor. When Hellenization takes over the land, the liberal Greek views lead the Jews to a rethinking of some of their values. While upholding the covenant, Ben Sira includes in his teachings the value of individual responsibility. Another reaction during this period was apocalypticism, which emphasized "land in hope" as opposed to "land in possession."

MICHAEL PRIOR'S VIEWS

Michael Prior challenges Brueggemann and other scholars for their lack of attention to morality and particularly the morality of taking or occupying other people's land.[12] Present-day concern for indigenous peoples has, Prior feels, only minimally been discussed by scripture scholars. He points out that little if any thought, especially from a biblical perspective, has been given to the understandings and rulings of international law concerning sovereignty, as well as to contemporary understandings of human rights as portrayed by international conventions. His approach to this lacuna is through a renewed understanding of the role the Bible plays regarding the impact that conquest and settlement have on indigenous populations—be they ancient Palestine, colonial empires, or modern Iraq. Views of a God who initiates and delights in the taking of other people's land suggests a militaristic and xenophobic God and due to this misconception, Prior feels a keener ethical analysis is necessary.

Prior gives a detailed account of biblical land possession from Genesis to the end of Joshua and a more general view that covers its second-millennium history. He describes the threefold divisions of the Old Testament as first, the *Torah*—the primary category in which divine revelation and the subsequent laws in relation to this revelation are laid out; second, the *Prophets*—writings that call people back to the Torah's vision; and third, the *Writings*—these deal with the daily living out of the Torah. Prior suggests that there is no one view of land in the Bible and suggests, in line with certain scholars, that the land of Canaan became Israelite territory only gradually and through a process of infiltration that led toward integration. "Running consistently through the theories which respect the archeological evidence is the affirmation that the Late Bronze-Iron Age transition was marked by peaceful, indigenous change." He suggests that the patriarchal stories give no reliable evidence of a historical kind for the period depicted and are better seen a literary fictions. "Instead we have a succession of family events and highly charged religious episodes, with Abraham functioning as an example of faith."[13] He sees the Abraham tradition reaching its final redaction after the Babylonian exile, with the trauma of exile giving Israel its identity and emerging tradition. The conquest of the land of Canaanites/Israelites by Assyrians and Persians helped further to peacefully coalesce these disparate peoples into a group whose national identity emerged slowly over centuries.

Unlike the Zionist movement of today, Prior draws attention to a rabbinic tradition that largely lies hidden from view. Susan Niditch recounts how her grandfather (a Jew) wailed for the Egyptians and the plagues they had to suffer and suggests he reach out beyond the community of Israel to the community of humankind. "The joy experienced in the liberation of one's own people...is tempered by sorrow for the enemy."[14] From a Christian perspective, Prior makes the point that in the early church salvation was never perceived in terms of land possession but rather in the creation of communities of faith, hope, and love.

Clearly, Prior is concerned with the ethical dimension of land and the discordant note that arises in the connection between a God who is "merciful and gracious, slow to anger and abounding in steadfast love" (Ps 86:15) and a vengeful, merciless God, as shown when certain biblical passages are interpreted as factual history instead of as the writer's usage of a different literary form. The importance of morality in connection with places that are considered to have a sacred quality is basic.

New Testament—Ge/the Cosmos

Land in the geographical sense is not commonly named in the New Testament, instead, there is reference to "that district" (Matt 9:26), "darkness came over the whole land" (Mark 15:33). The land of promise, with its eschatological overtones, refers simply to the land being one's inheritance (see Matt 5:5). The old division of heaven and earth is considered as "the world"; a world that will pass away when God creates "a new heaven and a new earth" (Rev 21:1). It is this new heaven and earth that forms the entire cosmos.

The scandal[15] of Christianity's origins lies in its particularity, and of interest here is its particularity in relation to place. "The Word became flesh and lived among us" (John 1:14). Jesus was born and lived his entire life in one country. Then through his resurrection, his presence among the entire human family embraced cosmic proportions. I will examine an understanding of *place* from the perspective of the New Testament through two separate but intermingling concepts—the kingdom and the cosmos.

THE KINGDOM

The coming of a new image of *kingdom* is central to Jesus' teaching, especially as found in the Synoptic Gospels. There are many aspects that help further our understanding of the complex mystery of the kingdom, but of interest here is the "reference to new land arrangements."[16] Two categories emerge—those who have and must lose and those who do not have and bear the promise. Loss of land occurs through grasping, whereas land is given to those who wait in trust for the promises. This radical aspect of the gospel came as a big threat to landowners. Essentially, Jesus proclaimed that graspers lose and those open to gifts receive. Jesus in his own life experienced land loss in the sense of having "nowhere to lay his head" (Matt 8:20) and the most extreme form of homelessness on Calvary. His descent into death led to his taking up dominion over the entire cosmos through the power of his resurrection.

The Beatitudes, especially the second, indicate that it is the gentle who possess the earth (see Matt 5:4). In the light of this and other texts, Brueggemann says that land is a central theme also in the New Testament and summarizes the implications of this as follows: "The central movement of faith as understood here is a movement from secure land to gift land and the route from the one to the other is homelessness which is the sojourn of faith."[17]

The biblical notion of "placed history" has relevance for human living today. It points to the truth that grasping or misuse of land/place can lead to homelessness (the lesson of the exiled), whereas risking becoming homeless, in the Beatitude's sense of being nonpossessive, yields the gift of home. The latter is epitomized in its most radical form in Jesus' embracing homelessness and in a most extreme manner when on a cross; this embrace ultimately led to the awesome gift of home brought about through resurrection.

THE COSMOS

The cosmic proportions of the Christ event are highlighted in the Pauline literature. The hymn to Christ, the head of all creation, clearly says: "In him in heaven and on earth were created, things visible and invisible,...all things have been created through him and for him" (Col 1:15–16). A commentary on all perfection being found in God says, "the incarnation and resurrection make Christ head not only of the entire human race, but of the entire cosmos, so that everything that was involved in the fall is equally involved in salvation."[18] A passage in Romans also refers to cosmic dimensions: "We know that the whole of creation has been groaning in labor and pains until now; and not only the creation but we ourselves, who have been the first fruits of the Spirit" (Rom 8:22).

The Role of Place in the Early Church

Early Christianity—A Sense of the Global

While the Gospels were written with particular groups of people in mind and the letters were mainly directed to named local communities, there was early on in the apostolic era a move away from the local, from home, to the rest of the inhabited world. This movement is likely to have been influenced by Jesus' parting words: "Go therefore and make disciples of all nations" (Matt 28:19). People worshiped God in whatever place they found themselves, including in the early church conversions often taking place "on the way," for instance, the two disciples on the road to Emmaus (see Luke 24:13–35), Paul on his journey to Damascus (see Acts 9:1–19), and the Ethiopian on his way home from Jerusalem (see Acts 8:26–40). From then, up to today, the notion of pilgrimage has played an important part in Christian life, with many encounters with Jesus happening in transit. A modern example is C. S. Lewis's experience of getting on his brother's motorcycle as a pillion passenger en route to Whipsnade Zoo a nonbeliever and getting off a believer: "Jack wrote, 'When we set out I did not believe that Jesus Christ is the Son of God and when we reached the zoo I did.'" It was not an emotional conversion, nor was he aware of his reasoning. 'It was more like when a man, after long sleep, still lying motionless in bed, becomes aware that he is now awake.'"[19]

The early Christian community's apocalyptic element of future-oriented expectations gradually receded, with the localized notion of the Promised Land becoming symbolic. From early on what became significant was not so much places in general but rather what happened to communities or individuals in particular places. It was this fact that led to the notion that the holiness of people became the instigating factor in places associated with them being seen as sacred. Having stated, "Jesus is our holy place," Rowan Williams endorses and expands the above view when he describes Christian holy places as "places that recall to us a life in whose detail and movement Christ has been made visible."[20]

Teilhard de Chardin's Cosmic View of Christianity

Although a great deal has been written in recent times on creation spirituality, as well as theological writing concerned with the ecological movement, I have selected Pierre Teilhard de Chardin's writing as a way of offering a view on a Christian cosmological perspective. His mystical cosmic consciousness led him to become an outstanding proponent of Christ being at the heart of the evolutionary process. His understanding of the incarnation saw God descending into the depths of matter to become all in all through Christ. Teilhard de Chardin saw that if Christians wish to have communion with God, they need to be faithful to God and the earth. Communion with God through the earth comes about through the two movements of descending into matter as well as ascending from it, thereby following the pattern of Jesus' descent and ascent. Through "matter we are nourished, lifted up, linked to everything else, invaded by life."[21] Teilhard de Chardin insisted that Christians must love the world and that in daily life our love of God and the world must be united. This is to be achieved by the twofold processes of action and passivity, the latter, for Teilhard de Chardin, meaning the passivity of "diminishments."[22]

In a mystical and poetically moving voice, in "The Mass of the World," Teilhard de Chardin expresses his belief in the diaphanous nature of a universe that supports humanity. He finds himself one day without bread and wine and instead offers all the elements of the universe, both material and spiritual, to become consecrated into the one Cosmic Christ. This eucharistic moment was also for him a process whereby the evolving world is continuously being transformed from within through the immanent presence of the Divine.[23]

A Contemporary Understanding of Sacred Space

Despite the fact that God may not clearly be perceived as the referent from which all sacredness is derived, certain objects and places are described using the adjectival form of the word *sacred* and sometimes the verbal form, *sacralize*. Examples of items described as having a sacred quality include: sacred moments, sacred events, sacred writings, sacred music, sacred art, sacred dance, sacred geometry, sacred objects, sacred places, sacred space, and in a special way, the term *sacred mysteries* is used in reference to liturgical celebrations of the sacraments. In another sense, if *the Sacred*, God, is largely perceived as being mediated through holy or sacred objects or places that in some way elicit an awareness of Holy Mystery, then the adjectival use of the term *sacred* is appropriate and helpful in coming to know the Divine. A core question remains, however—what has *sacralized* these objects and places? Significance and recognition of the transcendence of Mystery seem likely answers.

The Role of Significance *in Relation to Sacred Places*[24]

A theology of place is becoming more central, a position until recently given to a theology of time. The foundation of a theology of place is that all divine-human encounters occur within the context of place. While early monastics sought out empty spaces in the wilderness as their path to finding God, as do those following the hermit way of life today, the normal route to the Divine is the ordinary placed existence of where we find ourselves. A sacred place is the point at which the Divine breaks into the world of the mundane, places where ordinary activities take place—workplaces, hospitals, law courts, homes, streets, in the air. The familiar things of life, however, can conceal or anesthetize the presence of the sacred contained within them. We cannot select such places; they are discovered rather than chosen. This requires an attitude of openness—to be surprised by revelations of the sacred in unexpected places. Developing a keener sense of wonder predisposes us to finding glimpses of the sacred literally in any *where*. This wonder is perceived more easily within Christianity's understanding of the incarnation through which the ordinary is no longer at all what it appears. Everything, every place carries within it the potential for sacredness because the holy has once and for all become ordinary in Jesus.

Places become qualitatively different from others due to the significance people give them. The nonreligious person will admit to *privileged places*, like one's birthplace or the place of one's first love. As such, these are not yet sacred places in the sense that the experience does not contain a numinous quality. "Privileged places," however, may contain certain predispositions that could lead to intimations of the Divine. Thresholds may also have particular significance. Such places could be the door of a church, a gateway, or a passage, which act as symbols of openings to a sacred space. The origin of the term *sanctuary* has an extended meaning of "threshold." The notion of sanctuary was understood as that space around a church or monastery at which the access of civil power ended. It was, therefore, a safe, privileged place.

Theophanies and hierophanies[25] are also ways of indicating that a place is sacred. Christian tradition has always specifically set places apart by the ritual act of consecrating spaces as sacred—the chief of these are churches and cemeteries. Churches are places set apart for gathering people for worship, for the rituals of baptism, Eucharist, and the other sacraments, and they offer space for personal prayer. Cemeteries are places for burying or cremating the dead body in a caring and respectful manner. While these places are consecrated for specific purposes, such places are not intended to become exclusive—an incongruous element in all things truly Christian.

The human endeavor of occupying, cultivating, and taking possession of space are activities of cocreating and transforming "chaos into cosmos." This work of "cosmicization" is what Mircea Eliade means by "consecration."[26] He gives the example that our home is not a mere object or "machine to live in." Rather, settling in a country, city, village, or personal dwelling is a decision that involves "undertaking the creation of the world that one has chosen to inhabit"—a task, he admits, that is often difficult. The idea of "cosmicization" described by Eliade, or of "consecration" of specific places within the Hebrew/Christian traditions, does not contradict the fact that a sense of the sacred can become manifest in and through any place; consecration merely names this truth in relation to particular places.

It is therefore by giving significance to places or finding significance within a particular place—such as presence, power, healing, solace, integrity, or beauty—that helps elicit a sense of the sacred. This significance can emerge from events that occurred within a place—not only the external happenings but also insights that occur, such as when a place furthers the discernment of meaning, heightens a sense of beauty, and most of all when it fosters a responsible growth in values, and especially that of love.[27]

A sacred place is a place where repetition is more easily allowable. This element can be foreign within today's culture where people easily get bored with what is not new, for example, with the constant search for new products that further "improvement." Such frenzied forms of searching can lead to a lack of awe unless people drop their attempts to always be in control of situations. A danger is that even recognized sacred spaces can become another commodity such as a therapy to relieve stress. The sacred is, and never can be, a means to an end.

Places are particularly determined by their association with the holiness of a person connected with that place. In the early church, a locus of the holy was the community of believers. As history unfolded in Christian tradition, the places connected with exceptionally holy men or women were said to have a sacred quality about them through association with human holiness. Such places could be the home or town where the holy person lived, for example, Assisi, his tomb, or some shrine connected with him after he died. This tradition started with the apostles, the martyrs, the ascetics, and monastic settlements and continues up to today. Present-day examples are Padre Pio's hometown of San Giovanni, and Pope John XXIII and John Paul II's tombs in St. Peter's in Rome.

Manifestations of this desire to visit sacred places are seen in the travel world, with tour operators offering tours to the shrines of France and other places and to the Holy Land (the very title indicating this land's special claim to being a sacred place), and have come about through the popular demand of people. The place itself is not the priority but rather what happened in it. The event in question often carries a salvific character for the believer who connects with it. From the great theophanies at Mount Sinai and the Upper Room, to present-day liturgical prayer, faith, and apostolic group meetings, as well as pilgrimages to varying locations, places can, as gatherings in the Lord's name, become special foci of the sacred through which God's presence is manifested.

The ideal of the Christian community has been and still is to cut across boundaries of separation and to particularly include those who are on the fringe of or even rejected from society. This inclusion encompasses sinners. Rahner points out the early church struggles about coming to accept that sinners are members of the church and that the church herself is a community of sinners.[28]

The Role of Recognition *in Relation to Sacred Space*

For recognition of the sacred to occur, it is essential to be present to a place. We can be in a place and not be there at the same time. We need to truly dwell in the place. *Dwelling* in a place of sacredness is more likely to lead to an encounter with the Divine Other. Such an encounter is a simple celebrating of the unique "is-ness" of what is occurring—in this instance, a revelation of God mediated within a specific place.

At a fundamental theological level, God is the "within-ness" of all things and that includes place. The immanence of the Divine is the ultimate reality behind all notions concerning the sacredness of place. The place of the inner self as well as the outer place we inhabit, or alternatively put, where we dwell emotionally and spiritually as well as the place where we dwell physically, are places where we can encounter Holy Mystery, precisely because the Divine is already in that place offering intimate presence.

The sacred becomes manifest when and where we recognize it. Certain instances and places can trigger/mediate a sense of awe. Coming unawares upon the divine whisper can happen unexpectedly when walking in the local park, in the countryside, or in an inner-city slum. Intensification of a sense of the sacred is more likely to happen on tops of mountains, while watching beautiful sunsets, in places with water, yet also in degraded spots. An example of a place recognized as having a sacred quality is Iona. George McLeod, the founder of the Iona community, described Iona as a "'thin place'—only a tissue paper separating the material from the spiritual."[29] A "thin place" can be likened to a thin veil that reveals that earth and heaven are not far apart. Daniel O'Leary extends the notion of sacred place to every spot in which we stand—"the sacred place we search for is the very ground on which we stand."[30] Hence, we can find sacred space literally anywhere.

How we recognize sacred places will somewhat depend on whether the cataphatic or apophatic approach is at the fore in our relationship with the Divine. The cataphatic religious imagination delights in the use of images (while remaining critical of their limits) and will rejoice in discerning the presence of God in the singularity and "this-ness" of places. This imagination is able to create places that become embodied means of experiencing the divine presence. Isaiah, for example, gives an abundance of images of the wonders through which God's glory is made manifest. The God of both Testaments is one who "tabernacles" with his people in a particular locale, hence revealing the Godself as one who is always here, and not here, in the sense of *not only* here. On the other hand, the apophatic tradition is critical of images. Even this approach, however, is not devoid of place images in describing the experience of

God. Such apophatic people are more attracted to places of emptiness, such as the desert, and are at home with vague images, such as
a dark cloud.[31] A distinctive contribution of Christian faith is its
affirmation of the material world no matter which approach to God
is taken, and as a consequence, it has always inculcated a deep
respect for place.

In the empty moments of our lives, such as those of tragic loss, the
need for sacred space can become intense. For instance, after the collapse of the World Trade Center in New York or the Beslan school
killings, where people were profoundly wounded and lost, many felt a
need for places to mourn, to share feelings, to find comfort, and to
make sense of what happened. What happened, as was shown after
September 11, 2001, was that recognized religious places both local as
well as worldwide became the social places where people gathered.
Such places became spontaneous *ecclesia*, where individuals felt free
to express their grief and to join together spiritually. People went to
churches almost instinctively in their bewilderment as somewhere
where they felt safe and held. While the sacredness of the building gave
this support, the very coming together of people created the truest
form of *ecclesia*, or sacred happening, as people united in their sorrow.
In the desire to keep the memory of events such as this alive, one thinks
also of the twentieth century's most horrific event—the Holocaust—
and the need for memorials. As has been learned in the case of the
Holocaust, it is nearly impossible to find a suitable space and way to
do this that speaks to all involved. Another incident, Princess Diana's
death, led to the spontaneous setting up of mainly temporary memorials outside Kensington Palace—through flowers and candles, both
items that contain a religious significance.

The Necessity of Ethical Values
in Relation to Sacred Space

There can be a danger of "cheap sacredness"—a faking of a
sense of the sacred. This can be overcome by contending with what
is estranged, flawed, or damaged in material existence, by approaching place with an ethical perspective, and by having a sacramental
sensibility. The latter allows for the particularity of a place to point
beyond itself to the mystery of God. Michael Prior has shown how

insisting on fundamentalist interpretations of Old Testament texts prevent this "sacramental sensibility" from showing through.

The significance of place depends on interpretations, and difficulties arise when interpretations vary greatly even to the extent of their having opposing meanings. A classic example of this is Jerusalem, the most sacred city in the world, where particular sacred places are seen by the three monotheistic faiths in very different lights. The modern political Zionist movement and certain Jewish Orthodox fundamentalist groups insist on land conquest and possession, including Jerusalem, without showing moral concern for other peoples' rights.

The effects places have on people have moral implications. One of these implications is it calls for the spaces in which people live and work to have a human quality inherent in them. The design of towns and cities, for instance, affect human relating, and their designs can either enhance or prevent them from becoming places that foster human encounter. An exhibition of contemporary Japanese architecture affirmed this point, noting that apartment buildings should avoid uniformity and instead be variegated, clustered at different levels, have open spaces and thus be human in scale.

A lack of attention to human needs could be partly due to cities and towns no longer having a spiritual center—a center that gives meaning to the city. Public spaces can be sterile and treated in unimaginative ways. This can lead to a lack of respect and even to vandalism. Facilitating a sense of the sacred in relation to places can only flow from a respect for the sacredness and transcendent capacity of individuals and communities.

The darkest of all places is given the name *hell*. As Christians, especially through the revelation given in the mysterious event of Jesus' descent into hell, no one and no place is excluded from God's redemptive love. The Divine can break into any place, including those that seem utterly inhospitable, dark, and empty abysses—even including the dark place(s) that may exist beyond death.

The Interconnectedness of Place and Hospitality

Locations can exude hospitable or inhospitable "vibes." Obvious inhospitable places to the human person are those that have severe climates; as a result of this the landscapes are often barren and harsh due to, for instance, a lack of water or vegetation or to an abundance of water in the form of ice. Human-constructed places can, by their design and other features, also prove hospitable or inhospitable. The added dimension that helps make a place hospitable is often the human element when a sense of welcome and possibly a personal greeting are present. Attempting to make people feel comfortable—even at home—in a place can be manifested in a range of ways, but occurs when people feel respected and free to be themselves.

A tradition of hospitality is inherent both within the Jewish faith and within Christianity. Jesus himself loved to share meals with people. In Acts, we see the early church sharing hospitality in each other's houses. Preeminently, eucharistic celebrations lie at the heart of Christian hospitality, with all forms of hospitality pointing to or leading from this supreme form of celebration. Paul writes, "extend hospitality to strangers" (Rom 12:13) and Peter says similarly, "be hospitable to one another without complaining" (1 Pet 4:9). The author of the letter to the Hebrews adds, "Do not neglect to show hospitality to strangers, for by doing that some have entertained angels without knowing it" (Heb 13:2; cf. Gen 18).

The Mamre incident (see Gen 18:1–15), when three visitors come to visit Abraham in his tent, has become particularly famous through Andrei Rublev's well-known depiction of this scene in an icon. Rublev's painting not only illustrates Abraham's three visitors having a meal but also symbolizes the three persons of the Trinity. The icon's design draws viewers into that meal thus inviting them to become participants in the inner trinitarian life. David Ranson, influenced by that icon, sees Christian ministry as a call to become "agents of hospitality," meaning serving others with trinitarian qualities that foster widening circles of community relationships: "Hospitality always tends towards communion....Hospitality is the journey by which the stranger becomes a friend rather than an enemy [and] is open to the possibility that the stranger might bear blessing."[32]

Another writer takes up the Abraham story and elucidates further on its significance. Pierre-François de Béthune focuses on hospitality from an interfaith perspective.[33] His ideas on hospitality spring from Clement of Rome's Epistle to the Corinthians (c. 100 CE), where he remarked that it is by faith and hospitality that Abraham became the son of the covenant. The addition of hospitality as a requisite to becoming a son of the covenant is borne out in the biblical texts that refer to welcoming the stranger both in, and into, one's midst.[34] The stranger is viewed as having a right to sanctuary and this stranger-become-guest also provides a special way of meeting the Sacred. Hospitality starts with Abraham "our father in faith,"[35] who at Mamre gives an example of his gracious and generous hospitality. He welcomes, shelters, and feeds in his own home three strangers whom he clearly understands to be special. He "ran from the tent entrance to meet them" (Gen 18:2) showing reverence as he bows to them, and then invites them to stay in his own home. He takes their needs to heart by washing their feet and sharing his food and drink with them. He meets their wishes without them being expressed and finally accompanies them by showing them the way as they set out on their onward journeying.

For de Béthune, hospitality is based on a consciousness that we are all members of the human family and that however much of a stranger a person may seem they are to be received as a brother or sister. It is about "letting the other in, of ourselves entering another's space....It is essentially an experience. Therefore time, and warmhearted attention, must be given to it."[36] This type of sacred hospitality comes from a desire to receive guests. He quotes from Cardinal Danielou: "civilization took a decisive step, perhaps its most positive step, on the day the alien, the enemy, became the guest. That is to say the day when the human community came into being. Until then, there were human species and animal species."[37] He warns against too early a familiarity that would be unlikely to take into account differences and notes that true hospitality is a process that moves from receiving the stranger into the "hallway" of our hospitality, to receiving visitors "from the hearth" of our faith life.

De Béthune was obviously influenced by the founder of his order, Benedict, the father of Western monasticism. Followers of his order, through the Middle Ages and up to today have always emphasized the importance of hospitality as part of their way of life. The position of guestmaster is still considered a significant position within contemporary monastic life. Also today not only the monastery but also their gardens are being made available to visitors. For example, Downside and Worth Abbeys in England and Glenstal and Rostervor Abbeys in Ireland express their hospitality by sharing both their monasteries and their gardens.

Gardens are the topic of the next chapter but their hospitable quality is noted here. A striking example of garden hospitality can be found in the Quiet Garden Movement. Started in 1992 by Rev. Philip Roderick, a parish priest in the Diocese of Oxford, this movement is now worldwide. At present 230 gardens are involved covering seventeen countries. A Quiet Garden is a space that responds to the movement's vision for stillness and prayer. Occasional days that offer opportunities for reflection include the gardens of private dwellings, monasteries, religious institutions, schools, colleges, hospitals, and retreat centers. Brigid Boardman says that while these gardens vary greatly in size, location, availability, and outward characteristics, each has in common their offer of "spiritual and physical renewal and refreshment in a safe environment and free from stress...They help to focus the mind and heart and so create that mood of receptive peace when prayer comes more readily."[38]

Writing about this now worldwide network, Esther de Waal says these gardens have become "places in which to draw aside in order to encounter our own selves and encounter God in an oasis of calm with space and time for silence, prayer and meditation."[39] She notes the movement's suggestion of taking time to slow down, coming with one's senses alert and aware and in a state of mindfulness that is open to the vision of the garden. The Quiet Garden Trust's brochure describes itself as follows: "Quiet Gardens and Quiet Spaces: A Ministry of Hospitality and Prayer."

By way of conclusion a question is offered: Where are today's sacred places? Churches hold that position for some. Also helpful is a trend today to set aside quiet spots to facilitate prayer within one's home, as well as the older tradition of various shrine spots that still speak to some people. Yet it would seem alternate places other than churches and shrines are needed for private and shared communing with the sacred dimension of people's lives. Because of Western society's prevalent antireligious stance, some people do not know how to articulate their inner hunger for depth within human living or how to find places where this need could be somewhat met. Hospitality, encouragement, and at times a gentle form of facilitation toward quieting the inner self can be facilitated when the above supports are offered in beneficial places that offer stillness, beauty, exposure to nature. This book suggests that the countryside and in particular gardens afford a way of answering this new need.

Gardens as Context
of the Sacred

Gardens have had a place in history since the beginning of civilization. They are essentially enclosed plots of land that vary greatly in size, type, and the features they exhibit. Since earliest recorded history the sacred nature of gardens within different civilizations has been visible. From the beginning of biblical history, gardens have been seen as a symbol of divine blessings—as places where chaos and barrenness are replaced by a fruitful garden.

Gardens have the potential, as private or public spaces, to become places of significance or places of recognition that allow for openness to the transcendence of Holy Mystery's becoming a reality within personal experiencing. They have offered and continue to offer the possibility of becoming sacred spaces. A reality today is the awakening of a genuine concern for the environment, accompanied by fears around its threatened survival. This has led to greater attention and appreciation being given to gardens and landscapes in general.

Gardens are radically influenced by the culture of their time and place. They are dependent on climate, landscape, and soil, as well as on human interests that vary according to taste, function, affluence, for their contemplative and healing qualities. As a result, the role gardens play in society has been, and still is, varied. The range of their roles extends from supplying survival needs for food, shade, and shelter, to providing spaces for entertainment. Over the centuries, the different uses of gardens have included: pleasure, play, prayer, relaxation, celebration, ritual, therapy, education, profit, personal struggle, lovemaking, enhancing plant and wildlife, extending one's home, remembering people or events, burying the dead. Some examples of specific gardens whose uses are as listed above include: children's playgrounds (play); botanical gardens (education); sensory gardens (therapy); "garden rooms" (extension of one's home); roadside memorials (remembering those killed in accidents).

Gardens have tended to be seen as oases, whether they exist in the middle of a desert or within cities. Gardens can become sanctuaries, places set apart from the noise, rush, and stress of life. They can offer glimpses of paradise as well as become a space where humanity, nature, and the Divine meet in a harmonious way.

Gardening is essentially "the work of human hands"[1] that tames and enhances nature in some way. Penelope Hobhouse writes, "From earliest times people laid out gardens in order to counteract the lack of order in their environment; gardens developed as enclosures."[2] Over time, different types of gardens have emerged, such as tended and wild (often with a degree of tending), formal and informal, public and private; varying forms have also emerged, such as parks, groves, orchards, and allotments. Gardens can also be divided according to type, such as monastic, country, tropical, spring, flower, or vegetable gardens. Today in the West, gardening has become more popular as a leisure pursuit, partly as an antidote to the harsh aspects of city living and partly from the desire to "green" our living. Also in recent times, gardens and parks are being given a more prominent place by urban planners.

Gardening is an encounter with nature through the use of the body as well as the mind and feelings. It is an activity that has the potential to instill a sense of humility and awe as we notice the different vegetations' strengths and fragilities as the seasons unfold. Garden centers are more numerous and those that already exist are expanding. Gardening books, magazines, newspapers articles, as well as television and radio programs are proliferating. Increased wealth in the West has something to do with this expansion, but is there something deeper that lies behind this phenomenon?

Gardening has never been so popular, nor the spiritual quest so broad. Is there a link? Martin Palmer and David Manning suggest practical links—both involve "hard work, proper preparation of the ground, consistency, imagination and endurance."[3] There are also deeper links when gardens are perceived and used as places for reflection and contemplation. The latter idea is growing, as seen in the Quiet Garden Trust organization, whose aim is to alert people to the existence of gardens where people can rest, be nourished spiritually, and be helped to discover their true path.[4]

History of Gardens—Part 1

The following history of gardens focuses particularly on how the theme of the sacred has been present from early beginnings right up to today.

Garden Origins

The dawn of civilization began in the northern hemisphere after the end of the last great ice age, approximately twelve thousand years ago. Following this change, sea levels rose, climate became warmer, and precipitation increased. This led to the flooding of rivers and plant life reviving, which resulted in gardens growing in Mesopotamia, Egypt, and Persia almost simultaneously. Scientists today say this climatic change happened over a short period of time and led to great fecundity and variety—a "Garden of Eden" type of experience—alongside fears of flooding. A belief in benevolent as well as terrifying gods and goddesses emerged as a new relationship with nature and the Sacred came into being.

Christopher Thacker commences his history of gardens as follows: "The first gardens were not made, but discovered. A natural spot—a clearing in the forest, a valley opening up in a barren mountainside, an island in a remote lake—made pleasant by a belt of trees, flowering, fragrant, and bearing fruit. No one tends this garden; it grows of its own accord."[5]

Cultivation of the land developed alongside the growth of civilization. Nomadic hunters began settling in villages, then towns, and finally cities, and with this development gardens emerged. Nature became less threatening and the god or gods of nature were gradually understood as more benevolent. Jericho's origins are dated at 10,000 BCE and archaeologists discovered that plants were cultivated in the Jordan Valley before 7000 BCE.

Middle Eastern Gardens

Mesopotamian gardens appeared around 3000 BCE. Learning how to harness water and establish irrigation and drainage systems were the first essential steps. Following success in this field, the Sumerians developed hunting parks and collected new plants. The area between the Tigris and Euphrates Rivers became known as the Fertile Crescent.[6] Wild flowers, fruits, and spices were turned into domesticated plants grown for interest and pleasure as well as for offerings to the gods.

In parallel, *Egyptian* gardens began (c. 2500 BCE) when again engineers learned to build water channels. Their sole water source, the Nile, and the ability to conserve its yearly high level, are vital for all their vegetation. Pharaonic gardens were mainly built around temples and tombs. Egyptians' funeral rituals led to temples being surrounded by orchards containing sacred trees. Gardens were used for growing grapevines, olives, and vegetables; growing trees for incense or fuel, as well as for festivities, religious processions, and funerals. Nature fascinated Egyptian artists, whose artwork is found on the floors and walls of temples, palaces, and tombs. The earliest known pictorial record of a garden is a 1400 BCE Egyptian garden. It illustrates a pond and fruit trees. Their gardens were integrated with their buildings and each garden was given a name, usually after one of their gods. Their gardens contained many elements that would be taken up by other cultures, such as terraces (before the Persians used this method) and atria (which the Romans later copied at Pompeii). They also had sculptures—note Alix Wilkinson's remark, "the meaning and the message of the garden was frequently found in the sculpture."[7]

Persian gardens commenced around 2000 BCE, largely in the area between the Tigris and Euphrates Rivers. Geometric layouts, water systems, terracing, as well as remnants of mosaics, curbstones, and drawings, illustrate their skill in artificial landscaping. The phrase *paradise gardens* had its origin in Persia, thereby predating the biblical usage of this image. The great sand desert of Persia lies below sea level and part of it is considered the hottest desert in the world. The inhospitable nature of the harsh and desolate landscapes of desert when contrasted with water and vegetation made gardens apt representations of paradise. They were enclosed spaces containing water, trees (especially desirable were fruit trees), and flowers. It is easy therefore to conceive of gardens as a haven, a bit of paradise. The idea of enclosed spaces for gardens with orderly planting of trees and flowers spread throughout the Middle East. The most famous garden of the ancient world, the Hanging Gardens of Babylon, was built by Nebuchadnezzar II (604–562 BCE). Ancient descriptions of these gardens exist, and Iraqi memory has kept knowledge of their existence alive. One of the great influences of gardens on other arts in Persia was in tapestry designs and later in carpets.

Throughout the Middle East the notion of gardens is found in the contrast between oasis and desert, and even today a place where there is water and a tree is considered a garden. Refreshment and shade are essentials. Another essential in the Middle East was and is olive trees, often grown in groves.

Many mythological stories concerning creation came from the Middle East. For the three Abrahamic faiths (Judaism, Christianity, Islam), God chose a garden for his creation of humanity and it was in a garden that humanity had its first encounter with God. Gardens were therefore considered special places where God, humanity, and nature coexisted in an intimate way. This idyllic picture is for Judaism, Christianity, and Islam a story of sacred harmony, which since the Fall remains aspiration. The image of this perfect garden has for the three monotheistic faiths remained a metaphor of paradise.

The Significance of Gardens in Old and New Testaments

From the Bible's first book, Genesis, to its closure in Revelation, gardens hold significant place. Attempts are made in the following sections to keep close to modern biblical scholarship's interpretation of texts and to omit theological interpretations that are overly free in their use of analogy. The exception is the Song of Songs, which is recognized by scholars as an allegorical work.

Old Testament

Two Old Testament texts have been chosen—the Genesis 2 creation account and the Song of Songs—since both books give gardens a central role. To begin, however, I refer briefly to "Noah, a man of the soil...[and] the first to plant a vineyard" (Gen 9:20), who became the first tender of *haadamah* mentioned in scripture.

GENESIS 2

It was from images of the luxuriant gardens in Mesopotamia and Egypt that the Sumerian and Babylonian creation stories developed. These stories existed prior to biblical creation accounts, and they included the idea that humanity's task was to make the land fertile.

The original secular Hebrew word for garden, *gan*, was used, for example, in reference to "the king's garden" (Jer 39:4), "a watered garden" (Isa 58:11), "a garden locked" (Song 4:12). The term for garden was lifted from its secular usage to the religious sphere when the Septuagint (LXX) largely replaced *gan* with the foreign word *paradeisos*, "paradise," which became in Hebrew *pardes*. The Iranian word from which the Greek and Hebrew terms were derived also came into Latin and was used by Jerome in the Vulgate, where it also became the more common term used in the phrase "the garden of God." In Genesis (2:8) the LXX uses *gan* for the first garden of the world which Yahweh himself planted according to the Yahwistic account of creation (see Gen 2:8f., 3:1–3, 8, 10). Despite the secular term *gan* being used to describe this first garden, it is clearly God's garden since the phrase "garden of Yahweh" in Genesis 13:10 also uses *gan* as opposed to *pardes*.

Yahweh plants his garden in *Eden*. This word suggests a direction toward the east and possibly the name of an actual territory that later became the name of the garden itself. *Eden* became a term for a beautiful, fruitful, well-watered garden possibly due to the author recalling a similar Hebrew word, *eden*, which meant "pleasure" or "delight." This fact, combined with the lush description of the garden, indicated God's Garden in Eden as a symbol of divine blessing.

The garden in Genesis 2 is described in terms of its close connection to God, in a relationship that is independent of the human person. Humankind is created in a garden, is allowed to live in this garden, and is sustained by it, with the proviso that men and women take care of it. The primary work given by God to humanity is to be caretaker and developer of our environment. Living in this garden in a manner that is in tune with God's intentions enables men and women to live in close communion with God. This intimate relationship between God and people is revealed in the image of "God walking in the garden at the time of the evening breeze" (Gen 3:8).

The main feature of the garden of Yahweh was the divine presence and his people entering and dwelling within that presence.

Gardens also provided the imagery for the coming messianic age. This is well described by prophets such as Isaiah (41:17–20; 43:16–21) and Amos (9:11–15) in terms of abundant vegetation. A modern example of the desert blooming is found in the lush botanical gardens of Kibbutz Ein Gedi. Fed by the waters of the Ein Gedi spring, this paradise desert/tropical garden near the Dead Sea contains over one thousand species of plants and trees and includes a unique cacti garden.

THE SONG OF SONGS

This is a collection of love poems. Although it has been attributed to Solomon, the style and vocabulary of the Song suggests it was written in the fifth or fourth century BCE. Its five songs express the love of two human lovers: the Lover and a Shunammite woman. While this work may have been secular in origin, from earliest times, it has been seen in Jewish and Christian literature as having religious links. It depicts in allegorical form the love between God and his people expressed in a story of longing, searching, losing, and finding.

The references to garden appear in the third poem—summer of the wedding. In this poem, there are five references to a garden—first two, "A garden locked is my sister, my bride" (4:12)[8] and "a garden fountain, a well of living water" (4:15); then two by the bride—"blow over my garden" (4:16); and "let my beloved come to his garden" (4:16), followed by the bridegroom—"I come to my garden" (5:1). Roland Murphy suggests that "the garden locked" (the word *pardes* is used) refers to the bride reserved for the beloved.[9] The invitation by the bride to the wind to breathe over the garden is quickly extended to the bridegroom to come himself. This dynamic is immediately followed by the joyful cry of the bridegroom who comes and takes possession of his bride.

Arminjon gives the following summary, setting the garden in the Song of Songs within the context of the significance of gardens throughout scripture:

It can be said that the theme of the garden runs through the entire scriptures: the garden of creation in the first chapter of

Genesis; the garden where the prince of life will be buried and where Mary Magdalen will come on Easter Sunday; the garden of the new world in the last chapter of Revelation; the garden of the Bride at the center of the third poem of the Song, of the whole Song itself, and of all the Scriptures. Five times, the Bride is admired here as the garden from which life draws its source and triumphs (4:5:1).[10]

Dianne Bergant comments on the importance of gardens in the love poetry of the ancient world both as places for meeting and as a metaphor for fecundity and especially for female sexuality. The erotic association of the fruits mentioned in the Song, the exotic plants, the pungent aroma of the spices and flower fragrances, and above all, the dynamic bubbling, living water of the fountain and the rush of movement it offers in contrast to the static descriptions of profusion, make the garden in the Song a fantasy garden that suggests "the exceptional beauty of the woman" and her "life-giving potential." After the bride has given the bridegroom access to the garden, it then becomes "his garden." Bergant suggests that this reciprocity offers an image of "the total reciprocal self-giving and the acceptance by and of the other."[11] This book does not, however, end on the note of love finally consummated. The final chapter concludes with the notion of separation accompanied by a longing for union, illustrating that relationships in this life, be they with other people or with God, are always ongoing and never complete.

New Testament

There is very little reference to gardens in the New Testament until the gardens of the passion. I explore the opening and closing scenes of the paschal event and the context of garden in which they are situated.

GETHSEMANE

Jesus crosses the Kidron Valley and enters "a place where there was a garden" (John 18:1).[12] John is the sole evangelist to specifically set this scene in a garden. This garden was an enclosed area—he "went into it" and "came out of it." It was possibly the private garden of an unnamed friend and, as John suggests, it was probably the place where Jesus hid from his enemies during Holy Week. Mark (14:32) and Matthew (26:36) name the place Gethsemane.[13]

In the New Testament, the Greek word for garden is *kepos*, which refers to a plot of land where vegetables, flowers, or trees are grown. The non-use of *paradeisos*—with its inevitable linkage to Genesis and further paradise associations—seems to have been intended by John, since the term was known and used in Johannine writings (see Rev 2:7). Raymond Brown sees no link between the Gethsemane garden and the original paradise garden and neither does he allow for a link with Zechariah's reference to the Mount of Olives (14:4).[14]

This book cannot delve into the theological implications of this event other than to draw attention to the fact that it was a simple garden, a plot of land that was chosen by Jesus for this agonizing happening. It was in this place that he knowingly and with love embraced "his hour," realizing that it had finally come in the intense form of a suffering-servant path that included betrayal that ultimately led to death. Noteworthy is Jesus' closing statement: "I am" (veiled within the "I am he" remark). This suggests, in Brown's view, an awareness of a divine power over the forces of darkness.[15]

A BURIAL GARDEN

The word *kepos* is also used for garden in the Johannine text (19:41). Brown says it is not clear what kind of garden John envisaged. The site of the crucifixion was a quarry from the eighth to the first century BCE. In the first century CE, it was filled in to serve as a garden, with the quarry floor some thirty feet below revealing caves that were used as burial places.[16] The fact that Golgotha and the garden were in close proximity suggests that Jesus' execution took place just outside the north wall of the city. This is not improbable since tombs of the Hasmonean high priests were known to be near this area, and the text does say that Jesus was buried in a prestigious place (John 19:38)—a place belonging to Joseph of Arimathea.

GARDEN OF RESURRECTION

A third use of the word *kepos* occurs in John's story of Jesus' appearance to Mary of Magdala. Misunderstanding pervades the scene. The *gardener* could mean the owner of the garden or an overseer or caretaker—therefore someone who would have known who disturbed the tomb. Brown remarks that the word *kepouros* ("gardener") is the only biblical reference using this term, yet it was not an uncommon word in secular papyri.

M. E. Boismard, in contrast to Brown, makes reference to patristic writers who saw the garden setting of the resurrected Jesus, the new Adam, as a repossessing of paradise and the opening of the possibility of entering this paradise on offer to everyone.[17] The scene thus carries echoes of the earthly paradise of Genesis 2—3, from which humanity was driven because of disobedience. Sandra Schneiders also links this resurrection garden scene with the second creation account in Genesis and with the Song of Songs. Mary's "peering" through her tears into the tomb is an instance of a rare term in scripture—*parekypsen* ("peering"). That term is also found in the Septuagint version of the Song of Songs, in the context of searching for the beloved. For Schneiders, this search for the loved one alerts "the reader to the fact that this garden setting is intended to evoke both the creation account in Genesis, where God walks and talks with the first couple in the garden (see Gen 2:15–17; 3:8)" and the Song of Songs, which was understood in the New Testament period as the hymn of the covenant between Yahweh and Israel.[18]

Before the dialogue with Jesus begins, we see Mary, clouded by her grief, in search for Jesus. She first recognizes him as someone who is playing a recognized role in that place—be it gardener or someone who officially tended that place. The place and the tending of the place are linked. When the conversation with Jesus commences he initiates it by probing the depth of her discipleship while Mary sees in a veiled fashion someone whose role is to care for the place. Similar to the beginning of John's Gospel where the disciples were asked, "*what* are you looking for?" (John 1:38) Mary is asked "*whom* are you looking for?" (John 20:15). Mary's failure to *see* Jesus is overcome when she "hears" Jesus pronounce her name.[19] She already knew that he was Lord because of his life, but now she understands that title more profoundly when she responds with her single word: "Rabbouni." Schneiders understands this scene as the resurrected Jesus inaugurating the new covenant, with Mary portrayed as the symbol of the new people of God, the church.

The scene focuses on the central component of Christian faith: coming "to know Christ and the power of his resurrection" (Phil 3:10). The core element within the appearance of Mary of Magdala is the emergence of a faith that recognizes the Risen Jesus. A consequence of this faith is mission—"*go* to my brothers and *say* to them I am ascending to my Father and your Father....Mary Magdalen *went*" (John 20:17). Mary, complying with this call, became the first proclaimer of the resurrection.

By way of summary to this section, it is important to reiterate that the primary interest here has been to focus on the garden as the context in which the passion commences and above all where the resurrection—the most momentous moment in history—is announced. Gardens are now redeemed places, as are all places; significantly, the beginning of this redemption of place occurred in a garden setting.

History of Gardens—Part 2

Islamic Gardens

The Persian garden particularly influenced Islam following the newly converted Muslim Arabs' takeover of Persia in 637 CE. Their garden style became the source of all Islamic gardens and remains present within the Muslim tradition up to modern times. One of the best examples of this style today is found in the Alhambra in Granada, Spain. Hobhouse writes: "Islamic gardens in Persia developed as a high form of art where religious meanings and poetic imagery combined a love of flowers and beauty."[20] The presence of water as a life-giving symbol was considered essential, and it was often arranged in canals representing the Rivers of Life. Water was often left still in order to reflect the sky as well as buildings, thus providing an oasis of calm. To Muslims, a garden is more than an earthly reality—it represents an anticipation of heavenly paradise. Their ban on images and their love of numbers led them to geometric designs in their planting.[21] A profusion of plants, often scented with roses, which were particularly held in high regard, added to the beauty of this art form. The Arabs became learned botanists as well as skillful gardeners. In addition to vegetation, a Muslim garden is not complete without birds, bees, and insects.

The theological significance of Islamic gardens was highlighted by their frequent mention within the Qur'an. A common image of union with God is that of dwelling with Allah in a garden. Islamic gardens were also built to complement and enhance buildings, especially mosques. Islamic gardens spread also to the east, and one of the most famous is found, strangely, in India—the Taj Mahal (1632)—erected in memory of Mumtaz by Shah Jehan.

Asian Gardens

The art of oriental gardening began in China around the third century BCE and two centuries later spread to Japan, which later developed its own styles.

CHINESE GARDENS

Early Chinese gardening paid great attention to the soil to the extent that Maggie Keswick called it "a religion of agrarian fertility."[22] The Chinese were modest about their own position in nature since humanity was seen as not essentially different from other created things. As a consequence, happiness depended on successful adjustment to natural forces. This harmonious adjustment to nature did not make them passive since human beings were considered the agent through which the potential of nature could be fully realized. The Chinese aim was and is to learn from nature and to fit into the beautiful, sometimes awesome, nature of one's landscape.

Chinese gardening is about delighting in and using what is already there, with an emphasis on the importance of space. Walking in and listening to the place, sensing its energies, flows, contrasts, the feel of hot and cold areas, are essential before establishing a garden. A Chinese saying states, "The wonder of the garden is in the use of scenery, not in the creation of it." Taoist philosophy is based on the unity of creation and is essentially, according to Confucius, about discovering the way of nature and replicating that in all aspects of human living. This includes gardening, the pursuit of which is to search for "the nature of nature." Noteworthy is the fact that "landscape painting is closely connected with gardening in China; indeed so much so that the four arts of poetry, calligraphy, gardening and painting are thought of as interdependent, each requiring an under-standing of the others."[23]

Gardening is seen as an act of reverence, as well as a delighting in the order and harmony that lies at the heart of creation. Intuitive, tranquil receptivity enables those who meditate to arrive at enlightenment. The symbolism of rocks, paths, water, trees, and flowers, and the way they are combined in a yin-yang manner, are critical.[24] Finding a significant (usually expensive) stone or rock for the garden is a central issue. Stones are to be contemplated since they contain a message-bearing quality. "A garden without stones would not have the name garden."[25] Paths of sand or pebbles have played a crucial role in drawing one into the garden as a participant rather than an observer. "The path should lead you from encounter to encounter until you reach the still nothingness of the center, where what you find is your own self reflected back....The path is the very essence of the garden."[26] Ancient gnarled trees (especially the gingko and pine) are considered particularly significant, as are magnolia trees. Bamboo, chrysanthemum, and lotus plants are also prized due to their qualities of resilience and longevity.

Chinese Taoist gardens are not formal, yet at the same time, an emphasis is placed on restraint and harmony. The heart of gardening, like all other human activities, is to find a correct balance between yin and yang life energies. Individuals are revitalized through the outflow of energies from the elements. Gardening is seen as a sacred activity in that it draws nature out by allowing each element to contrast with, highlight, and balance one another. The gardener's role is more about being a balance keeper than an innovator. In China one *builds* a garden whereas in Europe one *plants* a garden. This building is achieved by a type of "planned disorder" combined with the use of both hard and soft materials. The use of space is considered of utmost importance. Martin Palmer, a specialist in Chinese culture, says that the heart of a Taoist garden is emptiness. This may express itself in a lake or pond that provides a calm reflective center, similar to traditional Chinese rooms that leave the center empty.[27] In Taoist gardens, the space between objects, in other words absence, is as important as presence, and the gardener's task is to learn from nature—to enhance it but to keep in mind leaving empty spaces rather than trying to fill everything. Keswick summarizes all of the above when she writes: "The aim [of Chinese gardens] was always to represent nature's infinite change and mystery."[28]

One of their oldest surviving gardens is that built around Confucius's tomb soon after his death in 479 BCE. Its form is that of a sacred grove and is composed of trees and rocks. The sacred grove is a partially tamed wilderness. Sacred groves were significant in many ancient civilizations, particularly in India and later in Greece.

JAPANESE GARDENS

Japanese gardens were greatly influenced in the early stages by the Chinese. Japan comprises mainly mountains, rivers, and forests. Even today 67 percent of the land is forest, showing the restricted space left for the size of its population. This sparseness of habitable space has led to the striking quality of compactness in Japanese gardens. "Small is beautiful" is a truism since their gardens are viewed not as isolated entities but rather as "a condensation of all nature."[29] Gardens are an intrinsic element of Japanese culture and as in the older civilizations of Korea and China gardening is seen as an art form. In the past and up to today the Japanese have had a sense of awe and reverence for nature and particularly for stones and trees.[30] Daivetz Suzuki says, "The Japanese love of Nature, I often think, owes much to the presence of Mount Fuji in the middle part of the main island...its beautiful formation, always covered in snow. The feeling it awakens does not seem to be all aesthetic in the line of the aesthetically beautiful. There is something about it spiritually pure and enhancing."[31] The creation of microcosms is an aspect of Japanese culture and is seen in ikebana (flower arranging), bonsai, tea ceremony, and especially gardens.

In the third century BCE wet-rice agriculture began. The beginning of gardens was the creation of open spaces, *niwa*, in front of Japanese houses, which when purified, became a place to welcome visiting deities. Particular stones (taken from the seashore or the mountains) and trees were seen not as the abode of the gods but rather as elements through which deities could be encountered. When such stones or trees became part of a *niwa*, deities were considered in some way to dwell in these gardens.

Since gardens represented nature and nature was regarded as sacred, this made gardens—both in Shinto, the indigenous religion, and later in Buddhism—sacred places. This understanding of human-ity's ability to contact its deity through nature was the beginning of the garden. Gradually over centuries Chinese influences became more marked, and this included the introduction of Buddhism in the sixth century CE. It was, however, not until the thirteenth century, with the arrival of Zen Buddhism, that this way of life became acceptable throughout the country. In the intervening period, due to the dampness of the climate, moss (which represents land spread), gravel or sand (raked to indicate the movement of water), and later actual water elements became features of many gardens. A garden culture began to take prominence through the gardens that sur-rounded the new growth of temples and emperors' palaces. Buddhist monks became the great garden designers. During the fourteenth century some of these gardens were known as paradise gardens.

While small Shinto shrines—surrounded by a garden of moss, with an azalea or bamboo tree, and usually containing a wooden temple, sacred gateway, path, stone lantern, and a bell—are dotted around the country, more Zen-type gardens have become the norm. Pure Zen gardens pare everything down to a minimum. According to Shunmyo Masuno, "the path to simplicity in a Zen garden, whether ancient or modern, is to express nature in a pure form, without plants and without water."[32] The purpose of Zen gardens, for Teiji Itoh, is that they "strip all nonessentials from nature and strive to discover the transcendent meaning of life."[33] These "dry gardens" of stones, which are placed in different patterns, and sand, which is raked into different designs, have both an aesthetic function as well as a use in Zen practice in awareness. A select number of prominent upright stones complete such gardens. These stones are chosen for their microscopic effect. Their aesthetic element, if there is one, comes about through "the aesthetic of discovery." Three stones in a garden "in a sense are the classical Chinese triad of heaven, earth, and man."[34] Some see the Zen garden as an expression of the empti-ness of reality.

Small courtyard gardens (tsuboniwa) are very common and are found in homes, offices, and public buildings. Kyoto, the ancient capital of Japan, is considered the birthplace of such gardens. An enclosed space containing just two rocks is considered a garden. The striking quality of a courtyard garden is its simplicity. Another noticeable feature is the way the garden is integrated with the building. This is often achieved by a single pane of glass reaching down to ground level acting as an invisible divider. An overarching principle is making more out of less. This is realized by having a focus on one object or by capturing a distant or borrowed view. These are seen as ways of summoning one to a simpler way of viewing the world. The lack of private space necessitates using the space one has responsibly and in a spiritual manner. Masuno describes a garden as a "spiritual space," a space that celebrates nature and acts as "a kind of balm" that enables one "to become acutely sensitive to the simple, small matters that are often blanketed by daily life."[35] Other modifications, accretions, and less purist Zen elements of Japanese gardens include "dry waterfalls," stepping stones, lanterns, and water features.

In the seventeenth century "stroll gardens" appeared. These were larger and designed for walking around and observing views. Such gardens go with the flow of the landscape while at the same time transforming it. The path linking the garden's attractions, including ponds, waterfalls, or pavilions, is considered essential and its main function is to lead one toward the various spots where vistas are opened up.

Of special significance in Japan is the *tea garden*. The tea ceremony is based on Zen philosophy, which maintains that "everything a person does can be regarded as religious."[36] The epitome of Japanese gardening, in the sense of its style as well as its potential for symbolism, aesthetics, and ritual, is revealed in these small gardens that link the house and the tea ceremony room (sometimes referred to as a hermitage).[37] The tea garden is essential to the tea ceremony.[38] The garden's purpose is to prepare those who are about to partake in this ceremony. The tea garden assists in this event in a twofold way: by providing "an atmosphere consonant with participation in the tea ceremony" and by providing the space and utensils for the cleansing ritual.[39]

The tea garden is always a special small section of the main garden, more a passageway or alley, hence its name *roji* ("dewy path"). Its essential features are stepping stones, lanterns (preferably lit by candles), a waiting bench, a low stone basin (a *tsukubai*—over which the participant needs to bend in a spirit of humility when cleansing hands and mouth), and fences, usually made of bamboo. The stepping stones are designed for a type of walking meditation where one concentrates on the business of walking. There may be some larger flat stones on the path, which invite visitors to pause and look at the beauty around them. The tea ceremony is considered to have commenced once a guest enters the tea garden. "The important thing about it is in the influence it has on the minds of those who walk through it and discover beauty in a sequence of experiences."[40] Before the guests arrive the host sprinkles water on the *roji* to create the mood of cleanliness, freshness, and welcome.

European Gardens

GARDENS IN GREECE AND ROME

These gardens are known from their mention in classical writings such as those of Pliny and Virgil. The emphasis in garden design was on balance, proportion, and good use of space. The first record of a Greek garden is found in Homer's *Odyssey* (eighth century BCE). It was a royal garden surrounded by hedges and contained all kinds of trees and flowers and two springs. In Athens, gardens were used as meeting places for poets and the peripatetic philosophers as they debated while walking under the shade of plane trees. As Hobhouse points out, however, the Greeks were not gardeners, maybe because the land itself is arid and mountainous and therefore difficult to garden.[41] An alternate reason could be that their landscape was so beautiful it sufficed as a backdrop for the temples and other buildings. Trees and shrubs were, however, grown around sacred places and groves of trees were even found in city sanctuaries. The Greeks were keen botanists and many wild flowers flourished in Greece. Hippocrates (d. 470 BCE) used plants in medicine, and Aristotle (d. 322 BCE) studied plants scientifically. Plants were also appreciated for their beauty. The Greek and Latin names of plants and trees listed by Pliny in his *Naturalis Historia* (first century CE) are largely the names used in the gardening world of today.

Roman gardens were both of a small as well as of a larger villa variety. Small gardens were uncovered by archaeologists in Pompeii. Most significant, however, was the Roman villa style of gardening, Hadrian's villa being a prime example. Country estates with their farm and garden became popular as did the commencement of market gardening. Improved technology allowed the Romans to have elaborate fountains and ponds in addition to sculpture (some are still in situ in Pompeii) and the art of topiary. These and other factors added to the elaborate nature of some villa gardens. Alongside the grander side of gardening, Alicia Amherst takes note of Pliny the Elder's remarks: "the garden constituted of itself the poor man's field and it was from the garden that the lower classes procured their daily food."[42] She also remarks that the rich indulged in luxury and extravagance in the garden, and vegetables and fruits were raised at great cost for their by the rich use but were not enjoyed by the community at large.

The Medieval Period (including Monastic Gardens)

Little took place in the gardening world following the final fall of the Roman Empire, apart from the Islamic gardens in Spain and the emergence of monastic gardens. There is little knowledge of gardens apart from monastic ones throughout the medieval period (500–1500 CE). Medieval towns started with the disadvantage to gardening that they had to be protected by strong outer walls with as many houses packed in as possible. Later, when danger of attack lessened, people moved outside the walls. Large houses and castles tended to have moats. The only gardens that did exist would have been plots of land around one's cottage to grow vegetables. There was not much difference in those days between agriculture and gardening.

Gardens, however, played a significant part in the early Christian monasteries, starting with Benedict at Subiaco in Italy (early sixth century). Sylvia Landsberg, writing about English monasteries, says that such gardens were not only for privacy, study, and contemplation but also for recreation and refreshment, for the production of foods and medicines, for ornamentation, as well as for burying the dead.[43] Due to the Reformation, however, none of these gardens remains except for some in their cloisters. A monastic ideal was to be self-sufficient and therefore gardening became a necessity.

Benedictine monasteries in particular emphasized hospitality, offering refuge to travelers (usually pilgrims), whose food and drink was provided for by a guesthouse as well as by a cellarer's garden.

This hospitality also extended to tending to the needs of the sick. Another of the Benedictine monks' good works was disseminating medical and botanical knowledge through their writing, collecting, and illustrating of many manuscripts. The focus of the major orders differed—the Benedictines' focus was hospitality, the Cistercians' agriculture, and the Augustinians' care of the sick.

Varying types of gardens existed within the monastic enclosure, which often housed large numbers of people in addition to the monks. These gardens included the cemetery orchard, the infirmary garden (which included the herbarium, whose plants were grown for medicinal purposes and could be applied to every complaint), the green court (something like a village green with the bakery, granary, fish house, brewery, and candlestick maker), the obedientiary gardens (private gardens for the abbot, prior, almoner, and other officials), the cellarer's garden (for vegetables, flowers, honey, and for pasture for cows, horses, and sheep). The cloister held a preeminent place at the heart of the monastery. It was usually a plain lawn, with occasionally a single tree and sometimes a fountain. The grass was always cut short to keep the green color prominent because green was considered to have a tranquilizing and refreshing effect.

Celtic Gardens

Little is known about gardens within Celtic traditions, although a general love of nature was a core characteristic of this tradition. Enda McDonagh substantiates this view regarding the poverty of knowledge about the Celtic tradition and cautions against applying the term *Celtic* too liberally to different fields. This free use of the term *Celtic* may be suspect since it can be "at once too broad and too narrow."[44] I agree and hence do not concur with the term *Celtic* being applied to gardens.

I will mention, however, the Irish monk Fiachra and his contribution to gardening, herbs in particular, which led him to become patron saint of gardeners.[45] He was born c. 590 CE to a noble family in North Connacht. He established a hermitage near Graiguenamanagh, where nearby today is found Fiachra's holy well. His pilgrim path took him to Meaux in France, where he lived most of his life until his death (c. 670). The newly established public gardens in Kildare are named after him.

From Renaissance to Mid-Twentieth-Century Gardens

The Renaissance spread throughout Europe in the sixteenth century. This new flourishing affected gardens, and gardeners made the most of the new influence of mathematics and perspective, adopting natural-looking planting designs.

The move from utilitarian monastic gardens to ornamental-style gardens occurred first with the Italian villas in the fifteenth century. Some of these gardens took their inspiration from Greek and Roman gardens, with nature and art often being combined in ancient classical styles. Proportion and balance were important. Geometric designs became popular and these were enhanced by topiary, labyrinths/mazes, trellis work, and arbors. In some gardens, sculptures were added, usually placed in grotto-type settings. During the sixteenth and seventeenth centuries exotic plants brought from travels abroad became fashionable.

In the seventeenth century, highly stylized gardens developed in France. Versailles, probably the most famous of all European gardens, was created by the designer André Le Nôtre in 1661. The emphasis shifted to gardens as symbols of humanity's power and our control over nature. This was accompanied by gardens becoming displays of wealth. Stephanie Ross suggests that eighteenth-century gardeners in France and in England developed an elevated view of gardening as an art form and that gardening itself was operated as a trade that was passed down from father to son. Gardens of this period, according to Ross, "conveyed moral, religious, political, and philosophical messages to viewers strolling through them."[46] Guidebooks were developed to unpack the garden's meaning. She also notes the increasing body of gardening literature, which goes back to the seventeenth century.

This movement of formal, symmetric-style gardens began to change in the nineteenth century in England, when a more natural form of landscaping appeared. Although specific gardeners are not often named in this work, I mention here the English garden designer Capability Browne, whose natural approach contrasted to Le Nôtre's stylized designs. Parklands, with sheep and cattle grazing, became the ideal and this was often associated with the country retreat style of living. This new landscape style spread slowly back to Europe.

The beginning of smaller private gardens was also developing at this time. The attitude toward gardens also changed. In the words of Penelope Hobhouse, "man's sublime reactions to a garden became of increasing importance, rather than the measure of man's control over it."[47] As more and more plants were introduced from abroad, flowerbeds and herbaceous borders came more to the fore, particularly during the Regency and Victorian periods, and with this style more labor-intensive gardening became necessary. Greenhouses and the invention of the lawnmower transformed gardening.

In the last century both formal and natural styles have been used separately and together. The U.S. contribution was the development of public gardens for urban inhabitants, cemetery gardens, as well as open-plan front gardens for private houses. "Walls, high fences, belts of trees and shrubbery" can be means "by which we show how unchristian and unneighborly we can be."[48]

As way of both summary and emphasis, it can be said that the early history of gardens showed that many gardens were perceived as sacred places. The frequent references to paradise gardens in Middle Eastern cultures is particularly striking. The use of gardens to surround places of worship such as temples and the association of orchards with cemeteries reveal a clear linkage between gardens, a divine presence, and the afterlife.

The importance of gardens in biblical history highlighted their significance as the setting of key happenings in both Testaments. The continued history of gardens emphasized the reverence that the Chinese and the Japanese had for nature and specifically for aspects of nature such as stones and trees and also indicated the significant role that gardens play in evoking a sense of awe or mystery. A reverence for the earth was seen also in monastic gardens, through the discovery of new methods for the growth of grains, vegetables, and fruits and also in the understanding of the medicinal as well as the culinary uses of herbs. These developments were generously shared with others through monastic hospitality and writings. The monks spent time in prayer and reflection several times a day in the cloister garden. Apart from the church building, the cloister's simple and well-maintained grass area helped to make this garden a central and hallowed spot in the monastic enclosure.

Over the centuries, therefore, gardens have historically been places that offer the possibility for the revelation of the Sacred across varying cultures and religions. Each garden, private or public, offers in different ways a location in which we can appreciate our own place in the universe and also be brought in touch with the Creator of the wondrous beauty that is around us. Gardeners have the privilege and responsibility of enhancing this beauty.

Contemporary Gardens

As has been shown, gardens have over the centuries been places that offer the possibility for the revelation of the Sacred across varying cultures and religions. Contemporary gardeners, who have the privileged role as well as the responsibility of enhancing the beauty of the universe, carry forward history in their own unique way. No two gardens are ever alike. Modern gardens are now viewed in a broader manner than in the past, which includes parks and landscapes.[49] The landscapes could be connected with road networks, public buildings such as museums, educational and health care institutions, business parks, and so on. When the settings of such places are creatively thought out, they offer great potential for human enrichment, including enlivening individuals' and communities' aesthetic and religious sense. This is more likely to occur when people truly experience, dwell in, these spaces as opposed to merely viewing them as an external onlooker.

New styles of private, semiprivate, and public gardens abound. For example, Alnwick Garden in North East England is a large twelve-acre garden and one still in the making.[50] Alternatively, Shekina Sculpture Garden, in County Wicklow in Ireland, provides an example of a small one-acre garden.[51] A common mission of these two gardens is that they deliberately set out to offer reflective space to their visitors.

Gardens today are often seen in a broad context. For instance, in contemporary gardening, the dividing line between ecology, landscaping, and gardens overlaps. This has occurred because of the movement of "greening," beautifying and caring for the environment. This phenomenon is occurring nationally, locally, and in people's own backyards. This happening, combined with the enrichment and enchantment that gardens uniquely offer, provides the possibility of gardens acting as a lifter of the human spirit. This lift can become an inner movement from "ah" to "awe."

Since gardens are visual entities, they foster engagement with what is perceived. David Brown specifically sees such engagement as offering a "sacramental sense of divine engagement."[52] Contemporary living, with its functional approach to life leading to instrumental values becoming paramount, can affect the way gardens are perceived. For example, they can be viewed as and cultivated merely for produce or health. Gardens can, however, be primarily seen as places where beauty is made concrete in an abundance of ways. Their richness, made more varied as the seasons unfold, makes them a pertinent metaphor for/sacrament of the Sacred revealed in and through this beauty. From the Garden of Eden up to the present, this manifestation of sacredness, while always containing a concealing quality, can at the same time reveal the beauty of Holy Mystery's immanent and transcendent presence within creation and within the human heart that appreciates such beauty.

The focus throughout this chapter has been on the potential that gardens have for human enrichment and in particular for their ability to enliven individuals' and communities' aesthetic and religious sense. The emphasis is on experiencing and dwelling in these gardens as opposed to merely viewing a garden as an external onlooker. The following hackneyed yet truth-bearing phrase states this fact: "One is closer to God's heart in a garden than anywhere else on earth."[53] Gardens can truly be oases for the spirit, roads toward the sacred. This is particularly due to their exceptional ability to orient people to beauty, to interiority, and to intimations of an awareness of a divine presence, an ability that has been present from earliest civilizations up to today.

I offer a final conclusion in the apt words of Nicholas Lash:

In the beginning, the story of the world is told as God is producing it, as it ought to be but, as yet, is not: God's garden. Then, in the end, the story of the world is told as it will be, when God's peacemaking is complete. And in between, there is another story of the garden as a place of sweat and blood, and pleading, and betrayal; a place of darkness, of the night, which is, however, also a place of most mysterious appearance, a place of freshness and unexpected recognition. This is the story of the time between and of the way in which the wilderness is made to be what it both should and will be: paradise, God's garden.[54]

Personal Experiences in a Sculpture Garden

Shekina Sculpture Garden

The context of the practical research that formed such an important background to this book is Shekina Sculpture Garden. This one-acre garden is situated in the center of County Wicklow, a county known as the Garden of Ireland. The County Wicklow Garden Festival Committee requested that Shekina be involved in their first festival (1992) and since then has been a listed venue in each year's festival. Shekina Sculpture Garden became the property of the state in 1995. Following the handover, Irish Government Publications produced an attractive book on the garden and its sculpture collection.[1]

In addition to the beauty of this garden's setting and its composition of a stream, ponds, shrubs, and trees, its unique feature is its sculpture collection. Over time, the sculptures have "grown" into the garden and the garden has grown around the sculptures, thereby giving a sense of a harmonious whole. All the sculptures are by recognized modern Irish artists: Fred Conlon, Michael Casey, Noel Scullion, Ken Thompson, Imogen Stuart, Alexandra Wejchert, Cliodna Cussen, Paul Page, Alexander Sokolov, Leo Higgins, James Gannon, Elke Weston, and Ann Murphy. The materials used in the sculptures are varied: bronze, wood, glass, enamel, metal (iron and stainless steel), and stone (granite, limestone, and reconstituted stone).

Research Carried out in Shekina Sculpture Garden

I adopted a qualitative research method based on semistructured interviews that lasted on average three-quarters of an hour. These conversations took place six months after participants had spent a reflective day in the garden. I left participants free in regard to their personal responses to thirteen questions. The initial questions acted as openers to the more in-depth ones, which gave people the opportunity to speak about their awareness, if any, of a sense of the Divine/God/Holy Mystery/Higher Power. I asked participants specifically to describe what *sacredness* might mean in their lives.[2]

A stratified random sample of thirteen people was selected by requesting one volunteer from each of the groups that participated in Time-Out Days during the summer of 2003. The social profile asked for age, religious affiliation, and occupation. Occupations included: mother, wife, counselor, bookkeeper, parish sister, secretary, nurse, chaplain, chartered accountant, textile engineer, researcher, residential care worker, campaigner, bus driver, childcare worker, priest, Montessori teacher. Some people listed more than one occupation.

Individual Profiles

A miniature vignette of each participant is given below, not with the intention of labeling people, but in order to make the reading of people's responses easier and more interesting. The names given are fictitious.

Paul (70–79), although retired, described himself as a businessman and a textile engineer. He is married and has both Irish and German citizenship and referred to his religious affiliation as Christian. He is a keen appreciator of art, noting that "real art has an element of spirituality in it."

Peter (60–69), a bus driver, is married and wrote under the section on religious affiliation "nil." He was aware of a "great feeling for nature" and beauty's calming effect. He particularly noticed the rain and said how much he enjoyed it.

John (40–49), a chartered accountant, married, described himself as a practicing Catholic. A frequenter of art galleries and museums, he particularly enjoyed the sculptures.

James (40–49), a priest, was looking for a day away from the city. He gave his religious affiliation as "a Catholic sinner!" He was aware of the moods of the seasons and noted how the liturgical season of Pentecost fitted with the time of his visit.

Miriam (30–39), a nurse, is married and defined her religious affiliation as a "spiritual Catholic." This was her third visit to the garden, which she described as a "great teacher" and "very nourishing."

Rachel (20–29), a Montessori teacher/childcare worker, gave her affiliation as Christian Catholic. She described herself as "a big water person" and found the day freeing.

Esther (70–79), coming on her fourth visit, is a housewife and grandmother and gives her affiliation as Roman Catholic. She sees a woman's great role as being a giver of life and discovered life-giving qualities within the garden.

Sarah (60–69) described herself as mother, wife, and researcher and campaigner on green issues and genetically modified foods, as well as French interpreter. She gave her religious affiliation as Christian.

Naomi (50–59) is married and a chaplain and described herself as being "profoundly ecumenical." A particular concern on the day she went was to further bonding among the group she brought with her.

Hannah (60–69), wife and grandmother, described her religious affiliation using the phrase "in love with God." She works as residential assistant in a school. On her fourth visit, she returned to reconnect with her special tree, to meet other people, and to experience the contemplative dimension that the garden offers.

Ruth (40–49) is a wife, mother, counselor, and bookkeeper. She stated that she was a nonbeliever and put as her religious affiliation "searcher in love of life." Her vibrancy became obvious in the interview and she remarked at its end "this student was ready and the teacher appeared!"

Deborah (60–69) was a teacher and is now a parish sister. She described herself as Catholic. As will be shown, the grass in the garden became a significant element in her day.

Eve (40–49) is a mother of three who works full time in the home looking after her mentally handicapped child. She stated that she returned to be a Roman Catholic and gave the reason why in the interview.

Participants' Responses

These responses are presented under six themes. I made an effort to keep as close as possible to the interview transcripts so that participants' voices can be heard in an unadulterated manner. Jeff Astley's views on listening and learning from the God-talk of the nontheologically educated person could prove helpful when reading these responses.[3]

Theme 1—Expectations

The comments expressed under this theme indicate people's presenting dispositions. Coming in a spirit of openness was described by Paul: *"being open in mind and to let it happen as it happens."* Others had less specific expectations, for example, they were attracted to the idea of a day out; some to being away from the city or from their routine; others to being in the mountains or the thought of simply being in a garden. On arrival Naomi was *"eager to get started on the day, to get a feel for the place."* Ruth remarked on the benefit of knowing that no one could contact her for the day. Rachel felt that there might be specific elements to the day such as self-development, while Hannah wondered if there would be meditation or whether questions might be asked leading to both coming with apprehension and feelings of *"would we be able for it!"* Hannah said that her fears were eased by a welcoming word and after meeting other people who seemed happy—she *"was prepared to take whatever came."*

Peter and John mentioned expecting a much larger garden; one imagined a formal garden with *"fabulous grounds, Powerscourt[4] at least!"* while Peter was pleased on arrival to find it smaller—*"it was more personal."* Peter also remarked on his sense of anticipation when journeying down to the garden and wondered if he would be disappointed or not. Eve said *"I prayed as soon as I came through those gates: 'Holy Spirit how do you want to speak to me?' I try so much to leave myself open to the Spirit."* Naomi came with a group perspective in mind. She felt the day might help her group *"to gel," "because I know sometimes if you do something out of the ordinary just like that, it just melts boundaries."* She added that early on she was aware that the day *"was fulfilling all my expectations—in fact more than doing that."* Ruth saw the day as a *"caring day, a minding-me day,"* where one relaxed and *"chilled out."* James specifically stated he was looking for *"a day when you'd renew your spirit."* Miriam came initially out of curiosity as well as having a sense of being "called" to this garden as opposed to the other gardens listed in the Garden Festival brochure because of its name, Shekina. She returned to do a Time-Out Day as a result of her previous two Open Day visits that had given her "a feeling of being at home" in this place.

Theme 2—Levels of Experience

This second theme is presented in the light of Lonergan's four "qualitatively different levels of experience," and studies how participants' experiences fitted into the four precepts: *be attentive, be intelligent, be reasonable, be responsible.* This approach enables readers to view the range and depth of participants' experiences.

BE ATTENTIVE[5]

Naomi's noticing began immediately after *"getting out of the car and breathing the silence, which was lovely"* and continued, *"I was prepared to go with the experience and get the most out of it. It was so soothing."* Similarly, Ruth remarked: *"it's a place apart, once you come in the gate—that's it"*; for Hannah, *"it's its own little unit, a haven, an oasis."* Miriam, after glimpsing her first view of the garden, exclaimed: *"it was breathtaking."* An initial reaction of Paul was to liken coming into the garden to entering a cathedral. This experience was heightened by the feelings of peace and harmony he became aware of when strolling around the garden. Eve noted *"the sense of orderliness and friendliness."* Others were conscious of particular features: for instance, Sarah described *"the hilly areas, the benches dotted around, and the lovely little areas including the overgrown bits, the creepers, and the gazebo."* Her attentiveness was also present in her comment: *"public sculptures are usually very big, people drive past them and don't take too much notice but here you have to look at them. It's lovely to see art with nature."* Returning to the gazebo, Eve said it gave *"a sense of coziness and being enclosed."*

Depending on the weather on the particular day, some focused on the rain, which "added to the day" (Peter) and Sarah also found it particularly enjoyable, while those who had sunshine on their day delighted in it (John). Eve referred to *"the feel of the wind in your hair and the sun on you."* Sarah said *"I didn't mind the rain but my shoes got wet so I just walked around the grass in my bare feet which I really liked."* James noticed the clouds and the sky, as did Ruth, who was struck by looking up and noticing the sky's grayness *"with bits of blue appearing. In the city you don't look up because there are too many distractions."*

Specific forms of attentiveness were shown in a variety of ways. The stream was noticed under its differing aspects, such as its mini waterfalls (James) or the water flowing from *Rebecca*'s jug (Miriam);[6] others were caught by its sound (Rachel), and Peter said, *"the tinkling of the water is like music."* The water stirred emotions: *"I just loved the water"* (Miriam) and *"the brook was very calming and made you feel good"* (Peter). Other things noted were *"the dog racing around"* (Naomi), the birdsong (James, John, Paul), the absence of noise (Sarah, Ruth) and the smells, particularly of cut grass (Ruth). Others enjoyed the trees (James), their *"forestlike appeal"* (Ruth) and the general scenery of the place. James and Deborah remarked on the *"sponginess"* of the grass. The varying sense of aliveness that was elicited by these experiences of attentiveness while in the garden is captured in Ruth's words: *"It [the garden] had it all. I've never been in a space that just had it all. If I want water, I go to the beach; if I want a forest I go to a forest; if I want grass I go to a park. But that space seems to have got it all."* Esther in a similar vein said, *"all of life is in that garden. And yet it is so simple."*

People's spontaneous gestures or activities also indicated their heightened awareness. Eve had *"a strong desire to touch everything. I was so relaxed I felt I could."* She also wanted to roll in the grass. Miriam liked to touch *Rebecca* and to walk in the stream, while Naomi found herself *"kneeling on the grass and looking into the water, just watching the leaves float and putting my hands into the water. That's profoundly moving. I think of the journey of life like water flowing. I like the metaphor of water flowing, the current, and the notion of pushing the boat out."* Deborah enjoyed walking carefully around *"the labyrinth. I think it is very centering."*

One major result of the time spent in the garden was the awakening of awareness of feelings. Some of the articulated feelings included: *"a great feeling of peace," "feeling safe"* and *"bubbly inside"* (Hannah), tranquility (Peter), harmony (Paul), serenity (Deborah), relaxation, friendliness and awesomeness (Eve), joy and *"feeling nourished"* (Miriam), excitement and a *"feeling of space"* (Ruth), *"feeling close to nature"* (Peter), *"feeling accepted for myself"* and *"feeling refreshed"* (Esther), *"feeling free"* (Rachel), *"feeling it was a precious, depth experience"* (James) *"feeling part of the place and feeling good in being there"* (Deborah), *"feeling it was meeting my expectations"* (Naomi), *"that feeling of wow"* (Miriam and Ruth).

On the negative side, John said, *"I didn't feel any great connection, despite the setting being special, 'absolutely idyllic.'"* He later described himself as *"constantly in the head with no movement in the heart whatsoever. I'm always looking for reasons,"* yet he also described the day as *"something special, something to be treasured."* Sarah cited feeling disappointed that no robins, snails, or worms were seen and that there were *"no nettle places for butterflies to lay their eggs."* Rachel expressed feelings of anxiety at the beginning of the day but these changed over the morning: *"I felt very comfortable in the garden and it became a freeing experience."*

Deep feelings were spoken in the sharing session at times but also were expressed in the quiet times alone. For example, Miriam commented, *"you see someone in a corner crying, in the little corner house crying, and the next thing you'd see them sitting down and happily talking. People said an awful lot of things; possibly it's the only place they would say it."* The interaction between people was a significant part of the day for several participants. For John, *"the essential part of the day was the sharing,"* which he enjoyed, admitting *"I get bored with my own company."* He particularly enjoyed the cups of tea and sandwiches.

BE INTELLIGENT[7]

Coming to understand, expressing what was understood, and tuning into the implications of these understandings frequently became part of Time-Out Days. Hannah, for example, commented at the end of her interview, *"the day got me thinking in a totally different way."* Several insights about meaning and significance came as a result of pondering the sculptures. Ruth commented: *"We all had dif-*

ferent readings on the sculptures. I found that very enriching for myself. I had never seen a sculpture until last year and wouldn't have looked for any meaning in them. I didn't know you could find a meaning in them, so it has opened up my mind on that."[8] An insight that occurred for John was: "What stayed with me was that first and foremost you go and have a look at it. You were given time to look at it, and then decide what's provoked in you about it, what appeals to you about it. I am always trying to relate it back to something I know." Esther discovered: "I found some of the sculptures spoke to me about myself. In one I saw the complexity of the work and it spoke to me of my own complexity."

A further comment on the value of shared reflection on the sculptures is: "It is fascinating and enriching and something you wouldn't get on your own when you sit in front of a sculpture and you hear six different things that happened to people. There's huge value in the shared reflection as well as in your own." Miriam found listening to other people's stories and life experiences "wonderful. It has broadened my horizons. I came away thinking I hadn't thought about that. It gives an appreciation of someone else's point of view." Similarly, Ruth said she came to realize there was no right or wrong way to look at sculptures, rather it was "about finding what it meant to you. I was comfortable in the knowledge that whatever I had to offer it would be okay."

A common experience was that both the garden and the sculptures aroused powerful associations, some going back to childhood. A sad incident of association was given in Naomi's interview:

An amazing thing happened at that bench that was split in two [Mother and Child sculpture]. There was a baby's head. One of the girls in our group had a baby die. That girl carries that pain every hour of everyday. She sat on that bench and another sweet girl came along. At some stage I joined them. She was crying a lot and I said we'll pray together. We just held hands, prayed, and that was the closest I ever got to that girl at that moment. It was just a thing touched into in that moment. That was powerful.

At that same sculpture Eve was touched, not by the sculpture itself, but by the stones that surrounded it:

What appealed to me most were the stones and I wondered why was I drawn to something so simple? I sometimes wonder is it something to do with having a disabled child because in looking after her your life is quite simple at a certain level because her handicap is severe. She loves simple things, a simple routine and when her life is not complicated she feels most secure. What I liked about those stones was their simplicity and yet they were so beautiful and so lovely to touch and the shape of them to have in your hand. I had to pick the stones up and touch them. I felt God was saying I left these beautiful things for those who can see to enjoy.

A third example of association was of a deeply personal, as opposed to an interpersonal, type. The intimate nature of the sharing necessitates that the account given was edited. Ruth felt drawn to the wooden sculpture but was shocked that her initial reaction was so negative, even finding it *"disgusting,"* knowing on reflection it echoed her views about her own sexuality. She was surprised and excited to discover that others viewed the piece as expressing positive aspects of male and female sexuality. Other people's positive interpretation led her to begin to see the piece as beautiful and to see her own sexuality in a different light.

BE REASONABLE[9]

A frequently used word that indicated this third level of experiencing was *realize*. Instances of this were shown in comments such as: *"that day I realized I had to mind myself"* (Ruth); *"I realized I was opened up"* (Rachel); *"I'm only realizing now that nobody can complete you that totally, they [husband and children] are not my whole life, I realize now I don't own them"* (Ruth); *"I realized that what I want to do is to spend more time with nature. I do more walking since that day"* (Eve).

A central truth/realization that was aroused in several people was the discovery and affirmation of oneself. For Ruth it started in this manner: *"When I went out I was conscious I didn't want to talk* to anyone, be with anyone. I didn't even want anyone crossing my path. I just wanted that feeling of space. I had a great feeling. And the garden had everything. Actually that day was probably one of the first days that I said I want this day for myself and I need this day." Esther commenced her interview by saying: "It [the garden] put me completely at my ease. I was just myself in the garden and I felt accepted for myself. Not many places I feel that. I feel in most places there is an agenda. You can't always be free, but in the garden I felt free." At the close of her interview the same theme was returned to:

> Welcome is like acceptance, and if you feel accepted there is nothing beyond that. One then moves out from that. I think if I accept myself as I am, I can then accept other persons as they are, not the way I would like them to be....The visit showed me how necessary it is to be at peace with oneself. I went back a different person. I can see my own growth, which is lovely.

And a final comment, "I would say to other people if you want to know about yourself, go to the garden."

Miriam, who also experienced a feeling of "great acceptance" in the garden, described in addition her sensation of herself as experiencer: "I had a feeling of meeting myself going around, if that makes sense. The feelings when I went around the garden were that of joy and happiness. Sometimes you have to stop and just be conscious of yourself listening [in this instance to the stream]. I had an awareness of myself listening. We are not conscious sometimes because we are so caught up in our own thoughts. I just sat down by the pools and felt my soul was listening to the flow of life." She also spoke of listening to the thoughts that came up from within "that you haven't looked at or maybe didn't want to look at," (which she termed a Garden-of-Gethsemane experience since it was so filled with pain and struggle). She also became aware of "how we get locked into a view, into situations and sometimes we won't move." She became aware of the need to "shift our perspective" through moving to a higher viewpoint and enacted this realization by actually walking up to a higher level within the garden. She noticed clearly that when you move higher you get a different angle, a better overview of things.

She likened her overall experience to a *"Promised Land/Garden of Gethsemane,"* and suggested that each side of the one coin was interiorly enriching in its own way.

BE RESPONSIBLE[10]

The fuller experiencing that occurs in the fourth precept was manifested in the decisions people made as a result of their day in Shekina. The importance of making and implementing decisions was spelled out by Ruth: *"Now I am very good at knowing that I need time for myself. I am making better use of my time for myself, I am better able to grab the moment. I also see nature differently and feel a great need to be out there. For instance, I now get more of a kick out of walking down the beach than I used to get out of walking around Marks and Spencers looking at clothes."* She also discovered in herself a new orientation toward life: *"I try not to label things anymore—it takes from the experience."*

Eve spoke more specifically about what taking personal time out meant in practice for her: *"I decided after the visit to spend more time quieter in myself and I do have opportunities when the children are at school in the morning. To look at what you do; where you are going; affirming myself; giving myself the kind of food I need—spiritual food I suppose—to have people positive around you; to go out into nature more"* became components of her newly found time-out moments. Rachel left with the resolve to *"not just keep pushing things to the back of my head but to try and deal with things as they happen and to take responsibility for what's happening in my life....I don't do this all the time but I do find it easier. I feel I have come a long way, even though it's only been a short space of time. I've grown up. It opened my mind and set me on the road where to go at the time. Since then I've done bits and pieces and allowed space for myself, like I did a psychology course. I think if I hadn't gone to the garden that day I'd be stuck in a place where I was."*

Esther felt more at peace with herself and went back home with a *"reenergized, rejuvenated self. It made me feel young and ready to take up the reins again."* She felt challenged *"to make a new start"* after her time in the garden and has since attempted *"to see things differently and to love more deeply especially in the situations that are difficult. It gave me a kick start."*

Deborah's heightened attentiveness began by her following a suggestion to take off her shoes. She then recounts the unfolding of fuller levels of experiencing in the following way:

The first thing that struck me was the soft feel of the green grass beneath my feet. It was so powerful and beautiful that I quickly made the decision to forget about reflecting about my surroundings because I felt this was something really good for me, of value, and to give my whole time and attention to it. I have very tender feet and that made it more beautiful. I can literally walk on nothing but carpet. So first of all I was absorbing the softness into my feet, but then into my whole person. Then any time during the day, if we had a moment, I walked on the grass because I felt I didn't have enough time to absorb what I was getting from it. As time went on I reflected on this softness, which was what my feet needed, and then later on how much I needed softness in my heart and in my life. My prayer during the day, without words, invited God to fill me with softness, fill my life, my heart, and all the areas in my life that needed softness. I reflected that there is a certain hardness in my person. It comes from a lot of things—my parents were hard-working, we lived on a farm. I was a teacher and I worked the students hard. This new awareness of my need for softness was an awareness that I hadn't got anywhere before. It started with the grass, then absorbing the experience, followed by the reflection on it.

A similar account of a growing range and depth of experiencing is echoed by Hannah's description of an experience she had in the garden.

When I saw this old battered tree, that's the way I felt—it was rotten and I felt that's why I am here. The tree shouldn't be here and I shouldn't be here. And yet when I looked at it closely, I thought "there is hope." In the middle it seemed much livelier and I thought "well, maybe there is something inside that can start growing and overcome all this trouble," because I had had a lot of trouble. I had had a rough child-

hood. I'd been abused and I felt if only something could happen. And I think I thought then something could happen. It was a symbol of hope and new life. The branches were coming out in three branches. But the piece in the very center was a darker green. And there was life in that. And that's what spoke to me. There was hope and maybe there was something in this shattered life. I was just fed up getting knocks everywhere. I thought I could get over this, could start living again. It was kind of a conversion, and just amazing things happened after that.

The story continued in too personal a way to relate, but this part of her history was dramatically resolved some weeks later—*"Definitely there was something happening, I don't understand it, but I know I had been given forgiveness. A few weeks later, a sense of peace came, it is now something just gone away and doesn't trouble me anymore. It was things like that [that] started to happen. It started in the garden."*

Theme 3—Aesthetic Experience

This theme involves the ways in which individuals were affected by the backdrop of beauty that surrounded them. This was sometimes consciously recognized and sometimes not, as is borne out by Rachel's comment:

The scenery and where it was set was just amazing. The beauty maybe allowed me to go into myself. I didn't take it on board that I was in such a beautiful place. But now, obviously, it did have a huge impact because I was able to do something I hadn't really done before.

The comments on beauty varied. For instance, Peter, who had lived in the city all his life, remarked, *"beauty calms, has a calming effect. If you see trees, you kinda feel you are where you should be."* James commented, *"beauty lifts my heart. You forget about everything else and swim in it. You enter it—in the garden it was that sort of experience."* Both John and Paul spoke similarly of the garden and its setting as *"very very beautiful."* Deborah elaborated further by mentioning specific things, including *"the blue sky overhead and the lovely trees, shrubs, and sculptures. Just to be there. You imbibed the beauty from the place,"* and then she turned to herself, *"maybe I am talking nonsense, but it all made you feel beautiful."* She also found that *"the space was just beautiful, it was just empty of all the things that clutter up your day."* Ruth began by saying she had no garden, just a backyard, then spoke of her excitement as she initially looked out on the garden from the sunroom: *"I was so cold when I arrived I thought I would feel better tucked up in bed, and then I looked out into the garden and it seemed to be alive. Looking out, finding things in the garden and the beauty, it all became bigger than I was feeling. It took me out of myself completely."* Paul made the general remark that appreciation of beauty/art *"depends on your depth of perception."*

Others referred to specific items in nature or the sculptures that they found particularly attractive. Paul referred to *"the birds—beautiful. It was June, after Whitsun, and I was amazed how many birds there were to be heard. That's an experience for me. It's funny with summer solstice they withdraw."* Then he carried his experience of beauty to two *"of the various pieces of art. I was very much taken by one that I quickly realized contained a female shaping. I was also much attracted to the piece of bog oak across the little stream. I think that's very very beautiful; the setting of that is superb."* He did not like the metal frames (which depict the first creation story). He saw them as a construction and, according to his taste, not a piece of art. He felt it disturbed the harmony of the others. Interestingly, John, who used the word *beautiful* many times throughout the interview, waxed lyrically about *"the absolutely beautiful day, unseasonably beautiful"* from a weather perspective, the garden setting, *"the trilling of the birds and their singing was absolutely beautiful."* He also thought, unlike Paul's comments, that *"the work in the wrought iron piece was very beautiful and incredibly intricate and detailed."* Peter also found this sculpture beautiful.

The beauty of nature and the beautiful garden setting were a constant refrain. For example, James said, *"I feel it's like a work of art, something precious."* For some, this sense of beauty was not spelled out further. For instance, Naomi referred to the quiet, pervasive nature of beauty within her overall experience of the day: *"I think when you see beautiful things—God is in all things—you have a sense of the presence of God. In fact it wasn't a sunny day. From where I was sitting on the patio there was a hill and it was misty. It was one of those quiet really soft days. I just love beautiful things. Those shapes were so lovely in the garden. A softness in the air and maybe a softness in the surroundings.*" Rachel and Eve had somewhat similar experiences, showing as Naomi did the close link that can exist between religious and aesthetic experience. "*Everything was so beautiful in the garden that the first thing I thought about is God in creation*" was a remark of Rachel's whereas Eve elaborated further, "*There was the beauty of the place and the beauty of the mountains in the distance. Always looking at something very beautiful like that, I find it calming and peaceful. It adds to that feeling and brings out in you a desire to praise God. It was so beautiful, the whole setting.*" Paul, a keen appreciator of art, said, "*real art has a profound element of spirituality in it.*"

Ruth, while stating that the garden was beautiful, was more aware of the atmosphere in the garden having a beauty-filled dimension. "*It's just the general feeling here. You feel safe. It's hard to explain—it is just calming and peaceful. You can sit anywhere in the garden and it's a different place. Each place you sit is just totally different and there is peace everywhere you go.*" Only Esther and Eve mentioned color in any of their comments. Esther was aware of subtle shades, remarking, "*the colors, the colors of the trees, they take on a stronger hue. All the different leaves and yet each one is so clearly defined. You can see a yellow one, and a red one, and a green one. It centers you on beauty. You know its all there, but you can't take it all in.*"

An awareness of beauty was also experienced in the interpersonal dynamic that unfolded as the day progressed. Paul discovered that he went away "*personally enriched. I thought it very beautiful that we did speak about it; the way we got to know others better, touching on aspects that we maybe would never have talked about.*" Hannah exclaimed, "*it's the friendship of total strangers that hit me most. It's wonderful, an unusual experience, something I've never experienced anywhere else. It is beautiful.*" "*The loveliness of the togetherness that was generated*" was remarked on by Deborah, who continued, "*there was a great sense of inclusiveness. People looked shy, like myself, but said the most beautiful things. That was won-*

derful. So was the sitting around the table while we had lunch. I think the table was round. If it wasn't we would have ended up sitting in a circle."

Theme 4—Religious Experience/Experience of the Sacred

Attempts to explore the manifestations of religious/faith experiencing that occurred were diverse. Intimations of such manifestations were elicited by dwelling on the words *wonder*, *depth*, and *mystery*, and then on the term *sacred*.

To commence with a negative comment: John, in response to the question on wonder, depth, and mystery, said he experienced none of these things, but then immediately added, *"it [the experience] wasn't shallow. I am sure I did pray on the day but don't recall it specifically."* James described his overall experience of the garden as *"transcendent, inviting one to the mystery of God."* He went on to say that he experienced wonder, depth, and mystery and that these words *"very accurately summed up the day"* for him. His further elaboration focused on the word *mystery—"life is a mystery, I am a mystery to myself, other people are mysteries, nature is a wonderful mystery. I don't mean an unsolvable mystery, but a mystery where there is depth, [it] will never be explored but invites to exploration."*

Sarah, who was the most negative about her overall experience, due to her seeing everything through, it seemed, one lens—ecology issues—admitted, *"I think people could have an experience of the non-concrete and that if someone [was] searching,…had lost their way a bit, I think it would have the effect of bringing them back."* Deborah said, *"Mystery for me is the Spirit, the Holy Spirit. Wonder, wonder and awe together were definitely in the garden."*

The word *depth* had an appeal, particularly for some of the women and especially in regard to the discoveries they were making about themselves. For instance, Ruth's general experience of the day was in the depth category and said this depth experiencing was *"awesome."* *"It's like falling in love—you can't describe it. I had to go inside myself to look at what it was saying to me."* She then continued: *"I have no God, I have no prayer life. My God, I think, I am finding inside myself. The more of this work I do, the more I am finding this God inside in myself. I don't have a prayer life but I have focus."*

Naomi also spoke of *"depth"* then added *"mystery and wonder too"* in relation to that discovery. For Eve, that day meant discovering value in her life and feeling affirmed that *"what I am doing is right."* She mentioned wonder and mystery in relation to nature and then to *"the whole mystery of it all. I like the feeling of mystery. You are not putting everything in a little box and explaining it."*

Peter claimed at the beginning of the interview that he did not believe in God, yet in another part of the conversation, remarked spontaneously, *"I remember praying the circle"* as he walked around the Celtic Zen walk. He expressed experiencing mystery in relation to the sculptures, which *"gave you something to think about,"* and also to nature, specifically the changing of the seasons, which means that things never stay the same and therefore one could never be bored.

In response to a question about an explicit connection with the Divine, *wonder* and *amazement* were expressed reactions. For example, Hannah described how *"I could come into this place so negative and go out so full of the joys."* She found that the moments alone in the garden led her to a depth that brought her an awareness of *"God's love, deeper than I'd ever experienced. The depths of God's love you can be drawn into on being alone. It's easy here. I think there is prayer around, it is just hovering over us. It's a sanctuary really."*

A further comment made by Deborah:

> *There was the depth of feeling rooted in the story of creation and of my own story being part of that story. There was depth to the whole day. I felt all we were doing had a value and there is a depth to that. I've already touched into mystery, the mystery of God that we can't understand. I love mystery; mystery lifts me out of the mundaneness of life. Hopefully it brings me closer to God. I prayed down there, asking God to give me gentleness, softness, touch my heart, to "change my heart of stone into a heart of flesh." I handed over to the Lord my lack of gentleness, understanding, softness, and asked him to make up to all the people I had offended in this way.*

Esther remarked toward the end of the interview, *"I have discovered the wonder of myself and I wouldn't have discovered that, only God has given me that—of seeing myself as he sees me—insofar as I* can understand it. I am the person God has created and that's the wonder of me."

Mystery was a particularly appealing term for Miriam:

I try to understand everything, like where I am in life, how I've got to where I am. There is a mystery to that. There is mystery as to who comes into our life and the route we are taking. I think it's a spiritual mystery. It's like the mystery of the rainbow—there is a plan for where we are going but we don't always see where we are going. The mystery of life is that we each have our own unique journey to take. We can't take that for each other, we have to enter the mystery on our own. It opens up your awareness that there is a great Presence there; it's a feeling you are not on your own. There is a feeling that maybe sometimes we don't need another human being to understand because there is that feeling that someone understands me. I find it almost as though there is somebody standing by my side. It's a Presence.

In her concluding remarks, she said, "We are so caught up in technical things. That's not all we are or all we need. Again it's about going for mystery."

Two sculptures in particular elicited a sense of mystery. Both pieces are by the same sculptor—Fred Conlon. The large untitled one drew varied comments. For instance, Rachel said simply, "I remember the shell—it was like around you." A fuller account was given by Hannah: "There is one with a circle and an inner circle. There's something about that circle—it brings me to the presence of God, draws me closer to him. It's like going through a tunnel or something. In his presence there is safety. When you are in his presence, then you understand things that you can't understand in the bustle of life. I think there is something about that circle, going through to something very special."

Peter mentioned this sculpture three different times during the interview. "I remember the granite one. My first impression was that it was like someone giving a hug. It felt as though it was something you could hold, a place where you could be and get a big hug. This one had a big effect." Later he added, "I liked it. It was like a mother and child kind of thing—birthing; a round kind of thing; somewhere *you can hide."* His final comment referred to it as *"the granite twisted one, it was a warming sculpture—a thing you could think about a lot."* Deborah said very simply about both this and the other piece (discussed below) *"I was just happy imbibing the mystery of these rocks."*

Sarah, who previously mentioned wanting to see *"a few snails marching around,"* likened this piece, it would seem with affection, to a snail: *"I particularly liked the circular sort of one. I could see it going on past itself. It was a bit like a snail. I just felt it was going on silently and invisibly. The solid physical bit was here but I just felt it went on at least a yard and a half on, just privately on its own. If you had eyes to see this you would have seen the invisible bit. None of the others spoke to me as much as this snail one."*

Two people were particularly drawn to Conlon's second sculpture—*Ni Mar a Shiltear Bitear* ("things are not what they seem"). James, after referring to it by the nickname of *"a square in a round hole,"* said *"it spoke to me of mystery; maybe the round being the infinite, then the change to the square. It caused me to delve into the mystery of the sculpture—leading to explore the infinite if you like."* Naomi was profoundly touched by this sculpture and gave a lengthy description of the geometric complexity of this piece, its roughness and smoothness, its dark and light shades, and how her powerful association with this piece connected her with her present struggle in all that she was undergoing. This led to her exclaiming: *"It was overwhelming. It epitomized the way I was feeling that day. But it also spoke to me of hope. There was hope because the outlet was smoother. That image is so vivid even to me now. It sort of gave me courage. Okay, there is going to be struggle, it will be painful, but not to give up. There is a way through that hole, there is another side."*

A traditional way of referring to religious experience is by stating one's awareness of being in God's presence. Naomi said that as a child she had a strong sense of God's presence in nature and in the family garden and that it was moving and precious to get in touch again with something familiar. She had a sense of *"going very deep into the center, where God is. I can articulate it now, whereas as a child I couldn't. There is something comforting in having made the journey to be able to put words on something that has always been there."* She also remarked that her experience in Shekina made her feel connected with the whole of creation.

The idea of finding God within creation was mentioned by others. It happened in a veiled way for Ruth, who said, on looking out at the garden, *"It was like there is more than this. Like I just felt there was more than....No man is creating this. As I was looking at it I just said 'it's heaven.' It seemed to be alive; the beauty became bigger. It took me out of myself completely. I felt I was opened up."*

Rachel said very simply, *"everything was so beautiful in the garden that the first thing I thought about is God in creation—but I don't think it inspired me to want to pray."* John had a single sentence: *"It [the garden] was full of nature and to me close to creation and the Creator."* While Peter said somewhat ambiguously: *"I like nature just because it is there. It is part of you and you are part of it. It's as much part of you as you are part of it."* Esther was more explicit and clearly saw God in nature, in all things: *"One can see the divine in it, see God in it. I think that seeing God in nature or in a person does not necessarily need a religious context. If I didn't see God in it I wouldn't see the other thing. I think God is the kernel. I would be incapable of certain thoughts without God being behind or God being the giver. God is revealing himself at all times, in all things, even in bad things, dreadful things."*

Experiencing the closeness of God, being in God's presence, was clearly a reality for Hannah:

> *It opened contemplation rather than prayer. It was more being able to sit in the presence of God. You are in some great presence and you can be at peace. You don't have to communicate, say, or repeat a lot. It's there in the closeness that you know you are safe; you know somebody is with you. That taught me a lot. You don't have to say words—I don't think I would have done this before. You don't have a start, you don't have a middle, you don't have an end. The time you are there, the time you walk away doesn't matter. It's not about words, it's about being in his presence. It was a profound experience.*

People linked the word *sacred* to many things—people, places, moments, memories, also God. Sarah, who had problems entering into the day, seemed to have less difficulty in directly focusing on this question about the sacred. Referring to a *"sacred place"* she said, *"it's a place that you would feel reverence for. It's a place where something happened, maybe where someone lived or [has] done something wonderful. It's somewhere where you'd lose yourself a little bit to something else."*

Rachel said, *"sacred to me means something that is just very, very, very special—at a higher level than ordinary things. It's the most special something could be. I've never had cause to use the word* sacred *I think—only in prayer, Sacred Heart. I wouldn't use it as an everyday word—it's the highest you could go with special. Definitely the garden had an element of the sacred about it. I can understand why people might call it a sacred space—it is just a space to be yourself."*

Peter, who said he was an unbeliever, answered the question about the meaning of the sacred by turning to mystery. He started with: *"It's the magic in life."* He continued, *"There would be an element of the sacred in the garden in the sense of its mysteriousness. It's something you think you know and there is still mystery there. I think that's what life is about. We all have a mystery. I hate using anything, like the word* religion, *it's bigger even than that. There's no answer, it's like the universe, there is no answer. You can think about it. It's there and it is vast, but you'll never know."*

John referred to sacred moments, such as reaching the top of a mountain, *"where you'd have to feel closer to God,"* and to other special places, such as *"churches built for the honor of God and graveyards for the honor of man."* He spoke of special buildings or places—*"countless yearnings and efforts have gone into something and these all being handed up to God makes it pretty sacred for me."* He was also aware of the sacredness of special moments such as *"the birth of your children."* Hannah also spoke of the sacred in relation to moments: *"I think the word* sacred *describes special moments in your life, when you are touched beyond anything you expected to experience. I think sacred is being touched by God, by the Holy Spirit. It's beyond special, it's beyond anything you could create for yourself. When you recognize a sacred moment time stands still. When I was within one of these moments I would be happy to die."*

Paul took up the phrase *"sacred space"* and said *"it could be an experience with a human being—something that is deeply meaningful to you. It may even be negative, something that has hurt me deeply, but I'm grateful looking back that I have had the experience.*" In the context of the sacred, he described a recent encounter with a stranger with whom he *"within minutes had a very deep conversation going."* He longed for deep conversation and said, *"I would love, for example, to have a conversation about the Lord's Prayer."*

Shekina *"is a sacred place," "I had a feeling of sacred ground"* were comments of James, Miriam, Hannah, and Rachel.

Some quotations follow that are lengthier due to the richness and sacred quality of their content. The first of these gives James's thought on the meaning of the sacred:

> *Sacred means precious, dear (not expensive) in the heart. Sacred maybe touches the depths of the human being and of the divine being, of course. And maybe the touching of the two would be sacred. Demeaning people is the exact opposite to that. Solzhenitsyn's* Archipelago, *the Nazis who slaughtered the Jews, the war in Iraq lead to dehumanization. It cheapens people, makes them so low, removes the sense of the huge worth of the individual person and their capacity for God and infinity. The sacredness of the human person and their capacity for God, for infinite love—that's where I would put the sacred. The sacred and the holy are part of the same. For me someone with integrity, who is living the mystery and who has integrated the sacred into their daily life is holy. A holy person is not someone removed from life, but rather someone who is living life and living it very well. I do think everyone has a sense of the sacred. It may be just hunches. Even those who demean others may not be in that place yet, but the potential is still within them. I feel the garden is sacred, has a sacred quality about it, but it has to be kept sacred. The same is true of the church. Some have a sense of the sacred, while others don't have room for it; the sacred is squeezed out.*

Finding the sacred within oneself was one way Ruth described it:

> *The sacredness I feel is coming from inside myself in the beauty of whoever has provided it for us; that feeling there is more than this. I don't know what it is. The God word or the*

man word does not sit right with me. The sacredness is, or the God is, to continue towards that much more than I have ever thought possible. It's like someone has changed my light bulb from a zero watt and now I'm burning on a hundred watt and I want it to be a thousand or more. It is a very sacred feeling. I won't use God, but it is a sacred feeling and I feel very humbled to have experienced this. I feel happier inside myself, more peaceful, than I have ever done in my life. And I know there is more. It has to be other than me because I couldn't do this on my own. Is it the God I'm meeting inside myself and in the people I'm meeting on the journey? I don't know. This mystery within—it's wonderful and I wish I could give it out to everyone! I know I have it and I hope in the light of what I have it will spill out somewhere. Something has happened inside me. It's like I was asleep and I've wakened up.

The sacred meant for Naomi that the Sacred, meaning God, was in everything:

The sacred can be anywhere, any place. It is an awareness of God breaking through and this can happen in very ordinary situations. It is something to do with attentiveness, an awareness. It's very much a heart thing. To be aware of the sacred there needs to be an openness in one. We can easily ignore the sacred. I am sure it passes us by all the time. Any encounter can be sacred. I've had very sacred moments in my work—very sacred, holy ground. Just when something happens, a word, a look, a touch, and God is in it. Time-Out helps that awareness—this awareness of the divine. I wonder does the initiative come from God? It's a connection made somehow between the divine and yourself. I suspect it is opening ourselves to what is always there. I think probably everywhere is sacred. I am reminded of one of my favorite passages "if only you knew..." [said by Jesus to the Samaritan woman]. I think that veil is so thin. I expect the sacred is just around us all the time. I think the garden is a very, very sacred place—I think sacredness is anywhere. Some things immediately speak their sacredness, but it's harder to find sacredness in some situations. God is everywhere and God is in all things I do believe.

Deborah commenced her thoughts on sacredness with reverence, and links sacredness to one's awareness of God:

Sacred is a lovely word and what comes up around it is reverence. You immediately think of God. You think of being drawn into another place when it's a sacred place. It's a place or state (by state I mean a way of being), that draws one to another level, awareness, living. It's a place where I can more easily be brought in touch with God. I love being in a sacred space, it's out of the ordinary. It is the ordinary but it is more than the ordinary; it's where I'm more aware of being in God's presence; it's where I can be at a different level of living and more in touch with God. God is the Sacred One and all sacredness comes from God. We just try to create a sacred place (with cloths, candles, shrubs, or whatever) but really it is God who makes it sacred.

For Esther, "*Everything that is good is holy. Holy can be holy or wholly; there is little difference between the two. It is something to be revered, to be respected. Sacred is something you'd hold very close to you, is something that is part of you. It's not trivial. It's not something that appeals to the senses. The work of the garden, the creation of the garden comes from the sacred.*"

Miriam started by saying:

Shekina is a sacred place, a sacred ground. It's a place apart. It's to be honored and respected and is calling us to honor and respect ourselves as well as the people who are on the sacred ground with you. The idea of sacred ground—it's a great feeling of love that we actually have inside ourselves and it comes up. It's a feeling of connection between ourselves and the Mystery. People are searching because the day-to-day stuff isn't enough—they try to escape. Sacredness is life giving, but the sacredness in people can die. The sparkle has gone. The sacred is the sparkle.

Hannah said that when difficulties arise she turns to sacred places:

If anything is wrong I go to sacred places because I seem to experience the presence of God more there. There is a feel-

ing of prayer and presence. My tree [mentioned earlier in this analysis], to me that's sacred ground, holy ground. I have only to go to certain places and then everything is alright. I think sacred for me is mainly a place. When I'm in his presence, it's then I put a different slant on things and that to me is sacred. I feel God is here and that I am close and that he understands. There are sacred places where I immediately know, I've arrived, he is here. I'd say this garden is a sacred place. All of a sudden you feel, Oh...we're here. You are in here in the center of it, at the heart of it.

The final sharing in this section is given to a description of a moving scene where sacredness is expressed and experienced in the loving gestures of both mother (Eve) and daughter within their two different forms of giving and receiving:

Sacred would have a feeling that God is present. It would lead your mind to the whole area of God and the wider picture of your life—to deeper questions. My daughter [who is very intellectually disabled] has poor circulation in her legs, and her feet are so cold I massage them. Sometimes I feel I am massaging the feet of Christ [many tears]. I scratch her back because I feel it might be itchy and she loves you to do it. I feel so honored at times. I'm not saying it's all rosy. But the words of Christ, "when you do this to the least of my brethren..." I wasn't actually a particularly spiritual person...I stopped practicing after the death of my father and then my daughter was born. When she was about two or three I tried to have a reason or purpose for her in life. Why is she here? What has she to offer? You can only get those positive answers in religion. I remember starting to pray, asking God that I might see a way, some value to her life. That it wasn't just going to be all pain and suffering for her. I remember feeling a very strong voice, it was really God speaking to me saying: "to me she is perfect."

And then I realized she loves unconditionally. She behaves in a way that is Christlike. She has never sinned, will never sin, because of the level of her disability. She just loves to love people, to hug and to pour out her love. Of course many people miss this. You feel she is very Christlike. Her sight is extremely poor and I often think she would never have seen anyone hug anyone else so she would never have learnt it, yet she loves to do it. At night when getting ready for bed she will reach out and grab you and hug you. It's amazing, it's in her nature. I feel so very much at times that she is so near to God. Even people who come into the house say there is a lovely sense of peace in the house. I often think my daughter brings this—her gentleness, these qualities about her that are so Christlike. She would never hurt anyone. You feel she is so Christlike because she would never set out to hurt or destroy people.

So, sacred is more than a feeling—its being in the presence of something wonderful; it's a mystery, something you can't understand, but it is energy giving. Working with her keeps you very close to and grounded in reality, the present moment, taking things one at a time, slowly. Living in the present I suppose is all sacred. I feel with my daughter that the best thing has happened to me and the hardest.

Theme 5—Effects after the Visit

The comments that arose pertaining to this theme give a clear indication of what the day meant to the participants. Two forms of effects were noticeable—lasting effects, namely, those that affected the participants personally, and permeating effects, effects that led people to tell or to not tell others about coming to visit the garden.

"What stayed with me really was the atmosphere" said James, while John said very simply that what remained was *"the whole idea; the fact that it was such a pleasant day."* What strongly affected Eve was her insight into self-affirmation, including affirming herself about her present tasks in life. In a similar vein, Rachel took away a desire *"to be more in control of my life and not to feel I'm doing it for other people."* For Miriam, the effect was acknowledgment of a new awareness of *"being opened up to who I am,"* as well as *"accepting things if I can't change them"* and *"letting things go, especially negative stuff."* Hannah said, *"it got me thinking in a totally different way."* She also said she left *"carrying away some of other people's pain while my own pain was eased."* Esther took away the

value of encouraging others, as well as receiving healing for herself, which led her later to be more forgiving toward a family member. *"Finding time for myself to do nothing and not feeling bad about it"* was the garden's effect for Ruth.

Naomi began with laughter, stating, *"the fact that it is so fresh now—probably nine months later"* showed her how significant the visit had been and then added *"it not only stayed with me, but kept me going."* Similarly, Sarah said, *"it must have been special to me to have remembered it so clearly. Other people's gardens you visit, you just go through and then out. It's a funny thing how this one has stayed. There must have been more to it than I thought at the time. Yes, it must have been since I can see everything so clearly. It's only now that I am remembering that I remember that garden more than any others. Other gardens would just go through my head and I wouldn't think of them."*

The four male participants gave more general comments. For John, what stayed was *"the whole day"* and *"the pleasantness of the day."* Similarly, James remarked that it was *"the sum total of everything"* that lasted. For Paul, it was just the wish to visit again and Peter said he went away with a good memory.

Wanting members of their family or friends to visit was a common response to the garden. Some discretion was needed about this, however, for instance, Ruth said, *"I would be particular about whom I would recommend it to. I wouldn't take my sisters. They would just have wanted a party. Five years ago I wouldn't have understood it, I wouldn't have been able to be with myself."* James expanded on Ruth's view:

> *I would recommend it to people who would value it because I feel it's like a work of art, or something precious. I don't think you'd give that to someone who is just there to chew gum! I think you choose people who have a hint of the ability to appreciate God and nature, beauty and sculpture and that sort of thing. I think people who were just going to zip in and out wouldn't get the value of what is there. It's a bit like love. You can't force love. I think it's a precious, depth experience and is one I wouldn't bandy around.*

Naomi said that it would depend on whom she was talking to as to whether or not she would recommend the garden. *"I would talk about the opportunity for reflection, quiet, relaxation and for getting in touch with the spiritual—a day of refreshment."*

Deborah took up the same idea. After saying how *"I was very 'with' everything, I was absolutely undistracted,"* she said she would recommend the day *"as a day apart for yourself in a lovely space, giving time to reflect."*

Rachel suggested, *"Everyone should do it; be able to turn off totally and listen to oneself. I think it's an important thing to do and most people don't do it,"* whereas John was less enthusiastic, *"I would say if you are in the vicinity drop in. I think it is something to be discovered rather than forced."*

Peter was more specific and said that he *"would recommend it to anyone who had a bit of trouble, to go down and reflect on themselves."* Esther echoed this by saying, *"if you want to know yourself, go to this garden. You know we talk about going to the Holy Land. I think everything I would find in the Holy Land I have found in this garden."*

The experiential element was central for Miriam. She recommended that people come in a spirit that is *"open to experience the experience."* The final comment is given to James: *"I would recommend this place for quiet reflection for individuals and groups. I did suggest this to a group."*

Theme 6—The Significance of Place in Relation to Shekina Sculpture Garden

I left this theme to the end because of the overarching influence the context of place had on the participants' entire experience. In general, three types of comments were made, with some of these echoing previous remarks. Comments in the first category referred to the need of taking time out in "places apart" from one's normal environment. Ruth referred to the need to *"make space for yourself,"* to which she added *"in order to be in touch with the Spirit."* Deborah spoke of the garden as *"a lovely kind of empty space, an empty vessel for God to fill,"* whereas for Esther, it *"was refreshing just to sit there."*

Comments in the second category spoke of the garden's physical aspects—its setting and features. For James, *"The whole area was just very pleasant, very pastoral, very rural; the beauty of nature, the beautiful setting, the water features, and everything in it."* Paul pointed out early in his interview that *"two key elements that contributed greatly to the garden were its sloped ground and the water flowing through it."* Eve said, *"I was surprised that a place could be so beautiful with so little color, so few flowers."* A more negative remark about the place came from John: *"it was a beautiful day and the company was good, whereas the garden itself didn't speak to me or move me."* He did later say, however, that he found the place *"extremely welcoming."*

This sense of experiencing *"a welcoming place"* was referred to by several participants and leads to the third type of comment—one's referring to the "atmosphere" in the garden. It was, for instance, the garden's atmosphere that gave Rachel *"a chance to reflect and think about the things that were going on for me at the time."* She then added *"if it wasn't welcoming I wouldn't have been able to wind down the way I did."* This welcoming hospitable quality helped people relax, which for Miriam meant *"no fears, no worries, no brooding,"* and for Eve, to feel free: *"I felt very free in the garden. I felt you could touch anything and that you didn't have to be careful at any stage."* For Hannah, this spirit of feeling at home in a place was manifested in being given *"absolutely full access to the garden, you could walk anywhere, I felt part of the place."* Peter commented, *"the place itself has a surrounding type of feeling,"* and Naomi appreciated that *"we had time to explore and if you wanted to be on your own you could be on your own."* A final comment from Ruth, *"for me, my welcome was first to myself, to be able to be myself."* The cup of tea on arrival and departure as well as the picnic lunch helped engender a spirit of hospitality as people shared food, conversation, laughter, and tears with one another. The option was also there for people to go off on their own if they so wished.

It is a combination of this atmosphere and hospitality that has led to Shekina being perceived as a reflective place. Esther, when asked at the end of this third visit what she would want if she came again, said:

> *The garden puts me completely at my ease. I am just myself in that garden and feel accepted for myself. All those lovely*

things I experience in the garden—who would not want more of that. I just feel there is so much "more" than where you are at any given moment in your life. What I don't know excites me! You know God, Jesus, and you think you know all about him. But when I think what you don't know and can be revealed to you....I get really excited about the idea of the "more." I think it would be awful if that were all there was to be learnt about God was what I knew. It's not just knowledge, it's to get close. He has much more arms and much more depth that one can get to. Being able to get closer to the depth of Jesus must be wonderful. Maybe it's like holding babies. It's important for people to be held. I think that's what Jesus does but it goes beyond the physical. Going to the garden you would learn so much. There are not many places like the garden in your life, so the garden fills a great need I think. It is a sacred place, a holy place.

Conclusion

One remarkable fact that shone through was that participants' accounts of their experiences in the garden were so fresh and detailed even though the interviews took place six to eight months after their visit. The accuracy of their descriptions of the garden, and in particular of the sculptures to which they were attracted, as well as their recall of inner feelings and insights revealed a depth of memory that was truly surprising, thus revealing how deeply imprinted the garden experience had become. The generous way that people gave their time to come to be interviewed, despite inconveniences of work for some and travel for others, indicated that participants felt they had something worthwhile to share. Noticeable too was the reflective way people shared their experience—none were reluctant and many seemed particularly eager to do so.

10

Concluding Reflections

The overall aim of this work is to understand in greater depth the meaning of human experience and the Sacred and the intimate relationship that exists between both. Included in this aim was the recounting of experiences in a garden to discern whether they contained an awareness of sacredness. This discernment was carried out practically by listening to people's descriptions of their experiences after spending a reflective day in a sculpture garden. The interviews that followed their garden visit further enabled people to be more intimate in talking about themselves. In modern Western culture it can be difficult to find people and places where individuals feel free to talk about deep issues and especially matters concerning personal faith experiencing. If conversations about faith do take place, the approach tends to be either overly intellectual or overly emotional. In this work, a middle path emerged. In line with Jeff Astley's thinking, trust was placed in the validity of people's experiences. In conjunction with this, I relied on the trustworthiness of ordinary human conversation.

Conclusions

The *first conclusion* was the significant role places play as enhancers of fuller experiencing. This role is an undervalued entity, especially from the perspective of the ability places have to foster reflection and to act as a locus for the Sacred. Recognizing the effect places can have on experience requires a keener valuing of their potential. As nonplaces proliferate there is a need to discover or create alternative places that nourish people's inner life. Gardens, particularly due to their uniqueness, their beauty, and their ability to bring one close to nature, offer a contrast to the sameness, repetition, and functionality of nonspaces.

The *second conclusion* is that experiences are enhanced when aesthetic and numinous dimensions of human experience are awakened. Aesthetic experiences were aroused from spending time pondering nature's wonders and symbolic sculptures. Those who intimated an experience of the Divine described it as a real experience and did so largely in terms of having had an experience of Presence or Mystery.

The *third conclusion* relates to the depletion of the symbolic world by the present-day materialistic culture of the West; this can, however, be awakened by exposure to nature and art. The artwork in the garden and participants' reflective responses to these artistic symbols awakened a new understanding and appreciation of both art and symbol. Human imagination and its expression through nature and art open people up to the discovery not only of beauty but also of truth and meaning. Imagination also elicits wonder, a quality that particularly disposes people to the presence of Holy Mystery. The theoretical sections on aesthetics and symbols and the necessity of certain dispositions showed the desirability of heightening the use of the imagination as an adjunct to both deepening understanding and fostering creativity.

The *fourth conclusion* suggests that the term *sacred* could be a more helpful term than *religion* or *spirituality* when referring to the Divine. Opening up people to the possibility of the existence of the sacred by naming it, by alerting them to signs of its presence, and by fostering awareness of such happenings was an aim of this book. In the light of what has unfolded, the use of the terminology of *the Sacred* or *sacredness* to reactivate people's faith life, particularly for those who say they have left the church but who know (maybe only in a nebulous way) that they still have faith, could prove beneficial. For many today, the term *religion* tends to be associated with denominationalism and outward practices. Alternatively, the term *spirituality* is perceived almost solely interior and private in both its affects and its effects. The notion of sacredness could become a path that alerts one to the mystery element in life and could encourage a respectful reaching out to this mystery that could ultimately lead to a surrendering to Holy Mystery's gentle beckonings.

The *fifth conclusion* was that dispositions that orient people to interiority, beauty, and the Sacred can be nurtured by reflective and attractive venues such as gardens. Acquiring appropriate dispositions helps counteract the modern diminished view of reality where trends toward exteriority dominate. This latter view has detrimentally led to individual's interiority remaining largely unexcavated. Dispositions that aid as well as emerge from reflection can be elicited and fostered by places such as gardens.

The *sixth conclusion* is that, in the light of previous conclusions, depth experiences were fostered by creating reflective spaces for personal experiencing. The fact that people had significant depth experiences was shown by the accounts given of people's experiences in a garden. While the garden and the sculptures evoked immediate depth experiences these experiences also evoked memories of previous depth happenings. For some, it was experiences of difficulties and suffering that were recalled; while for others, it was other significant moments in life that reentered awareness. Such experiences were of a nontheistic nature for some, while for others these experiences mediated an awareness of the Sacred.

Suggested Ways of Implementing the Conclusions

The *first suggestion* relates to place. Since places affect experience—sometimes profoundly—new types of places that particularly aid reflection are required. The fact that people enter churches less frequently necessitates the discovery or creation of alternative venues. While gardens have been the focus in this work, other recognized places that are aesthetically pleasing, foster a reflective spirit, assist inner healing, and provide space for the celebration of significant life events need to be discovered or created. Such places are further enhanced when they offer an environment that is hospitable. Educating those in charge of public or semipublic places of the need to establish spaces that facilitate reflection should become a priority. Such places could also be set aside by faith, interfaith, or nonfaith groups as well as by individuals. The outdoor precincts of churches or other religious institutions could be developed further as sanctuary-type places.

The *second suggestion* relates to the terminology of sacredness. Since the term *religion* is often seen in a rigid and narrow fashion and *spirituality* has become a broad and nebulous term, the use of the term *sacredness* could prove more beneficial. Sacredness is a helpful way through which one can perceive the divine presence, transcendent yet immanent within created reality and especially within the human heart. Recovering, naming, and spelling out the numinous quality contained in experiences of sacredness, especially the experience of creaturehood, could prove beneficial in a world where personal autonomy has become the great value. Specifically facilitating people to activate their innate capacities and fostering the acquisition of dispositions that predispose one to sense the sacred should be encouraged.

The *third suggestion* relates to symbolic/sacramental reality and metaphorical language. I strongly suggest the implementation of educational processes that develop a more adult faith. This will involve deepening understanding of symbolic reality, enhancing a sacramental perspective, and enlarging an appreciation of metaphor. Unless symbol, sacramentality, and the use of metaphorical language are more profoundly understood and used when communicating matters related to faith, fundamentalism is likely to be resorted to. Some Christian symbols and sacraments have lost their meaning, while others, due to impoverished understanding, may present difficulties in the modern empirical world and thus appear irrelevant.[1] Also required is the creation of new secondary symbols and other images to replace those that are presently seen as unhelpful, possibly distorted, or even meaningless. Increased contact with nature and works of art enrich the imagination, foster creativity, and also nourish faith. A way forward in eliciting new images or symbols is by searching for artwork that evokes resonance, depth, and an awareness of the Sacred. Commissioning artists who work with integrity in their effort to expand a sense of truth, beauty, or even love needs to be encouraged. Such artists need not necessarily have a faith background.

A Concluding Reflection

I began in the introduction with the inspiration offered by comments of a theologian and of an artist. This concluding reflection ends also with the words of another author, Adrian van Kaam:

Fascinated by the Presence of the Holy in all creatures, I can look on in silent wonder....I know that my experience is limited, but I still ready myself for new revelations. I live in a sense of wonder, of respectful anticipation and expectation.[2]

This quotation sums up some of the themes outlined in this book: experience, the fascination of the numinous, and wonder. These sentiments express my personal desire to live in a spirit of readiness, awe, and "respectful anticipation and expectation." Working on my thesis and on this book has given me the graced insight of appreciating more profoundly that human life and all that is created are grounded and impregnated by the Sacred. Gifted with this deeper knowing, I move forward, attempting to live more fully with the two intertwined, indeed inseparable dimensions of life—the human and the Divine. I also wish to be an instrument in enabling others to become aware of that same reality in their lives, and it is my hope that this book will somehow enrich readers in a similar fashion.

Glossary

Consciousness is closely related to the word *experience*. It describes experiences in which we are aware of ourselves in relation to the activities that we carry out, for example, sensing, feeling, knowing, or loving. This awareness can also include an awareness of oneself as the activator of body, mind, and/or spirit. The quality of consciousness expands through growth in awareness of ourselves as we operate on the four different levels of human experience. This consciousness is manifested in a twofold manner—either when we relate to something *out there*, or alternatively, when we relate to ourselves as the operator. When these twofold modes of awareness take place the result is an experiencing, a being conscious of a richer self and a more expansive world. This richness is added to through our perception of not only different levels of awareness within consciousness but also different realms or viewpoints such as aesthetic or religious realms of consciousness.

Divine is a term used in this text in a generic way. It includes the words *God, Holy Mystery, Ultimate Other, Transcendent Other, the Sacred.*

Grace. This term essentially refers to the gift of the Godself. According to the *Catechism of the Catholic Church,* "grace is a participation in the life of God" (no. 1997); "grace is favor, the undeserved help that God gives us to respond to his call to become children of God" (no. 1996); "the grace of Christ is the gratuitous gift that God makes to us of his own life...it is the sanctifying or deifying grace received in Baptism" (no. 1999); "grace escapes our experience and cannot be known except by faith" (no. 2005).[1]

Mediate/Mediation. Chambers dictionary defines the word *mediate* as "middle: intervening, indirect, related or acting through something intervening." Lonergan uses the word *immediate* to describe anything that is a source, basis, or ground and the term *mediate* to describe what is a result, consequence, or outcome, insofar as it manifests or expresses its source. He gives the example of an immediate feeling of anger, which is then mediated through thoughts, images, and body language that flow from this feeling. The concepts *mediation, mediator, mediate* are significant when used theologically. Lonergan uses the phrase "mediated immediacy" in relation to the experiencing of God. In the Old Testament, people of God were aware that their relationship with God passed through intermediaries. For the Christian, the fullest expression of mediatorship between God and the human person is found in Christ.

Mystery is a term that refers to a real experience within consciousness of the Divine. It is a word that ultimately refers to God. According to Karl Rahner, "God is the mystery in human experience,"[2] and *Holy Mystery*[3] is his preferred term for God. An experience of mystery is a dynamic experiencing that is conscious yet without knowledge, in the ordinary understanding of the term *knowledge*. Mystery is experienced most explicitly when we surrender to the gift of God's love flooding the center of the self. It is a state of being in love. The *not-knowing* element is experienced as a positive fullness since it is born of a relationship with the incomprehensible, Unnamable Other—Ultimate Mystery.

A *mystic* is a person who lives a mystical life, someone who has surrendered to being in love with *Mystery*. This gifted state is an intimate human experience of God emerging from deep within the self. Such an experience is open to everyone and can be revealed in a myriad of ways, including in the events that occur within ordinary everyday living. It is never dependent on parapsychological phenomena or any other "thing," including our own knowing and/or loving.

Sacrament is a term derived from the Greek *musterion*, meaning "mysteries" or "secrets." Christianity's sacraments of baptism and Eucharist were originally seen as the two key mysteries. Over time, the word *sacrament* referred to the mediation of God's presence through a material reality. This sacramental mediation was viewed not merely in an instrumental way but rather as if the material component itself said something about the Divine. For instance, Augustine saw the Our Father, the sign of the cross, and blessed ashes as sacraments. *Sacraments/sacramentals* by their very nature contain the element of divine initiative and are always implicitly open to mystery, possibly to Holy Mystery. Sacramentals such as the rosary, pilgrimages, and other pious practices sometimes have more impact on people's faith than the seven sacraments. Since Vatican II, the term *sacrament* is used not only in relation to the seven sacraments but in a broader sense. This usage includes understanding the church as the sacrament of Jesus' presence with "the people of God" and also viewing the humanity of Jesus as the supreme sacrament of God's presence with humanity.[4]

David Brown advocates reclaiming the first millennium's broader sacramental perspective and suggests that it be "the primary way of exploring God's relationship to our world."[5] A diminished sacramental attitude/sensibility, he suggests, has led to a vacuum opening up within various spiritualities and therapies, with this leading to the emergence of "a retreat to magic." John Inge also endorses a reclaiming of sacramentality, noting how consistent this approach is with an incarnational faith.[6] A sacramental outlook does not mean that the world is indiscrimately revelatory of God but can become the place of God's self-revelation. Inge also sees sacramentality in relation to events—to moments when "rents" occur in the "opacity of history."

Spirit. When this word is used with a lowercase *s*, it refers to all interior movements of the person such as understanding, judging, and deciding. The human person is created with a spiritual nature that manifests itself through the processes of mind as well as feelings. The activities of the mind are spiritual functions similar to the way the operations of the body are physical functions. These mental activities are human phenomena and do not necessarily contain a theistic dimension. Due to the open-ended structure of the transcendental movements of consciousness, however, the human spirit is ultimately oriented to the Divine. It is precisely in the human spirit's unrestricted desire to know and to love, manifested through an insatiable longing for further transcendence, that the conscious in-breaking of the Spirit (Holy Spirit) within the human spirit is made known. This is always a graced happening.

Derived from the word *spirit* is the term *spirituality*. This refers to the actual living out of one's interior/spirit life. For some people today, this term is used in broad, woolly, and ambiguous ways. In addition, it has led to an understanding of an interior life that is private and self-centered. Because of such interpretations, this term is rarely used in this book. Instead the terms *sacredness* and *the Sacred* are preferred when exploring the divine-human relationship.

Symbol. Symbols have the ability to be not only their own reality but they can also represent a further reality and in some real way make that other reality present. If however the reality symbolized by the symbol is not recognized, it remains merely a sign. Alternatively if the symbol is seen as the full reality as opposed to seeing what it is the expression of, then the symbol can become an idol. It is only through symbols that some invisible essence can be expressed, and hence the function of a symbol is to open up levels of reality, especially its depth dimension, which cannot be grasped in any other way. Symbols are born and can also die when they no longer convey relevant meanings within changing cultural contexts. An example of this is when patriarchy is solely connected with one's image of the Divine. Symbols are more than indicators. They convey meaning, at times even presence, when we dialogue with them and surrender to what they offer. This symbolic form of knowing demands levels of participation/indwelling and has the potential and powerful ability to open us to Mystery.[7]

Transcendence. To transcend means to move beyond: to move beyond present limits. It comes from the Latin *scandere* meaning "to climb," and the Latin *trans*, meaning "across," "beyond." The human experience of transcendence is a natural phenomenon. *Self-transcendence* takes place as we move through the different levels of human experience. We constantly yearn, reach for something *more* in personal living, and it is the inner dynamism of this transcendent movement that draws us toward what lies beyond our world of immediate experience. Although we must remain firmly anchored in this world, an awareness of reaching beyond ourselves can become an experience of openness, which when elevated by grace can contain an awareness of the *Transcendent Other/the Sacred.*

Notes

Introduction

1. All biblical quotations are taken from the New Revised Standard Version, unless stated otherwise.

2. The notes largely refer to the key authors used in my thesis. It was deemed essential to keep certain quotations within the text for clarity purposes. By naming authors and their relevant works, and by giving the briefest biographical details of those considered most significant, I hope to offer further enrichment to readers.

3. Jeff Astley, *Ordinary Theology: Looking, Listening and Learning in Theology* (Aldershot: Ashgate Press, 2002). Astley, an English theologian, highlights the importance of listening to and learning from the God-talk of the nontheologically educated person.

4. Nicholas Lash, *The Beginning and the End of "Religion"* (Cambridge: Cambridge University Press, 1996), 5. Lash is an English theologian.

5. Nicholas Lash, "We need more than mitres," *The Tablet* (13 December 2003), 32.

6. Postscript to Hokusai's book *One Hundred Views of Mount Fuji*, written at the age of seventy-five.

Chapter 1

1. These are best outlined in Bernard Lonergan, *Method in Theology* (Toronto: University of Toronto Press, 1972). Lonergan was a Canadian philosopher/theologian who spent most of his working life lecturing at the Gregorium University in Rome.

2. Ibid., 9.

3. In addition are "unconscious" states, which are taken to mean a state of complete unawareness of reality, as occurs during sleep or due to some physiological brain disturbance.

4. Lonergan, *Method in Theology*, 20.

5. Both authors were Jesuits and spiritual writers. De Mello was Indian and de Caussade French.

6. Anthony de Mello, *The Song of the Bird* (Garden City, NY: Image Books, 1982), 22–23.

7. See Thich Nhat Hanh, *The Miracle of Mindfulness: A Manual on Meditation* (London: Rider, 1975).

8. Carl R. Rogers, *On Becoming a Person: A Therapist's View of Psychotherapy* (London: Constable, 1967), 64. Rogers was an American psychologist.

9. *Eureka* is taken from the Greek *heureka* meaning "I discover." In common parlance it means a moment when one suddenly discovers an insight and exclaims: "now I see!"

10. Bernard Lonergan, *Insight: A Study of Human Understanding* (1958; San Francisco: Harper and Row, 1978), 417.

11. Lonergan, *Method in Theology*, 13.

12. See the term *mediate* in the glossary.

13. Robert Doran, a student and then a colleague of Lonergan, expands more fully on the meaning of this term, which he insists is necessary in addition to self-transcendence. It includes self-knowledge, self-discovery, and self-understanding. It enhances our ability to know with some precision not only how we are thinking but also how we are feeling. Self-appropriation equips us with the added ability to judge ourselves more accurately as to the authenticity or inauthenticity of our understanding, evaluating, and decision making. See *Subject and Psyche: Ricoeur, Jung and the Search for Foundations* (Washington, DC: University Press of America, 1979).

14. Karl Rahner, "Christian Living Formerly and Today," in *Theological Investigations*, vol. 7, trans. David Bourke (London: Darton, Longman & Todd, 1971), 14. Rahner was a German theologian.

15. This study looks at the cultural and, indirectly, the social influences on experience in chapter 6. The importance of physical functioning, namely, human physiology, and, particularly in recent decades, the results of studies concerned with brain functioning in relation to the different levels of consciousness, are well noted by this author. However, while physiology is the fundamental *unconscious* innate capacity for all human functioning, this basic functioning is being taken for granted in this book. Helpful reading in this area are Eugene D'Aquili and Andrew Newberg, *The Mystical Mind: Probing the Biology of Religious Experience* (Minneapolis: Fortress Press,

1999); and Robert Forman, ed., *The Innate Capacity* (New York: Oxford University Press, 1998). The influence of physical factors on all forms of experiencing is accepted. Fatigue, pain, illness, and disability in its many forms can all alter experience. Mental disturbances and illnesses can profoundly affect experiencing.

16. Those who suffer from intellectual disability or from other psychological or physiological difficulties will have some form of diminished capacity.

Chapter 2

1. Today the words *religious* and *religion* evoke negative overtones and reactions and so the use of the term *faith* is preferred.

2. See Bernard Lonergan, *Method in Theology* (Toronto: University of Toronto Press, 1972), 101–3.

3. See the term *grace* in the glossary.

4. William James, *Varieties of Religious Experience: A Study of Human Nature* (New York: Longmans, Green and Co., 1913). James, an American, trained as a medical doctor but largely turned to psychology.

5. Nicholas Lash, *The Beginning and the End of "Religion"* (Cambridge: Cambridge University Press, 1996), 178.

6. Ibid., 173.

7. Abraham Maslow, *Religion, Values and Peak-Experiences* (1964; New York: Viking Press, 1970), see x–xvi. Maslow was an American psychologist.

8. Antoine Vergote, *The Religious Man: A Psychological Study of Religious Attitudes,* trans. Sr. Marie-Bernard Said (Dublin: Gill and Macmillan, 1969), 61, 13–14.

9. Dermot Lane, *The Experience of God: An Invitation to Do Theology* (1981; Dublin: Veritas, 1985), see 13–16; revised ed. (Dublin: Veritas, 2003). Lane is an Irish theologian.

10. See the terms *mediate/mediation* in the glossary.

11. Wayne Teasdale, *Mystic Heart: Discovering a Universal Spirituality in the World's Religions* (Novato: New World Library, 1999), 23. Teasdale is an American spiritual writer.

12. Arthur J. Deikman, "Deautomization and the Mystic Experience," in *Understanding Mysticism*, ed. Richard Woods (London: Athlone Press, 1981), 252–53. Deikman is an American psychiatrist.

13. See Lonergan, *Method in Theology*, 105–9.

14. Ibid., 109. See the term *mystery* in the glossary.

15. Ibid., 341, 106.

16. Lonergan formulates two distinctions that clarify how grace operates within the human-divine relationship. "One and the same grace is both operative and co-operative. It is operative when God alone acts and it is cooperative when both God and the will combine to produce an effect." Bernard Lonergan, *Grace and Freedom: Operative Grace in the Thought of St. Thomas Aquinas* (London: Darton, Longman & Todd, 1971), 127.

17. Lonergan, *Method in Theology*, 115.

18. Erich Fromm, *The Art of Loving*, centennial ed. (1956; New York: Continuum, 2000), 57. Fromm was an American psychoanalyst.

19. See Fromm, *Art of Loving*, 70.

20. C. S. Lewis, *The Four Loves* (London: Collins Fount Paperbacks, 1960).

21. Robert A. Johnson, *The Psychology of Romantic Love* (1983; London: Arkana, 1987), xi, xiii. Johnson is an English psychologist.

22. Gerald G. May, *The Dark Night of the Soul: A Psychiatrist Explores the Connection between Darkness and Spiritual Growth* (San Francisco: Harper, 2003), 77. May was an American psychiatrist and spiritual director.

23. Ibid., 192.

24. Louis Roy, "Can We Thematize Mysticism?" *Method, Journal of Lonergan Studies* 21, no. 1 (Spring 2003): 47–65, 54.

25. Bede Griffiths, *A New Vision of Reality: Western Science, Eastern Mysticism and Christian Faith* (Illinois: Templegate, 1989), 253. Griffiths was a Benedictine monk and a *sannyasi* ("one who has renounced the world").

26. Lonergan's earlier thought on the distinction between faith and belief can be found in "Belief: Today's Issue," in *A Second Collection* (Toronto: University of Toronto Press, 1996). In *Method in Theology*, he speaks about the *inner* word, the prior word of faith, and the *outer* word, which makes the inner word more explicit (119, 123–24). For the Christian, the *outer* word would be the Christian story/message.

27. A common example of this occurrence is when someone stops going to Sunday Mass, they are considered by some to have lost the faith. This intellectual-assent-to-propositions understanding of faith has been prevalent post-Trent to pre–Vatican II. The latter restored the earlier biblical understanding of faith as a deeply personal reality.

See *Dei Verbum* §§2–6, in *Documents of Vatican II*, ed. W. Abbott (New York: Guild Press, 1966).

28. Lonergan, "Religious Experience" (1976), in *Third Collection* (New York: Paulist Press, 1985). This article offers background to this paragraph.

29. Echoes of the latter could be heard in Jesus' poignant phrase: "If you, even you, had only recognized...[but] you did not recognize the time of your visitation from God" (Luke 19:42, 44).

30. See the term *sacrament* in the glossary.

31. Bernard Lonergan, "The Mediation of Christ in Prayer," in *Philosophical and Theological Papers 1958–1964* (Toronto: University of Toronto Press, 1996), 179–81.

32. Ibid., 189.

33. Ibid.

34. Lonergan, *Method*, 109.

35. Karl Rahner, *The Practice of Faith: A Handbook of Contemporary Spirituality*, ed. Karl Lehman and Albert Raffelt (London: SCM Press, 1985), 63; Margaret Smith, "The Nature and Meaning of Mysticism," in *Understanding Mysticism*, ed. Richard Woods (London: Athlone Press, 1981), 20; Richard Woods, "Introduction," in *Understanding Mysticism*, 6.

36. Louis Dupré, *Religious Mystery and Rational Reflection: Excursions in the Phenomenology and Philosophy of Religion* (Cambridge: Eerdmans, 1998), 138. Hereafter termed *Religious Mystery*. Dupré is a French theologian.

37. Ceslaus Spicq, *Agape in the New Testament, vol. 3, Agape in the Gospel, Epistles and Apocalypse of St. John*, trans. Sr. Marie Aquinas McNamara and Sr. Mary Honoria Richter (St. Louis and London: Herder, 1966), 33. Spicq is a French biblical scholar.

38. Hans Urs von Balthasar elaborates on this reality in many of his writings, especially in his five-volume *Theo-Drama: Theological Dramatic Theory*. For example, "He [the Father] is always himself by giving himself. The Son, too, is always himself by allowing himself to be generated and by allowing the Father to do with him as he pleases. The Spirit is always himself by understanding his 'I' as the 'We' of Father and Son" (von Balthasar, *Theo-Drama: Theological Dramatic Theory*, vol. 11, *Dramatis Personae: Man in God*, trans. Graham Harrison [1976; San Francisco: Ignatius Press, 1990], 256). Balthasar was a Swiss theologian. Mark McIntosh, an American theologian, says similarly, "Each of the three is only constituted by abandoning any claim to be at all apart from the eternal giving

away" (*Mystical Theology: Challenges in Contemporary Theology* [Oxford: Blackwell Publishers, 1998], 227).

39. The type of meditation referred to by the apophatic path is the attempt to empty the self of images and concepts. Cataphatic forms of meditation, as exemplified by Ignatius of Loyola and Teresa of Avila, take the opposite approach and focus on images of Christ and gospel scenes.

The significance of Ken Wilbur, the well-known writer on human consciousness, requires mention because his approach to meditation might be perceived as similar to the apophatic way. It is not clear if his search for "unity consciousness" means that human identity is absorbed within this unity. He refers, for instance, to the separate self as dissolving, not existing; all there is, is consciousness, "the source and suchness of everything that arises moment to moment." See *No Boundary: Eastern and Western Approaches to Personal Growth* (Boston: Shambhala, 2001), 141. These comments suggest that his spirit-life is nontheistic.

40. See especially Thomas Merton, *Zen and the Birds of Appetite* (New York: New Directions, 1968), 19–20. While Merton mentions no specific Vatican II document, presumably he had *Gaudium et Spes*—introduction and part 1—particularly in mind. Merton was an American monk and hermit.

41. This letting go, self-emptying, draws a person closer to the restoration of the human person as God's image since God's inner life is in essence a triune form of self-emptying.

42. Merton, *Zen and the Birds of Appetite*, 31.

43. For example, Alcoholics Anonymous, which refers to a "Higher Power."

44. Psychosynthesis is a transpersonal field of psychology that stresses the importance of meditation. See Roberto Assagioli, *Psychosynthesis: A Manual of Principles and Techniques* (London: Aquarian Thorsons, 1965).

45. See Harvey Egan, *An Anthology of Christian Mysticism* (Collegeville, MN: Liturgical Press, 1991), 267. Hereafter termed *Christian Mysticism*. Especially helpful is Teilhard de Chardin's *Le Milieu Divin: An Essay on the Interior Life* (1957; London: Collins Fontana Paperback, 1964).

46. Jürgen Moltmann, *Experiences of God*, trans. Margaret Kohl (1979; London: SCM Press, 1980), 73. Moltmann is a German theologian.

47. Gerald G. May, *Will and Spirit: A Contemplative Psychology* (San Francisco: Harper Collins, 1982), 23, 25.

48. Ibid., 53.

49. In the full biblical understanding of the meaning of "to know." See also Antoine de Saint-Exupery who expresses a similar sentiment: "It is only with the heart that one can see rightly; what is essential is invisible to the eye" (*The Little Prince* [London: Penguin Books, 1945], 84).

50. May, *Will and Spirit*, 155.

51. See Egan, *Christian Mysticism*, 616–27, 189.

52. The main Rahner sources that form the background to this section are his *Encyclopedia of Theology: A Concise Sacramentum Mundi* (London: Burns & Oates, 1975), in articles on "Mysticism," as well as his article "Experiencing the Spirit," in *Practice of Faith*.

53. Rahner, *Practice of Faith*, 64.

54. Veselin Kesich, "Via Negative," in *The Encyclopedia of Religion*, vol. 15, ed. Mircea Eliade (New York: Macmillan Publishing Co., 1987), 252.

55. Dupré, *Religious Mystery*. See the last two chapters.

56. Ibid., 138.

57. The first three periods are those chosen by Bernard McGinn. See his trilogy, *The Foundations of Mysticism* (London: SCM Press, 1991), *The Growth of Mysticism, 500–1200* (London: SCM Press, 1994), and *The Flowering of Mysticism, 1200–1350* (New York: Crossroad Herder Books, 1998). McGinn is an American theologian.

58. Merton, *Zen and the Birds of Appetite*, 19.

59. "The Universal Call to Holiness" chapter of *Lumen Gentium*, in Abbott, *Documents of Vatican II*.

60. *Meister Eckhart: The Essential Sermon, Commentaries, Treatises and Defense* (New York: Paulist Press, 1981), 183. Quoted in McGinn, *Flowering of Mysticism*, 14. Eckhart was German and a mystic.

61. The title of Walter Kasper's book, *The God of Jesus Christ* (London: SCM Press, 1982).

62. See Spicq's commentary on "Caritas Christi urget nos" (Vulgate), "the love of Christ urges us on" (2 Cor 5:14), in "The Driving Force of Charity" in *Agape in the New Testament*, vol. 2, *Agape in the Epistles of St. Paul*, trans. Sr. Marie Aquinas and Sr. Mary Honoria Richter (St. Louis and London: Herder Book Co., 1965), 187–94.

63. Evelyn Underhill, *Mysticism* (1911; London: University Paperbacks, 1960), 414.

Chapter 3

1. Hans-Georg Gadamer, *Truth and Method*, trans. Jack Weinsheimer and Donald G. Marshall (1960; London: Sheed and Ward, 1989), 150. Gadamer was a German philosopher.

2. The word *numinous* was emphasized by Rudolf Otto. More is said on this later in this chapter.

3. See Lonergan, *Method in Theology*, 28, 76–77.

4. Lonergan, *Insight*, 545; Sallie McFague, *Metaphorical Theology: Models of God in Religious Language* (Philadelphia: Fortress Press, 1982), 16.

5. Ben Rogers, "Introduction," ed. Ben Rogers, *Is Nothing Sacred?* (London: Routledge, 2004), 1.

6. Piers Ben, "The Idea of the Sacred," in *Is Nothing Sacred?* 119, 124.

7. Yair Sheleg, "The Return of God," in *Haaretz* (English ed.), April 13, 2005. Italics mine.

8. Dupré, *Religious Mystery*, 137.

9. Leon Dufour, *Dictionary of Biblical Theology*, trans. Joseph Cahill (London: Geoffrey Chapman, 1967), 207, 208 (italics by author). Dufour is a French biblical scholar. Enda McDonagh, *Vulnerable to the Holy: In Faith, Morality and Art* (Dublin: Columba Press, 2004), 122. McDonagh is an Irish theologian.

10. David P. Wright, "Holiness," in *The Anchor Bible Dictionary*, chief ed. David Noel Freedman (New York: Doubleday, 1992), 237.

11. Frederick L. Moriarty, "Isaiah 1—39," in *The Jerome Biblical Commentary* (London: Geoffrey Chapman, 1970), 270.

12. This term refers to a manifestation of God's presence.

13. Rudolf Otto, *The Idea of the Holy*, trans. John Harvey (1923; London: Oxford University Press, 1950). See especially chaps. 1–3.

14. Ibid., 6.

15. Ibid., 10.

16. Ibid., 10 n. 1.

17. Ibid., 12–13.

18. Ibid., 17.

19. Ibid., 27.

20. Ibid., 28 n. 1. See *Confessions* ii.9, 1.

21. Ibid., 20.

22. Ibid., 22, quoting James, *Varieties of Religious Experience*, 66.

23. Ibid., 23, 24. See meaning of "Energeia" in William Barclay, *New Testament Words* (London: SCM Press, 1964), 77–84.

24. Ibid., 31 (italics by author).

25. Ibid., 105.

26. Sean MacReamoinn, "Secularization, not Secularism," *Doctrine & Life* (December 2000): 658. MacReamoinn was an Irish journalist and religious writer.

27. Karl Rahner, "Christian Living Formerly and Today," in *Theological Investigations*, vol. 7, trans. David Bourke (London: Darton, Longman & Todd, 1971), 17–18.

28. McDonagh, *Vulnerable to the Holy*, 65. This task is open to the common priesthood of all baptized Christians.

29. Ibid., 66.

30. John Wilkins, "A Farewell from the Editor," *The Tablet* (December 20/27, 2003): 4.

31. See Jürgen Moltmann, *God in Creation: An Ecological Doctrine of Creation*, trans. Margaret Kohl (London: SCM Press, 1985).

32. Ibid., 2.

33. Ibid., 3.

34. While the word *Shekina* does not appear in the Hebrew Bible, it was a concept through which the presence of God among his people was made known. In early biblical history, the symbol of the cloud by day and the pillar of fire at night signified the Emmanuel nature of God's presence.

35. Moltmann, *God in Creation*, 150.

36. Ibid. Italics by author.

37. Ibid., 156–57.

38. Ibid., 15.

39. Ibid., 16.

40. Ibid., 19.

41. John Polkinghorne, *Living with Hope* (London: SPCK, 2003), 47, 53. Polkinghorne is an English scientist and theologian.

42. Lynda Sexson, *Ordinarily Sacred* (1982; Virginia: University Press of Virginia, 1992), 90. Sexson is American and a professor of humanities.

43. Ibid., 7.

44. Ibid., 8.

45. Ibid., 11.

46. Ibid., 24.

47. Taken from the fifth-century Preface of Christmas 1. See *Roman Missal*.

48. A Web site set up by the Irish Jesuits in 2004 (www. sacredspace.ie).

Chapter 4

1. The word *beauty* can be used in an inadequate way that conveys merely the decorative or pretty. In relation to art, but also applicable to other realities, Richard Harries says "there is also the searing, disturbing, haunting element which is present in many of the greatest works of art." He also says that beauty only reveals its full greatness when seen in relation to truth and goodness. See Harries, *Art and the Beauty of God: A Christian Understanding* (London: Mowbray, 1993), 47.

2. Augustine, *Confessions*, ed. John Rotelle, trans. Maria Boulding (New York: New City Press, 1997), book X 27–28, 362.

3. *Summa Theologiae, Existence and Nature of God*, 1a. 2–11.

4. See especially *Dei Verbum* in *Documents of Vatican II*, ed. W. Abbott (New York: Guild Press, 1966).

5. Gesa Thiessen, *Theological Aesthetics* (London: SCM Press, 2004), 6. Thiessen is a German theologian who currently works in Ireland.

6. Hilary Mooney, *Liberation of Consciousness—Bernard Lonergan's Theological Foundations in Dialogue with the Theological Aesthetics of Hans Urs von Balthasar* (Frankfurt: Verlag Josef Knecht, 1992), 262. Mooney is an Irish theologian who works in Germany.

7. Patrick Sherry, *Spirit and Beauty: An Introduction to Theological Aesthetics* (Oxford: Clarendon Press, 1992), see chap. 8.

8. Under *works of art* are included recognized Western expressions of art, for example, music; painting, pottery, sculpture, architecture; drama, dance, performing arts; literature, poetry; film. To this list can be added some less Western art forms such as gardening (especially in Japan) and fiber art (e.g., weaving, particularly in Africa).

9. John O'Donohue, *Divine Beauty: The Invisible Embrace* (London: Bantam Press, 2003), 3. O'Donohue was an Irish philosophical theologian.

10. Daivetz Suzuki, *Zen and Japanese Culture* (Princeton, NJ: Princeton University Press, 1973), 363. Suzuki is a Zen Buddhist.

11. Erich Fromm, *The Art of Loving*, centennial ed. (1956; New York: Continuum, 2000).

12. Nigel Ford, "The Playwright's Tale," in *Sounding the Depths: Theology Through the Arts,* ed. Begbie (London: SCM Press, 2002), 64. Ford is an English playwright; Rowan Williams, "Making It Strange: Theology in Other(s') Words," in Begbie, *Sounding the Depths,* 29–30. Williams is a theologian and Archbishop of Canterbury.

13. Bernard Lonergan, *Method in Theology* (Toronto: University of Toronto Press, 1972), 30–31.

14. Bernard Lonergan, "Prolegomena to the Study of the Emerging Religious Consciousness of our Time," in *A Third Collection* (New York: Paulist Press, 1985), 70.

15. Lonergan, *Method in Theology,* 273.

16. Bernard Lonergan, "The Analogy of Meaning," in *Philosophical and Theological Papers 1958–1964* (Toronto: University of Toronto Press, 1996), 191.

17. Susanne K. Langer, *Feeling and Form: A Theory of Art* (London: Routledge & Keegan Paul, 1953).

18. Ibid., 402.

19. Enda McDonagh, *The Gracing of Society* (Dublin: Gill and Macmillan, 1989), 137.

20. Thiessen, *Theological Aesthetics,* 1.

21. Hans Urs von Balthasar, *The Glory of the Lord: A Theological Aesthetics,* vol. 1, *Seeing the Form* (Edinburgh: T&T Clark, 1982), 18.

22. Ibid., 26, 118.

23. Ibid. Italics by author.

24. Ibid., 119.

25. Ibid.

26. Ibid., 37.

27. Ibid., 120–21. The last sentence links with Lonergan's four levels of consciousness—"see it" (experience), "understand it" (understanding), "make it his own" (judgment), "live from it" (responsible decision making).

28. David Tracy, *The Analogical Imagination: Christian Theology and the Culture of Pluralism* (London: SCM Press, 1981), 111–12. Tracy is an Australian theologian.

29. Martin Buber, *I and Thou,* trans. Ronald Gregor Smith (1923; Edinburgh: T&T Clark, 1937), 17. Buber was an Austrian Jewish philosopher.

30. Stephan van Erp, *The Art of Theology: Hans Urs von Balthasar's Theological Aesthetics and the Foundations of Faith* (Leuven: Peeters, 2004), 41. Van Erp is a Dutch philosophical theologian.

31. Enda McDonagh, *Vulnerable to the Holy: In Faith, Morality and Art* (Dublin: Columba Press, 2004), 19.

32. Lonergan, *Method in Theology*, 268.

33. *Sacrosanctum Concilium*, par. 122, in Abbott, *Documents of Vatican II*.

34. John Paul II, *Apostolic Letter to the Artists of the World*. See *L'Osservatore Romano*, no. 17, 1999.

35. *Catechism of the Catholic Church* (Dublin: Veritas, 1995), see nos. 2500–2503 on "Truth, Beauty and Sacred Art."

36. Irish Murdoch, *The Sovereignty of the Good* (London: Routledge & Keegan Paul, 1970), 65.

37. See McDonagh, *Vulnerable to the Holy*, 181.

38. Taken from his poem "Advent." Quoted by McDonagh in *Vulnerable to the Holy*, 184.

39. See Robert Wuthnow, *Creative Spirituality: The Way of the Artist* (Los Angeles: University of California Press, 2000), 274. Wuthnow is a sociologist interested in cultural sociology and the sociology of religions.

40. A "pod" group was established where two theologians, Alastair McFadyen and John Inge, engaged with Jonathan Clarke, the artist, with each member of the pod group respecting the integrity of the other in their mutual contribution to this work. See Begbie, *Sounding the Depths*. Begbie outlined this project of dialogue between artists and theologians in the creation of art. He refers to the project's "conviction that theology not only benefits from the arts but actually needs them" (6).

41. Vanessa Herrick interview with Jonathan Clarke in *Sounding the Depths*, 163.

42. Hamilton Reed Armstrong, "The Transmission of Faith through Art," *Communio* 28 (Summer 2001): 386–97, 393. The Hopkins quotation is taken from "Letter for Bridges," August 14, 1879.

43. See Laura Gascoigne, "Drawings of a Modern Visionary," *The Tablet* (November 29, 2003): 20. While the art by Norman Adams contains religious themes and is found in churches, "for him as for Blake, sacred and secular are not to be separated."

44. Alice Ramos, "From Literature to Philosophy," in *Faith and the Life of the Intellect*, ed. Curtis L. Hancock and Brendan Sweetman (Washington, DC: Catholic University of America Press, 2003), 210–30. Ramos is a philosopher interested in literature, especially the novel.

45. Gordon Strachan, *Chartres, Sacred Geometry, Sacred Space* (Edinburgh: Floris Books, 2003), 97.

46. John O'Donohue, "The Quest for Form," *The Way* (October 2001): 350.

47. See Emmanuel Levinas, *Totality and Infinity: An Essay on Exteriority*, trans. Alphonso Lingis (1961; Pittsburgh: Duquesne University Press, 1993). See especially John Wild's introduction, 11–20. Levinas was a philosopher who had a special interest in ethics.

Chapter 5

1. Sandra Schneiders, "Religion vs. Spirituality: A Contemporary Conundrum," *Spiritus: A Journal of Christian Spirituality* 3, no. 1 (Spring 2003): 163–85, 163. Schneiders is an American theologian.

2. Rudolf J. Siebert, "The Open Dialectic between Religious and Secular Values and Norms," in *Religious Innovation in a Global Age: Essays on the Construction of Spirituality*, ed. George N. Lundskow (Jefferson, NC: McFarland, 2005), 42.

3. Alice Ramos, "Editor's Note," in *Faith, Scholarship and Culture in the 21st Century*, ed. Alice Ramos and Marie I. George (Washington, DC: American Maritain Association, 2002), ix.

4. Michael Paul Gallagher, *Dive Deeper: The Human Poetry of Faith* (London: Darton, Longman & Todd, 2001), 7–9. Gallagher is an Irish theologian.

5. Ibid., 7.

6. Louis Dupré, *Religious Mystery and Rational Reflection: Excursions in the Phenomenology and Philosophy of Religion* (Cambridge: Eerdmans, 1998), 133. See 130–43 as background to this paragraph.

7. Ibid., 142. A well-received BBC Two three-part documentary entitled *The Monastery* commences with Abbot Christopher saying that this experiment of five men coming to share the monastic life at Worth Abbey for forty days aimed to appeal to people's dissatisfaction with life (despite present-day material riches) by offering answers "that could be potentially life changing."

8. "It is only with the heart that one can see rightly: what is essential is invisible to the eye" (Antoine de Saint-Exupery, *The Little Prince*, trans. Katherine Woods [London: Pan Books, 1974], 70).

9. Stephan van Erp, *The Art of Theology: Hans Urs von Balthasar's Theological Aesthetics and the Foundations of Faith* (Leuven: Peeters, 2004), 248 n. 27.

10. Bernard Lonergan, *Method in Theology* (Toronto: University of Toronto Press, 1972), 28.

11. David Tracy, *The Analogical Imagination: Christian Theology and the Culture of Pluralism* (London: SCM Press, 1981), 128.

12. Kees Waaijman, *Spirituality: Forms, Foundations, Methods* (Leuven: Peeters, 2002), 575.

13. William F. Lynch, *Images of Faith: An Exploration of the Ironic Imagination* (Notre Dame, IN: University of Notre Dame Press, 1973), 7. Lynch is an American theologian.

14. Ibid., esp. 92–102.

15. The quotations in this paragraph are taken from Ignatius's autobiography as heard and written down by Luis Goncalves da Camara (1553, 1555). See St. Ignatius of Loyola, *Personal Writings: Reminiscences, Spiritual Diary, Select Letters,* introduction and notes, Joseph A. Munitiz and Philip Endean (London: Penguin Classics, 1996), 14–17.

16. Gallagher, *Dive Deeper*, 124.

17. Taken from the poem "God's Grandeur." See *Poems and Prose of Gerard Manley Hopkins,* ed. W. H. Gardner (London: Penguin, 1963), 27.

18. David Ranson, "The Trinity: Source of Ministry," *The Furrow* 56, no. 5 (May 2005): 285–91, 286.

19. Jürgen Moltmann, *The Spirit of Life: A Universal Affirmation* (Minneapolis, MN: Fortress Press, 1992), 94.

20. Ibid., 287. Ranson refers to Moltmann, *The Spirit of Life: A Universal Affirmation,* 94.

21. Gerald May, *Will and Spirit: A Contemplative Psychology* (San Francisco: Harper Collins, 1982), 25.

22. *Intuition, hunch,* and *whim* are allied terms with the first two sometimes used in an interchangeable manner despite their denoting different realities. *Whim* is associated with the fantastic, fantasy, with *whimsical* defined as "delicately fanciful"; *hunch* refers to premonition, a hint—"acting on a hunch (as a gambler might)" (see *Chambers* dictionary). *Intuition,* also according to *Chambers,* describes "the power of the mind by which it immediately perceives the truth of things without reasoning or analyses; immediate as opposed to mediate." The basic difference between *hunch* and *intuition* for this book is that *hunch* is more superficial and is usually concerned with more trivial things, whereas *intuition* arises from deep inside a person, comes slowly, is

often the culmination of working through something, and is therefore more likely to be true. It can at times be nearer to inspiration.

23. With the above note's description in place, it can be seen that intuition does not disregard the cognitional process. Intuitions that arise, however, could be likened to Lonergan's understanding of love and especially of faith—"the knowledge that is born of religious love." Heart knowing is the fullest and most existential expression of knowing and therefore is most likely to occur at the fourth level of consciousness, where its fundamental manifestation is perceived in personal decision.

24. May, *Will and Spirit*, 27, 44.

25. Lonergan, *Method in Theology*, 157.

26. Gerard Hughes, *God in All Things: The Sequel to God of Surprises* (London: Hodder and Stoughton, 2004), 75. Hughes is an English spiritual writer.

27. Ibid., 77.

28. Ann Ulanov and Barry Ulanov, *Primary Speech: A Psychology of Prayer* (Louisville: Westminster John Knox Press, 1982), 13. See especially chapter 2, "Prayer and Desire."

29. "Disposition," in *Encyclopaedia of Theology: A Concise Sacramentum Mundi*, ed. Karl Rahner (London: Burns & Oates, 1975), 350.

30. Ibid.

31. A core longing of Jesus is exclaimed about this point: "*If only you knew what God is offering*" (John 4:10). Jerusalem Bible translation, 1966 ed.

32. See Michael Paul Gallagher, "Newman on the Disposition for Faith" (English version unpublished; published in Italian in *Civiltà Cattolica*, March 2001). Several of the Newman quotations are taken from this article.

33. John Henry Newman, *Grammar of Ascent* (New York: Image Books, 1955). See chapter 9, "The Illative Sense," 270–99.

34. Gallagher, *Dive Deeper*, 2.

35. See May, *Will and Spirit*. The first part of this section is influenced by May's thought.

36. Ibid., see 10–21.

37. May, *Will and Spirit*, 25.

38. Ibid., 325, fn 11.

39. Ibid., 30.

40. Sarah Coakley, *Powers and Submissions: Spirituality, Philosophy and Gender* (Oxford: Blackwell Publishers, 2002). Coakley, an English theologian, outlines the meaning of Christian kenosis as follows: "The word *kenosis* does not appear as a noun in the New

Testament at all, and the entire debate about 'self-emptying' goes back to an isolated appearance of the verb *keno* (I empty) in Philippians 2.7" (5). She says this text was originally a hymn that was used in liturgical settings such as baptism or Eucharist (6).

41. Ibid., 34.

42. A familiar phrase used in Adrian van Kaam's theology. See *In Search of Spiritual Identity* (New Jersey: Dimension Books, 1975).

43. Fraser Watts, *Theology and Psychology* (Hants, UK: Ashgate, 2002). Watts is English and writes on matters pertaining to theology and the natural sciences.

44. Arthur J. Deikman, "A Functional Approach to Mysticism," *Journal of Consciousness Studies* 7, no. 11–12 (2000): 75–91, 78.

45. Lonergan, *Method in Theology,* 237.

46. Ibid., 237–38.

Chapter 6

1. John Paul II described culture as "the ethos of a people" and saw beliefs as central to that ethos. These words were spoken in 1982 at the founding of the Pontifical Council for Culture. See Conor Ward's article "Intimations of Immorality: An Analysis of the ISSP [International Social Survey Programme]," in *Measuring Ireland: Discerning Values and Beliefs,* ed. Eoin Cassidy (Dublin: Veritas, 2002), 68.

2. Examples of such places would include recognized pilgrimage sites.

3. Bernard Lonergan, "Natural Right and Historical Mindedness," in *A Third Collection* (New York: Paulist Press, 1985), 171.

4. Bernard Lonergan, "Belief: Today's Issue," in *A Second Collection* (Toronto: University of Toronto Press, 1996), 97. Italics by author.

5. Examples of these encyclicals included Leo XIII's *Rerum Novarum,* Paul VI's *Ecclesiam Suam,* John XXIII's *Pacem in Terris,* John Paul II's *Laborem Excercens.*

6. See Karl Rahner, "Christian Living Formerly and Today," in *Theological Investigations*, vol. 7, trans. David Bourke (London: Darton, Longman & Todd, 1971), 3.

7. Thomas S. Kuhn, *The Structure of Scientific Revolutions* (1962; Chicago: University of Chicago Press, 1996), 23. Kuhn is an American professor of linguistics and philosophy.

8. Ibid., 25.

9. See Anthony de Mello, *The Song of the Bird* (New York: Image Books, 1984), 12–13.

10. Bernard Lonergan, "Belief: Today's Issues," 92.

11. Bernard Lonergan, "The Absence of God in Modern Culture," in *A Second Collection*, 115.

12. Bernard Lonergan, *Method in Theology* (Toronto: University of Toronto Press, 1972), xi.

13. Bernard Lonergan, "Transition from a Classicist World View to Historical-Mindedness," in *A Second Collection*, 6.

14. Ibid., 2.

15. This is a German term meaning "over."

16. Jacques Dupuis was a French theologian. See especially his work, *Toward a Christian Theology of Religious Pluralism* (Maryknoll, NY: Orbis Books, 1997).

17. The texts of the reports, "The Special Assembly for Asia of the Synod of Bishops," can be found in *L'Osservatore Romano*, no. 17 (1539) (April 29, 1998). The following quotation is from the synod fathers: "The church believes that Jesus Christ is not one of the many savior figures of the world but the unique Savior of all. On the other hand, the presentation of Jesus Christ as the only Savior must be situated in the context of God's universal plan of salvation and with deep respect towards other religions."

18. Jonathan Sacks, *Faith in the Future* (London: Darton, Longman & Todd, 1995), 117, 116, 120, 124. Sacks is chief rabbi of the United Hebrew Congregations of the Commonwealth.

19. John Cornwell, "Science's Modest Master," *The Tablet* (May 15, 2004): 9. This quotation was part of a conversation Cornwell had with George Ellis, physicist, Quaker, and the 2004 winner of the Templeton Prize for Science and Religion.

20. Antjie Krog, an Afrikaaner journalist and poet, was a previous contender for the Nobel Peace prize. The above thoughts were expressed in her Irish RTE Radio One interview on April 1, 2004.

21. Lonergan, "The Absence of God," 115.

22. Lonergan, *Method in Theology*, 44.

23. See Eoin Cassidy, "Religion and Culture: The Freedom to Be an Individual," in *Faith and Culture in the Irish Context*, ed. Eoin Cassidy (Dublin: Veritas, 1996), 35–54.

24. Aylward Shorter, *Evangelisation and Culture* (London: Geoffrey Chapman, 1994), 32. Shorter is an English theologian who has worked most of his life in Africa.

25. Paul VI, Apostolic Exhortation, *Evangelii Nuntiandi*, December 8, 1975.

26. Michael Gallagher, *Clashing Symbols* (London: Darton, Longman & Todd, 1997), 7.

27. Ibid., 92.

28. Gerald O'Collins, *Incarnation* (London: T&T Clark, 2002), 113. Collins is an Australian theologian.

29. Jim Corkery, "Does Technology Squeeze out Transcendence," in *Technology and Transcendence*, ed. Michael Breen et al. (Dublin: Columba Press, 2000), 11–21, esp. 12. Corkery is an Irish theologian.

30. Ibid., 17.

31. Ibid., 20.

32. Bryan Appleyard, "Beyond Belief?" in the *Sunday Times* [Ireland], Easter Sunday, March 27, 2005.

33. Paul Tillich, *The Courage to Be* (1952; London: Collins, 1977), 180–83. See also "The God above God," in *Paul Tillich, Main Works: Theological Writings*, vol. 6, ed. Gert Hummel (Berlin: De Gruyter, 1992). Tillich was a German theologian.

34. Tillich, "The God above God," 418.

Chapter 7

1. By *context* I mean the settings, surroundings, and circumstances in which something or some experience is situated. Settings can be cultural, religious, or social, and although each of these is a separate entity, varying contexts have an interweaving effect in real life experiences even to the extent of either fixing or altering the meaning of experiences.

2. Philip Sheldrake, *Spirituality and Theology* (London: Darton, Longman & Todd, 1998), 10. Sheldrake's *Spaces for the Sacred* (London: SCM Press, 2001) has also been used as background reading.

3. Belden C. Lane, "Landscape and Spirituality: A Tension between Place and Placelessness in Christian Thought," Supplement, *The Way* 73 (Spring 1992): 6. This article is a summary of his *Landscapes of the Sacred: Geography and Narrative in American Spirituality* (New York: Paulist Press, 1988). An expanded edition of this work is also published (Baltimore: Johns Hopkins University Press, 2002).

4. Walter Brueggemann, *The Land: Place as Gift, Promise, and Challenge in Biblical Faith* (Philadelphia: Fortress Press, 1977). Brueggemann is a biblical scholar.

5. Etty Hillesum wrote movingly just prior to going to the Auschwitz concentration camp: "There is a really deep well inside me. And in it dwells God. Sometimes I am there too." See *An Interrupted Life: The Diaries and Letters off Etty Hillesum 1941–1943* (London: Persephone Books, 1999/London: Alban Books, 2003).

6. This conversation took place in 2004. McGuckian is a Jesuit who works in communication.

7. Martin Heidegger, "An Ontological Consideration of Place," in *The Question of Being* (New York: Twayne Publishers, 1958).

8. Holocaust concentration camps stand out today as horrific places, yet places that for some contain meaning. See Etty Hillesum referring to Auschwitz: "One ought to be able to live without books, without anything. There will always be a small patch of sky above, and there will always be enough space to fold two hands in prayer." The places associated with September 11, 2001; the night club killings of over two hundred in Bali in 2002; and the Beslan hostage taking of school children and their subsequent killing in 2004 have become significant spaces because of the shocking nature of the incidents that occurred in these places.

9. Brueggemann, *Land*, see 15–17.

10. Ibid., 5.

11. Ibid., 14.

12. Michael Prior, *The Bible and Colonialism: A Moral Critique* (Sheffield: Sheffield Academic Press, 1997), 45.

13. Ibid., 219, 221.

14. Ibid., 283. Quotation is from Susan Niditch, *War in the Hebrew Bible: A Study of the Ethics of Violence* (Oxford: Oxford University Press, 1993), 150.

15. By *scandal* in this context I mean "shock" that tends toward disbelief.

16. Brueggemann, *Land*, 171.

17. Brueggemann, *Land*, 179, 180.

18. *Jerusalem Bible*, footnote g on Col 1:19.

19. George Sayer, *Jack: C.S. Lewis and His Times* (London: Macmillan, 1988), 135.

20. Rowan Williams, "Holy Spaces," in *Open to Judgment: Sermons and Addresses* (London: Darton, Longman & Todd, 1994), 103.

21. Pierre Teilhard de Chardin, *Le Milieu Divin: An Essay on the Interior Life* (London: Collins Fontana Paperback, 1964), 106. In the previous paragraph he refers to matter as "holy Matter" (106).

22. A frequently used term in *Le Milieu Divin*. For Teilhard de Chardin, there are two forms of diminishments—those whose origins lie outside us, "all our bits of ill fortune," and those that arise internally as a result of personal failings, intellectual and moral weaknesses, and illnesses, which can diminish enjoyment and vision (81). As Christians, no matter what our circumstances, the challenge is "the transfiguration of our diminishments" so that everything in life finds its place "in the milieu of God" (83).

23. Pierre Teilhard de Chardin, "The Priest," in *The Prayer of the Universe: Selected Writings from Time of War* (London: Fontana Books, 1965), 8.

24. The word *significance* is used in both its attributed and its derived/acquired sense. Derived significance is applicable through the realization that all place is sacred because of its being created by the Divine. In addition, place has been touched through the incarnation in some special way, as was illustrated by Teilhard de Chardin's perspective on matter. Places also have attributed significance due to their association with particular people or events.

25. People, places, or things become hierophanies when, by manifesting the sacred, an object becomes something else while continuing to remain itself. For example a *sacred* stone still remains a stone, for those to whom the stone reveals itself as sacred.

26. Mircea Eliade, *The Sacred and the Profane: The Nature of Religion*, trans. Willard R. Trask (1957; New York: Harper and Row, 1961), 29–32. This term would not apply to unethical activity such as taking territory that belongs to another. A Romanian by birth, Eliade was a philosopher, who was particularly interested in the history of religions.

27. A remarkable comment was made by an eleven-year-old schoolgirl who spent time with her classmates and teachers in Shekina Sculpture Garden: "We loved one another in this place."

28. See Karl Rahner, "The Church of Sinners," in *Theological Investigations*, vol. 6 (London: Darton, Longman & Todd, 1969), 253–69.

29. See the main page of the Web site: www.iona.org.uk/abbey/main. See also Ronald Ferguson, *George MacLeod: Founder of the Iona Community* (London: Collins, 1990).

30. Daniel O'Leary, "The Infinity of Now," *The Tablet* (August 28, 2004): 14. O'Leary is a spiritual writer.

31. See, for instance, the classic *The Cloud of Unknowing*. Author unknown, *The Cloud of Unknowing and Other Works* (London: Penguin Books, 1978).

32. David Ranson, "The Trinity: Source of Ministry," *The Furrow* 56, no. 5 (May 2005): 290–91.

33. Pierre-François de Béthune, *By Faith and Hospitality: The Monastic Tradition as a Model for Inter-religious Encounter* (Herefordshire: Gracewing, 2002), 3–14. De Béthune is a French Benedictine monk.

34. Examples include, "You shall not wrong or oppress a resident alien, for you were aliens in the land of Egypt" (Exod 22:21); "The Lord watches over the stranger" (Ps 146:9); "I was a stranger and you welcomed me" (Matt 25:35).

35. This phrase is used in Eucharistic Prayer I; see *Roman Missal*.

36. De Béthune, *Faith and Hospitality*, 2–3.

37. Ibid., 9. No reference to Danielou's quotation is given.

38. Brigid Boardman and Phillip Webb, *In a Quiet Garden: Meditations and Prayerful Reflections* (Bath: Downside Abbey Books, 2000), 4–5.

39. Esther de Waal, preface to Boardman and Webb, *In a Quiet Garden*, 1.

Chapter 8

1. A phrase used twice in the Offertory Prayer of every Eucharist; see *Roman Missal*.

2. Penelope Hobhouse, *Gardens of the World: The Art and Practice of Gardening* (New York: Macmillan, 1991), 36. Hobhouse is considered a world authority on the history of gardens.

3. Martin Palmer and David Manning, *Sacred Gardens* (London: Piatkus, 2000), 10.

4. See newsletter of the Quiet Garden Trust, issue no. 1, Summer 1995. The trust uses its newsletter as a form of networking that alerts people to various workshops in different places as well as to the new quiet gardens that are constantly being established worldwide.

5. Christopher Thacker, *The History of Gardens* (London: Croom Helm Publishers, 1979), 9.

6. Ur, the homeland of Abraham, was situated in the Fertile Crescent. From here he received the revelation "go from your country...to the land that will show you" (Gen 12:1).

7. Alix Wilkinson, *The Garden in Ancient Egypt* (London: Rubicon Press, 1996), 8.

8. Blaise Arminjon, an authority on this work, notes that the terms *enclosed* and *sealed* are repeated three times. They express the exclusive dimension of love and especially of God's love for his people. Yet, "the more the Bride is exclusively consecrated to him the more universal also is his opening to the world and its fecundity. The sealed fountain will therefore, freely and impetuously, water the universe with its living water, as Jesus promises to the Samaritan woman" (*Cantata of Love: A Verse by Verse Reading of the Song of Songs* [San Francisco: Ignatius Press, 1983], 227). Arminjon is French and is considered a master of the Spiritual Exercises of St. Ignatius.

9. Roland E. Murphy, *The Song of Songs: A Commentary on the Book of Canticles or the Song of Songs*, Hermeneia (Minneapolis: Fortress Press, 1990), 160.

10. Arminjon, *Cantata of Love*; see expanded commentary 223–33.

11. Dianne Bergant, *The Song of Songs* (Collegeville, MN: Liturgical Press, 2001), 55, 74. Bergant is an American scripture scholar.

12. This is the only New Testament reference to Kidron. See Raymond E. Brown, *The Gospel according to John XIII–XXI* (London: Geoffrey Chapman, 1971), 806. Brown was an American and world-renowned scripture scholar.

13. The Semitic name *Gethsemane* means "olive press." Olive groves were known to exist on the western slopes of the Mount of Olives. Edward P. Echlin says "A sustainable cultivated olive plantation is one of the most biodiverse fields on earth, including wild and domestic animals, insects, micro-organisms and a host of herbs and plants" ("Creatures and the Soil Community: The Peaceable Kingdom," *The Way* [July 2001]: 203).

14. Brown, *The Gospel According to John*, 807.

15. Ibid., 818.

16. Ibid.

17. M. E. Boismard, *St. Jean (Synopse III)* (Paris: Cerf, 1977), 464.

18. Sandra Schneiders, *Written That You May Believe: Encountering Jesus in the Fourth Gospel* (New York: Crossroad, 1999), 195.

19. Unlike the beloved disciple, who believed when he "saw" the empty tomb and the clothes rolled up (John 20:8–9). The perceptiveness of Mary and that of the beloved disciples were based on love. See Raymond Brown, *A Risen Christ at Eastertime: Essays on the Gospel*

Narratives of the Resurrection (Collegeville, MN: Liturgical Press, 1990), 72.

20. Penelope Hobhouse, *The Story of Gardening* (London: Dorling Kindersley Limited, 2002), 43.

21. The number four held great significance and the octagon was a favorite design. Two squares overlaid created a stylized circle; the square symbolized humanity and the circle the unity of God. Geometric design offered a symbol of the order of God.

22. Maggie Keswick, *The Chinese Garden: History, Art and Architecture*, revised by Alison Hardie (1978; London: Frances Lincoln, 2002), 39.

23. Thacker, *History of Gardens*, 43.

24. "The Yellow Emperor said, 'The principle of Yin and Yang is the basic principle of the entire universe. It is the principle of everything in creation.... Yang stands for peace and serenity. Yin stands for recklessness and turmoil. Yang stands for destruction, and Yin for conservation" (*The Yellow Emperor's Classic of Internal Medicine*, quoted in Palmer and Manning, Sacred Gardens, 88).

25. Pierre Rambach and Susanne Rambach, *Gardens of Longevity in China and Japan: The Art of the Stone Raiser* (New York: Rizzoli International Publication, 1987), 14. The art of stone raising has been practiced longest in China and as an art has only been recently appreciated in the West. It is now seen in museums such as the Metropolitan Museum of Art in New York. Today stone gardens are appearing more frequently.

26. Palmer and Manning, *Sacred Gardens*, 95.

27. *Feng shui*, meaning literally "wind water," is the art of balancing natural energies and directions with those created by human activity. See Palmer and Manning, *Sacred Gardens*, 89.

28. Keswick, *Chinese Garden*, 138.

29. Teiji Itoh, *The Gardens of Japan* (Tokyo: Kidansha International, 1998), 35.

30. Torikai Shin-ichi, "Woodlands in the City Center," *Nipponia*, no. 24 (2003). Most shrines today—a place where a god is venerated—are surrounded with trees as well as by "sacred plants and cordoned precincts of pebbled beds."

31. Daivetz Suzuki, *Zen and Japanese Culture* (Princeton, NJ: Princeton University Press, 1973), 332.

32. Shunmyo Masuno, introduction to *The Modern Japanese Garden*, photographs by Michael Freeman, text by Michiko Rico Nosé (London: Nutchell Beazley, 2002), 11. Masuno is a Buddhist monk.

33. Itoh, *Gardens of Japan*, 87.

34. Ibid., 35.

35. Masuno, introduction to *The Modern Japanese Garden*, 14.

36. Itoh, *Gardens of Japan*, 87.

37. This room is entered through "a sliding door only 90 cms tall, [which] obliges guests to bow their heads and crouch—underscoring the fact that worldly status or social position means nothing within these walls, where all participants are treated alike" (*Japan—An Illustrated Encyclopedia* [Tokyo: Kodansha, 1993], 1536). The heart of the tea ceremony is in drinking thick tea prepared in a single bowl from which all the guests drink. Later, light tea is served in individual bowls.

38. Sen'ō Tanaka, *The Tea Ceremony* (Tokyo: Kodansha International, 1998). The tea ceremony, known as *Chanoyu*, "which literally means 'hot water for tea? has as its objective a relaxed communion between the host and his guests....Its ultimate aim is the attainment of a deep spiritual satisfaction through the drinking of tea and through silent contemplation" (15). "The tea ceremony has influenced our outlook on life, it has colored our beliefs and attitudes as well as the standards that so rigidly govern Japanese people" (10). This ceremony became formalized in the sixteenth century. According to a Tea Master, the essence of the ceremony is learning to be content: "One learns to be content, and only then does one make fire, bring water, boil it and prepare tea by one's own labor. The tea thus prepared is offered to the Buddha, then to people, and finally is partaken of oneself" (Sen Soshitsu XV [Grand Tea Master], "A Disclosed Soul of 'Roji,'" in *The Tea Garden*, 6). Saito, Tadakazu, and Haruzo Ohaski (photographer), *The Tea Garden* (Tokyo: Graphic-sah Publishing Co., 1989).

39. Itoh, *Gardens of Japan*, 87.

40. Ibid., 88.

41. Hobhouse, *Story of Gardening*, 32.

42. Alicia Amherst, *A History of Gardening in England* (London: Bernard Quaritch, 1895), 2.

43. Sylvia Landsberg, *Medieval Garden* (London: British Museum Press, 1998), 5.

44. Enda McDonagh, *Vulnerable to the Holy: In Faith, Morality, and Art* (Dublin: Columba Press, 2004), 185. McDonagh concentrates on what is Irish, "rather than ambitioning the Celtic," when writing about St. Patrick's legacy. He notes emphatically that "the

celebration of nature in word and in ritual seems an essential element in early Irish religion."

45. Jane Fearnley-Whittingstall, *The Garden: An English Love Affair* (London: Weidenfeld & Nicolson, 2002), 11. This author reproduces a fifteenth-century manuscript that pictures the saint in full monastic habit. See also a history of Fiachra's life by Maire B. de Paor in the booklet *St. Brigid & St. Fiachra*, published by the International Celtic Congress, 2003.

46. Stephanie Ross, *What Gardens Mean* (Chicago: University of Chicago Press, 1998), 45. Ross feels that gardens today are no longer seen as an art form and suggests that "environmental art is gardening's avant-garde" and that gardening is the ancestor of this new art form.

47. Hobhouse, *Gardens of the World*, 55.

48. Ibid., 62. Hobhouse is quoting Frank Scott, *The Art of Beautifying Suburban Home Grounds of Small Extent*.

49. For example, some of the BBC's gardening programs in autumn 2006 included public parks.

50. See www.alnwickgarden.com. The vision of the Duchess of Northumberland, who initiated this garden, is "to create a beautiful public space of contemplation, a place of fun, a place of inspiration and education."

51. See www.shekinasculpturegarden.com.

52. David Brown, *God and Enchantment of Place* (Oxford: Oxford University Press, 2004), 10, 13.

53. This saying is addressed by Nancy Roth in her article "Close to God's Heart in the Garden" *The Way* (January 2001): 33–41.

54. Nicholas Lash, *Believing Three Ways in One God: A Reading of the Apostles' Creed* (1992; London: SCM Press, 2002). The final chapter, chapter 7, of this work is titled "Gardening," see 121–24.

Chapter 9

1. Jim Larner, ed., *Shekina Sculpture Garden* (Dublin: Irish Government Publications, 1997).

2. For example, no one was asked "Do you believe in God?" First, such a question would not be open-ended and could be deemed overly intrusive; second, and more important, *faith* in general was more of a concern than specific beliefs (an issue discussed in chapter 2).

3. Jeff Astley, *Ordinary Theology: Looking, Listening and Learning in Theology* (Aldershot: Ashgate Press, 2002). As opposed to academic theology, which studies other people's theology, an "about"

theology that can have a "distancing" effect, "ordinary" theology, Ashley suggests, is always personal, self-involving, and lived in the now. It speaks in a mother-tongue language using metaphors that emerge from personal life and relationships; it is concerned with significance and meaning in relation to God and the living of life. It is a tried and tested theology, which Astley likens to a shoe that is made to fit the person in life's varying circumstances—otherwise they would not hold onto it.

4. A nationally famous Irish garden that is attached to a stately mansion and laid out in a grand scale and style.

5. This is the level of experience "on which we sense, perceive, imagine, feel, speak, and move" (Bernard Lonergan, *Method in Theology* [Toronto: University of Toronto Press, 1972], 9).

6. *Rebecca* is a water feature in the garden and water continuously flows from her jug.

7. This is the level "on which we inquire, come to understand, express what we have understood, work out the presuppositions and implications of our expression" (Lonergan, *Method in Theology*, 9).

8. Since her visit to the garden, Ruth has started going to art galleries and sculpture exhibitions. She is bringing her husband with her and educating him on how to look at works of art and to ponder personally their meaning.

9. This is the level "on which we reflect, marshal the evidence, pass judgment on the truth or falsity, certainty or probability, of a statement" (Lonergan, *Method in Theology*, 9).

10. This is the level "on which we are concerned with ourselves, our own operations, our goals, and so deliberate about possible courses of action, evaluate them, decide, and carry out our decisions" (Lonergan, *Method in Theology*, 9).

Chapter 10

1. "The Church needs to find a language which can promote a 'Catholic sacramental imagination'" is a point emphasized in a recent paper entitled, "On the Way to Life: Contemporary Culture and Theological Development as a Framework for Catholic Education, Catechesis and Formation," published by the Heythrop Institute for Religion, 2006.

2. Adrian van Kaam, *Personality Fulfillment in the Spiritual Life* (Wilkes-Barre, PA: Dimension Books, 1966), 59.

Glossary

1. *Catechism of the Catholic Church*. See the section on Grace, nos. 1996–2005.

2. Rahner's lengthy description is significant: "'Mystery' is the inexplicit and unexpressed horizon which always encircles and upholds the small area of our everyday existence of knowing and acting, our knowledge of reality and our free action. It is our most fundamental, most natural condition, but for that very reason, it is also the most hidden and least regarded reality, speaking to us by its silence, and even while appearing to be absent, revealing its presence by making us take cognizance of our limitations. We call this God" ("The Need for a Short Formula of Christian Faith," in *Theological Investigations*, vol. 2, trans. Karl-H Kruger [London: Darton, Longman & Todd, 1963], 122).

3. Karl Rahner, *Foundations of Christian Faith: An Introduction to the Idea of Christianity*, trans. William V. Dych (New York: Crossroad, 1994), 65. For Rahner, the word *God* exists and says nothing more than that. Its existence is prolonged even by the atheist who says there is no God. "It [the word] refers to that which is wordless, because every word receives its limits, its intelligible sense, only within the field of words" (46). The word *God* is used to describe an experience, in the analogous sense that one uses the word *tree* to describe what is meant by the general understanding of that term. Since the word *God*, however, is "'without contour' it speaks to us 'of God.' It means the 'silent one' who is always there and yet can always be overlooked, unheard, and, because it expresses the whole in its unity and totality, can be passed over as meaningless" (46).

4. See E. Schillebeeckx, *Christ, the Sacrament of Encounter with God* (London: Sheed and Ward, 1963).

5. David Brown, *God and Enchantment of Place*. See his chapter, "Sacrament and Enchantment: Reconceiving the Sacramental."

6. John Inge, *A Christian Theology of Place* (Hampshire: Ashgate, 2003). See the chapter, "Place and the Christian Tradition: A Sacramental Approach."

7. See especially: Karl Rahner, "The Theology of Symbol," in *Theological Investigations*, vol 4, trans. Kevin Smyth (London: Darton, Longman and Todd, 1966), 221–52; Paul Tillich, "Religious Symbols and Our Knowledge of God" (1955) in *Main Works, Vol 4. Writings in the Philosophy of Religion*, ed. John Clayton, (Berlin: De Gruyter, 1987), 253–69; Avery Dulles, *Models of Revelation* (Dublin: Gill and Macmillan), see chapter IX, "Symbolic Mediation," 131–54.